*Jesus said to her, "Woman, believe me,
the hour is coming when you will worship God
neither on this mountain nor in Jerusalem."*

JOHN 4:21

The CALVIN INSTITUTE OF CHRISTIAN WORSHIP LITURGICAL STUDIES Series, edited by John D. Witvliet, is designed to promote reflection on the history, theology, and practice of Christian worship and to stimulate worship renewal in Christian congregations. Contributions include writings by pastoral worship leaders from a wide range of communities and scholars from a wide range of disciplines. The ultimate goal of these contributions is to nurture worship practices that are spiritually vital and theologically rooted.

Published

Touching the Altar: The Old Testament for Christian Worship •
Carol M. Bechtel, Editor

God Against Religion: Rethinking Christian Theology through Worship •
Matthew Myer Boulton

What Language Shall I Borrow? The Bible and Christian Worship •
Ronald P. Byars

Christian Worship Worldwide: Expanding Horizons, Deepening Practices •
Charles E. Farhadian

Gather into One: Praying and Singing Globally • C. Michael Hawn

The Substance of Things Seen: Art, Faith, and the Christian Community •
Robin M. Jensen

Wonderful Words of Life: Hymns in American Protestant History and Theology •
Richard J. Mouw and Mark A. Noll, Editors

Discerning the Spirits: A Guide to Thinking about Christian Worship Today •
Cornelius Plantinga Jr. and Sue A. Rozeboom

Voicing God's Psalms • Calvin Seerveld

My Only Comfort: Death, Deliverance, and Discipleship in the Music of Bach •
Calvin R. Stapert

A New Song for an Old World: Musical Thought in the Early Church •
Calvin R. Stapert

An Architecture of Immanence: Architecture for Worship and Ministry Today •
Mark A. Torgerson

God Against Religion

Rethinking Christian Theology
through Worship

Matthew Myer Boulton

WILLIAM B. EERDMANS PUBLISHING COMPANY
GRAND RAPIDS, MICHIGAN / CAMBRIDGE, U.K.

Published 2008 by

Wm. B. Eerdmans Publishing Co.

2140 Oak Industrial Drive N.E., Grand Rapids, Michigan 49505 /

P.O. Box 163, Cambridge CB3 9PU U.K.

Printed in the United States of America

13 12 11 10 09 08   7 6 5 4 3 2 1

Library of Congress Cataloging-in-Publication Data

Boulton, Matthew Myer, 1970-

God against religion: rethinking Christian theology through worship /
Matthew Myer Boulton.

p.   cm. — (The Calvin Institute of Christian worship liturgical studies series)

Includes bibliographical references.

ISBN 978-0-8028-2972-6 (pbk.: alk. paper)

1. Reformed Church — Liturgy. 2. Public worship — Reformed Church.
I. Title.

BX9427.B67   2008

264′.042 — dc22

2007046557

www.eerdmans.com

Contents

CONTENTS

Series Preface

The first time I read the sentence "A Christian worship service is not a hiatus from corruption, but an epitome of it," I thought I had picked up the wrong book. It is not pleasant to suddenly think of one's lifework as an exercise in the epitome of human corruption. But that bracing experience soon reminded me of the similar experience of hearing the persistent prophetic critique of worship offered throughout the Old Testament. "Away with the noise of your songs," the prophet Amos's message, is hardly an uplifting or encouraging word for a typical worship leader. (Imagine a worship conference beginning with a sermon on that text!)

Nevertheless, Amos's message is deeply life-giving. And so is the message of this book. This is true because so much of our worship is simply presumptuous; so much of our talking about worship alternates between cynicism and sentimentality. When we fall into these traps, we need a prophetic word to penetrate our presumptions and set us free. We need to hear again about the greatness and goodness of God and to bask again in the life-giving and freeing truth that worship is not about pleasing or manipulating God or attempting to earn or justify God's favor. We need the truth of the gospel, and we need to wrestle with this truth intensively enough to let its message of grace permeate every nook of our imagination. When we do, it forges not anxiety or despair in us, but rather a deep, quiet peace and poise.

Thus, contrary to my first inclination, I realized that I had not picked up the wrong book at all, but a book that has challenged and ultimately comforted me a great deal. Reading it has functioned for me much like a kind of spiritual detoxification process. I pray that it will for you, too. As I worked my way through the book, I developed quite a long list of hopes for what this book might accomplish. Here are several of them:

1. I hope that pastors, teachers, and scholars will interrogate our fondness for defining liturgy as "the work of people." While serving as a needed corrective for clericalism, that little definition can undermine our expectation and awareness of divine activity in worship. What if we were to make a concerted effort to replace the typical definition "the work of people" with "the work of people-with-God" (p. 122)? Or perhaps we might dare to define it as "a collective work of God-with-us."

2. I hope that we will recover gratitude as the foundation of genuine worship. Gratitude is so often treated as a spineless or sentimental bit of goodness. In fact, if one were to look at actual practices, one might think that the epitome of gratitude in North America consists of eating turkey and watching football. Instead, think of gratitude as the muscular spine of Christian ethics, the core of faithful ministry, the anchor of faithful worship, the central affection of the Eucharist, a ground-motif of the Psalter.

   It is simply true, I believe, that most worship is driven by fear, guilt, selfish ambition, or gratitude. Each one emits its own ethos, sometimes in subtle (or not-so-subtle) ways that frame (or undermine) the meaning of the words we speak. All four of those feelings live inside each of us. It is crucial that Christians, both as individuals and communities, learn not only to confess our guilt, set aside our selfish ambitions, and comfort our anxieties, but also that we learn how to cultivate gratitude—first to God, then to others. May worship be renewed through deep and profound gratitude for the wonders of creation and the new creation God accomplishes in Christ. May we truly be bold to pray: "Give us such an awareness of your mercies that with truly thankful hearts we may show forth your praise, not only with our lips, but in our lives, by giving up ourselves to your service, and by walking before you in holiness and righteousness all our days, through Jesus Christ, our Lord" (Book of Common Prayer).

3. I hope that this book will inspire more theologians to a closer linking of worship and theology. It is remarkable and heartening to see how

many books in the past generation have called for this kind of linkage. It is also heartening that very few of those invitations and calls for renewed linkage between theology and worship are publicly criticized. (Indeed, it is difficult to picture someone ardently defending the idea that worship and theology should be separated.)

Thus the problem is not that these calls are criticized; it is that they are so often ignored. It is still astonishing how few theologians take worship practices (prayers, sermons, hymns, gestures, and other practices) seriously. One result is that a good deal of writing and teaching about worship goes unchallenged by constructive criticism from theologians. May Boulton's twofold plea "for a more critical approach to Christian worship" and "a more liturgical approach to Christian theology" (p. 3) be taken very seriously.

4. More specifically, I hope that students of both theology and worship will recognize more consistently the conceptual overlap between the theology of worship and other central topics in theological discourse. Any disciplined attention to the theology of liturgy must account for how worship is both a free act of human beings and also one that is inspired and enabled by God, one in which God works to nurture faith. In this way, theology of liturgy is conceptually similar to any other of the theological loci that attempt the delicate task of understanding how divine and human action are related (e.g., the doctrine of faith, the doctrine of providence). Christian churches in nearly every tradition would benefit enormously from new efforts to match how a given tradition understands human and divine action in the act of faith with how a given tradition understands human and divine action in acts of worship—and then from efforts to practice worship in ways that are consistent with this view. This volume is a thought-provoking case study in precisely that kind of work.

5. I hope that this book will help to resuscitate life-giving, gospel-oriented practices of penitential worship. In various streams of liturgical scholarship, there is a persistent worry about an overly penitential approach to worship, which is often associated with medieval penitential piety that was largely unquestioned in various Protestant reforms. I share the concern that, for example, many Protestant celebrations of the Lord's Supper are too narrowly penitential, with little room for Easter joy or eschatological hope.

But I do not share a general uneasiness over anything penitential.

Repentance remains a fundamental Christian practice. And without penitential piety, we are so often left without an awareness of human sinfulness, and that, in turn, leaves us with a truncated view of divine salvation.

This book is certainly not enthusiastic about any penitential piety that attempts to impress God by its humility. But it does develop a provocative way of explaining a piety of "penitential jubilation" (p. 205) that keeps Christian worship grounded in both lament and praise, both Kyrie eleison and Gloria in excelsis Deo. I hope that this constructively paradoxical phrase, "penitential jubilation," will gain traction, and that along the way it will question the simplistic operating assumption in some churches that all music must be rendered without the use of minor keys.

6. Finally, I hope that this book will challenge the reigning self-congratulatory ethos and piety of worship conferences, publications, and other programs. Altogether too much worship-related programming is, to quote Boulton, "riddled with self-justification" (p. 200). Far too much is muddled by a kind of "pious haze that clouds much Christian writing about worship" (p. 4). In fact, this is one of the most significant work-related dangers of people (like me) whose work focuses on worship practices for most of the day. For some of us, working our way through this criticism may be a tad depressing at first. But the gospel itself invites us to a rich and abundant life before God's face that is devoid of all cynicism, sentimentality, and self-justification. May God's Spirit work in each of us to detoxify us of those troublesome burdens.

JOHN D. WITVLIET
Calvin Institute of Christian Worship
Calvin College and
Calvin Theological Seminary

Acknowledgments

Many people have helped me with this project along the way, and I am grateful to them for the help. Kathryn Tanner shepherded me at every stage of writing, with generosity and insight. David Tracy and Susan Schreiner gave crucial guidance and feedback and, through their teaching, provided the intellectual room within which I could work out the argument. Many others also read and commented on drafts of the manuscript, or parts of it, including S. Mark Heim, John Witvliet, Gregory Mobley, Paul Griffiths, William Wright, Jonathan Knight, David Albertson, Robert Saler, Bram Briggance, Benjamin Broadbent, Miriam Margles, Richard Rosengarten, Chris Gamwell, Jeremy Biles, Jonathan Rothchild, Greg Taylor, Kathleen Self, Rick Nance, Will Kiblinger, and the invitees to the 2000-01 Luce Seminar at The University of Chicago. Much of what is useful in these pages (and none of what isn't) is properly credited to them.

I am grateful to the William B. Eerdmans Publishing Company, and in particular to Jon Pott, Reinder Van Til, Linda Bieze, and Jennifer Hoffman, and also to John Witvliet, director of the Calvin Institute of Christian Worship.

Elizabeth Myer Boulton not only read and commented on drafts from first to last, but in every way made this book possible. I dedicate it, with thanks, love, and joy, to her.

Thanksgiving, 2007   MMB
                                      Harvard Divinity School

God Against Religion

From a Berlin prison cell in 1944, Dietrich Bonhoeffer wrote of his most celebrated theological teacher, Karl Barth: "Barth was the first to realize the mistake . . . of clearing a space for religion in the world." Instead, Bonhoeffer wrote, Barth "called the God of Jesus Christ into the lists against religion, *'pneuma* against *sarx.'* That was and is his greatest service."[1]

It is a remarkable assessment. By 1944, Barth's chief interpreters had all but left this "greatest service" behind, lapsing, as Bonhoeffer put it, into "positivism," and "from positivism into conservative restoration."[2]

---

1. Dietrich Bonhoeffer, *Letters and Papers from Prison* (New York: Macmillan, 1953), p. 198. *Pneuma* against *sarx:* i.e., "spirit against flesh." In fact, Barth was by no means the first to do so (see Introduction, n. 2 below). But among twentieth-century Christian theologians, Barth was certainly the most prominent and influential.

2. *Letters and Papers*, pp. 198-99. In Bonhoeffer's view, Barth himself encouraged and participated in the first lapse, a fall into what Bonhoeffer called a "positivism of revelation." As we shall see, however, if we keep Barth's expressly liturgical account of divine revelation in view (i.e., his account of divine revelation as addressed to the church, and as such, pronounced in biblical texts and liturgically proclaimed "in the form of preaching and sacrament"), the charge of "positivism" appears out of place. On the contrary, precisely because Barth portrays divine revelation as emergent in concrete human liturgical acts of ongoing communal interpretation (reading, preaching, sacrament), God's Word always resounds in utterly human "words," that is, God's Word always resounds in contestable, provisional fields of play, where ongoing interpretive criticism is humanity's proper *modus operandi.* For Barth, when it comes to divine revelation, the church invariably finds itself in this

Likewise, in the decades that followed, Barth's principal advocates and critics — conservative, liberal, and otherwise — have only rarely treated, much less featured, the idea that "the God of Jesus Christ" is a God "against religion." And yet for Bonhoeffer, this idea is the most important and enduring one of all in Barth's work.

These prison papers are interesting, too, because they include Bonhoeffer's preliminary thoughts on how he hoped to develop the idea himself. He wrote boldly of a "religionless Christianity"[3] — and precisely here, he parted company with his illustrious teacher in a way that helps illuminate both sides of an intriguing divide. For Bonhoeffer, Barth had correctly diagnosed the problem of religion, but in the end he remained caught up within its bounds, because he failed to provide a "non-religious interpretation of theological concepts."[4] Bonhoeffer believed, to put it succinctly, that religion is a "temporary form" of human life, that the world had "come of age," and thus that "we are proceeding towards a time of no religion at all." To thrive in this new stage of "being radically without religion," he wrote, Christianity had to change just as radically, becoming "worldly" and "secular" in ways as yet unimagined.[5]

In other words, in opposition to Barth, Bonhoeffer envisioned a "religionless" way of Christian life. He pictured religion as "no more than the garment of Christianity," and thus as something that could and would be cast aside — not traded for another (equally religious) vestment, but rather sloughed off altogether.[6] Bonhoeffer charged that Barth had not taken his own critique of religion to this "logical conclusion," and this charge, in turn, helps clarify Barth's distinctive case: as early as 1922, in

---

acutely vulnerable hermeneutic position; thus Barth's definition of Christian dogmatics as "Church dogmatics" (i.e., as ongoing criticism of "Church proclamation"). See Barth, *Church Dogmatics* (Edinburgh: T&T Clark, 1975), I.1, e.g., pp. 47, 14.

3. Bonhoeffer, *Letters and Papers*, p. 163.

4. *Letters and Papers*, p. 198.

5. *Letters and Papers*, pp. 162-64. For a later, North American version of this view, see Robert W. Jenson, *A Religion Against Itself* (Richmond, VA: John Knox Press, 1967). Responding both critically and sympathetically to what he describes as the "great fuss just recently about 'believing in the death of God,'" Jenson calls for a "secularized worship," and indeed a whole "program of antireligious worship, theology, and life" (pp. 11, 56, 116). For a more recent view, and one in a so-called evangelical key, see Mark D. Baker, *Religious No More: Building Communities of Grace and Freedom* (Downers Grove, IL: InterVarsity Press, 1999).

6. Bonhoeffer, *Letters and Papers*, p. 163.

the second edition of *The Epistle to the Romans,* Barth anticipated this kind of criticism and gave his answer.

His answer is twofold. First, he argues that there is no "religionless" way of life, and certainly no "religionless Christianity," available to human beings this side of Eden. Any simple and apparently radical "war against religion," as Barth puts it, is only "pseudo-radicalism," only a sideways step into another religious form.[7] For as soon as we begin to specify the protocols, values, and regulations of such "religionlessness," we thereby take up again the religious project, formulating and following a particular way of life, a program for righteousness, a new *torah,* "law," "instruction" — and therefore another perfectly religious form of Christianity. We may, Barth argues, quite triumphantly declare ourselves free of our neighbors' "religious" difficulties, but this declaration is, after all, the standard cry of a new religious sect. Therefore, Barth insists that any sound theological critique of "religion" must be a self-critique first of all, a careful demonstration that the lead defendant in the case we bring against religion is none other than our own Christianity — "worldly" or otherwise.

Second, Barth's answer is that God is "against religion" not by annihilating it or by establishing a human way of life beyond or alongside or outside it, but by transforming religion, so to speak, from within. For Barth, the good news of the Christian gospel is that God saves humanity from religion by undertaking religion in Jesus Christ. Religion is, in Bonhoeffer's phrase, a "temporary form"; for Barth, however, it will pass away not in some imminent historical "stage" of civilization, but only at history's finale, in the boundless daylight of God's redemption. In the meantime, Christians may receive a foretaste of religion's end in liturgies of the Lord's Supper, or in practices of Sabbath-keeping (and this means receiving foretastes of liturgy's end, and Christianity's end as well), but true "religionlessness" is, for Barth, an eschatological reality. In the New Jerusalem, Barth agrees, there will be "no temple" (Rev. 21:22); until then, however, today's Jerusalem teems with religious life.

Therefore, if religion is a garment, for Barth it cannot be cast aside by modern men and women in a world "come of age." Rather, it is a garment like the garments of exile in Genesis 3: first, a desperate, makeshift gar-

---

7. Karl Barth, *The Epistle to the Romans* (London: Oxford University Press, 1933), p. 241.

ment of shame, the sad camouflage of leaves sewn together into "loin-cloths" (Gen. 3:7); and second, a beautiful garment of care and good shelter, the clothing gracefully made and put on human bodies by God's own hand, covering and thus transforming the human veil into a divine gift of refuge and protection (Gen. 3:21). Both garments are signs of exile, negative reminders of a lost state of living, "naked and not ashamed" (Gen. 2:25). And in Barth's view, both garments are provisional, "temporary forms," transitory just to the extent that the exile itself is transitory. Religion is a pilgrim's garb that is shed only at the end of the journey.

In this book I outline this portrait and critique of religion and show how, at its heart, it is a portrait and critique of worship. It is worship, most fundamentally, that has this double aspect, both veil and clothing, "fall" and "reconciliation." And thus it is worship, finally, that God will cast aside. Along the way, I take cues from Karl Barth, John Calvin, and Martin Luther, and also from new readings of biblical texts that these cues open up. But my primary mode in these pages is constructive and theological. Like a carpenter in a lumberyard, I aim to build a house, and so I am not long distracted by the wood I cannot put to good use. Therefore, one should seek more comprehensive treatments of Barth's (and Calvin's and Luther's) work elsewhere. Here I build up from their ideas a brief, systematic, liturgical theology in the Reformed tradition, a case that "the God of Jesus Christ" is a "God against religion," a God who saves human beings from religion — that is, from Christianity, and most fundamentally, from Christian worship — by entering it, transforming it, and, ultimately, by ending it. At the last, in this view, there will indeed be a "religionless" new life for humankind, a new life without worship, and Christians today properly pray for it, call for it, and may get a foretaste of it — in Christian worship and religion.

Rethinking Theology through Worship
in the Reformed Tradition

Pray on! Pray on!
Some sweet day after 'while,
Prayin' time will soon be over,
O some sweet day after 'while.

African-American spiritual

Worship is the heart of Christian life, and "some sweet day" it will end. Liturgical work — thanks, praise, and prayer to God in word and sacrament — is provisional, temporary work. It will pass away. God will end it. And in Jesus Christ this ending has already begun.

These ideas are by no means new. Sometimes hidden, sometimes plain, they are woven through biblical and theological traditions in Christianity. In this book I bring a few of these threads together into a brief systematic theology. This theology is in the Reformed tradition, first, because it builds on groundwork laid by Martin Luther, John Calvin, and Karl Barth, and second, because it picks up on a distinctively (though not exclusively) Reformed tradition of criticism: the critique of religion. In Luther's work, for example, the epitome of human sin is not pride in general but rather *religious* pride, the audacious attempt "to obtain righteousness in the sight of God." Likewise, in Calvin, corrupted human nature is not abstractly degenerate but rather *religiously* degenerate, "a perpetual factory of idols." And in Barth, as we shall see, these lines of thought are extended and intensified.[1] "Religion," Barth proclaims, is no less than "the most radical dividing of men from God."[2] In this book I develop this sort of criticism into a systematic theological picture. In my analysis, religion, far from being the happy solution to the basic human crisis of separation from God, is rather the very occasion for that crisis in the first place.

But my argument is also continuous with the Reformed tradition in another way: it is, at bottom, liturgical theology. Though modern Protestant thought is perhaps not widely known for taking worship as its fundamental theme and framework, Christian life is, in fact, finally a life of worship for Luther, Calvin, and Barth. Thus all Christian theology is finally liturgical theology. Accordingly, in these pages I argue that each movement in the divine symphony of salvation — the glory of creation, the catastrophe of sin, the miracle of reconciliation, and the new glory of redemption — all is properly interpreted in liturgical terms: thanksgiving and praise, confession and prayer, water and bread. In this view, thinking theologically means thinking through worship. Thus I will argue that the catastrophe of sin is liturgy's original and continual work; the miracle of reconciliation is liturgy's decisive transformation in Jesus Christ; and the glory of redemption — foretasted "already" but nonetheless forthcoming and hence "not yet" — is and will be liturgy's end.[3]

1. Martin Luther, *Luther's Works,* ed. Jaroslav Pelikan and Helmut Lehmann (St. Louis: Concordia, 1960-1974), Vol. 26, p. 231; John Calvin, *Institutes of the Christian Religion,* ed. John T. McNeill (Philadelphia: Westminster, 1960), p. 108. In both Luther and Calvin, of course, the critique is leveled not against religion per se, but rather against religion as practiced by "papists," "pagans," and rival reformers. Barth's development of this critique, in short, is to universalize it: now every religion is arraigned, including Reformed Christianity, since "no religion is true." See Barth, *Church Dogmatics* (Edinburgh: T&T Clark, 1956), I.2, p. 325. Here Barth breaks from Luther and Calvin; at the same time, however, Barth represents and extends Luther and Calvin, because the universal version of the critique is still fundamentally cast in the same terms: religion as "works righteousness," "idolatry," "unbelief," and so on.

2. Barth, *The Epistle to the Romans* (London: Oxford University Press, 1933), p. 241. Barth's thinking here took shape under the influence of Søren Kierkegaard, Franz Overbeck, Fyodor Dostoevsky, the Blumhardts, and others; see Eberhard Busch, *Karl Barth: His Life from Letters and Autobiographical Texts* (Philadelphia: Fortress, 1976), pp. 115ff.

3. In this book, I use the terms "liturgy" and "worship" broadly and interchangeably, first because they are closely related in any case, overlapping semantically to a considerable degree; second, because I want to resist the sometimes clannish and always incoherent claim — particularly on the part of some Protestants — that while all Christians "worship" in one

*   *   *

Methodologically, then, this book is a twofold plea: first, for a more critical approach to Christian worship and religion; second, for a more liturgical approach to Christian theology. Christian commentators on worship are fond of pointing to the English term's origins: the Old English *woerth* ("worth") and *scipe* ("-ship"). They then write or preach as if worship itself is eminently worthy, and thus beyond critique. The closing sentence of one influential textbook, *The Study of Liturgy,* is typical: "Worship is totally worthwhile."[4] But this kind of claim, even if it refers strictly to worship at its best, creates significant problems for "the study of liturgy." First, the claim is uncritical and incredible: a simple, wholesale endorsement of what is at best a sundry, shifting set of complicated, interested human practices. It may also be more than this, of course, but not less. Second, the claim is theologically unsound, because it suggests that Christian worship is a practical realm somehow set apart from sin, "totally worthwhile" in its provision of goods: divine forgiveness, sacred instruction, and, above all, clear access to the divine presence — on earth and in heaven.

On the other hand, however, are not such goods exactly what Christian worship claims to provide? Do not countless Christian liturgies in-

---

way or another, "liturgy" is strictly the domain of, say, Roman Catholics or Anglicans or Orthodox (as if, e.g., Congregationalist Protestants do not worship in "prescribed forms"); and third, because this kind of broad usage is consistent with the broadly ambitious ways in which Luther, Calvin, Barth, and others write about prayer, praise, thanksgiving, confession, baptism, and so on, an ambition that is exemplary and promising for Christian theologians — and Christian churches — today. In what follows, then, the terms "liturgy," "liturgical," and "worship" refer not only to gestures and practices carried out during special ceremonies or inside officially designated sanctuaries, but also to versions of these gestures and practices as they occur in other circumstances. A Christian prayer of thanks to God, for example, may occur (1) in a church building during a Sunday morning service, or (2) in a private home during a Saturday evening supper. In either case, for my purposes here, I will call the prayer in question both a "liturgical" act and an act of "worship." Of course, there are other ways to understand and apply these terms, but this one is most helpful for thinking about liturgy and worship broadly as the fundamental form of genuine Christian life, as I wish to do here.

4. D. H. Tripp, "Worship and the Pastoral Office," in Cheslyn Jones, Geoffrey Wainwright, and Edward Yarnold, S.J., eds., *The Study of Liturgy* (New York: Oxford University Press, 1978), p. 532. This sentence — the final one in both Tripp's essay and the entire volume — is a fitting coda for the collection as a whole.

clude the *sursum corda,* for example, in which the congregation responds to the instruction "Lift up your hearts" by announcing quite calmly, "We lift them up to the Lord"? Indeed they do. But this kind of ceremonial talk, as "worthwhile" as it may be, is also utterly ambiguous and questionable from a theological point of view. Every liturgy Christians build, no matter how excellent (and indeed all the more so for its alleged excellence), is permanently open to the charge that it is also a Christian effort to "make a name for ourselves," as the author of Genesis 11 puts it, to "lift up our hearts to the Lord" so that we effectively "build ourselves a city, and a tower with its top in the heavens" (Gen. 11:4). Every liturgy Christians build, in other words, is permanently open to the charge of spiritual pride. Thus we may ask: Is any Christian worship service exempt from this charge? Is there any way to pronounce the *sursum corda* — or for that matter, to approach God at all in Christian worship — without building a Christian liturgical tower at the same time?

There is today a kind of pious haze that clouds much Christian writing about worship, and it typically obscures the possibility of pressing these kinds of critical questions. But the questions arise anyway. They arise in biblical texts, from "Cain and Abel" to the "Tower of Babel," from the antiworship polemics in the prophets to the passion narratives in the Gospels. They also arise in theological texts, from Martin Luther to Karl Barth, among others. And these questions also arise, I hazard to say, in the hearts and minds of many Christians and non-Christians, both inside and outside the church, who are struggling to make sense of Christian liturgy. Therefore, I argue that we require a more critical framework for conceiving, assessing, and carrying out Christian worship, a framework open to thoroughgoing ambiguity and thus capable of more fully accounting for both the perils and the promises of liturgical life. In this book I briefly sketch one possible framework: a Reformed, liturgical, systematic theology.

And so my second methodological plea is a call for a more liturgical approach to Christian theological work. Too often in modern, Western Christian thought, worship has been featured as a kind of appendix to theology, a supposedly "practical" arena in which theological ideas are more or less helpfully dressed up, expressed, and inculcated among the faithful. Once appropriated, we are told, these ideas may then more or less effectively go on to influence life "outside the sanctuary." In these cases, worship is understood as an afterthought to theology, at best a handmaiden. Or alternately, worship has been featured in Western Christian theology as a more exalted — even quite piously and romantically revered — arena of Christian life, and yet ultimately as a sideshow to the allegedly main theological event, the serious hammering out of other doctrinal issues and their ethical consequences. Here worship is not quite a handmaiden, but not quite a mistress either. Liturgy is conceived of less as an appendix and more as a substantive theological chapter in its own right, but it is still hardly the central theme of Christian thought and work.

This is changing, of course, in a good deal of recent Christian writtng.[5] But the "appendix" and "sideshow" accounts of worship are still commonplace and, in many respects, normative, particularly in the late modern West, and particularly among Protestants. In this book, on the contrary, I put forward an example of a Christian theology in the Reformed tradition that takes worship as the heart of its subject matter: not only the heart of the Christian good life, but also the heart of Christian failings; not only the basis of our approach toward God in piety, but also the basis of our separation from God in sin. On the one hand, then, I propose a way of understanding sin in terms of worship, indeed, as occasioned precisely by worship itself; therefore, I propose a way of understanding worship as a form of life that God will one day put to an end. To put the case briefly: God is against religion, and preeminently against worship. Human salvation, in this view, does and will mean the end of liturgy once and for all.

On the other hand, however, I argue that, in Jesus Christ, God transforms worship from an event of fatal separation between humanity and

---

5. For relatively recent texts in which worship figures as constitutive and central to the broadest themes in Christian theology, see, e.g., William T. Cavanaugh, *Theopolitical Imagination: Discovering the Liturgy as a Political Act in an Age of Global Consumerism* (London: T&T Clark, 2002) and *Torture and Eucharist* (Oxford: Blackwell, 1998); Catherine Pickstock, *After Writing: On the Liturgical Consummation of Philosophy* (Oxford: Blackwell, 1998); Gordon W. Lathrop, *Holy People: A Liturgical Ecclesiology* (Minneapolis: Fortress, 1999) and *Holy Things: A Liturgical Theology* (Minneapolis: Fortress, 1993); Dorothy C. Bass, ed., *Practicing Our Faith* (San Francisco: Jossey-Bass, 1997); Don E. Saliers, *Worship as Theology: Foretaste of Glory Divine* (Nashville: Abingdon, 1994); B. A. Gerrish, *Grace and Gratitude: The Eucharistic Theology of John Calvin* (Minneapolis: Fortress, 1993); John D. Zizioulas, *Being as Communion* (Crestwood, NY: St. Vladimir's, 1985); Geoffrey Wainwright, *Doxology: The Praise of God in Worship, Doctrine, and Life* (New York: Oxford University Press, 1980); and Alexander Schmemann, *For the Life of the World* (Crestwood, NY: St. Vladimir's, 1963).

God into an event of saving reconciliation between them. That is, I contend that, in Jesus Christ, God undertakes and overcomes worship's disastrous choreography, renovating it into a way of vicarious participation in divine life, now carried out "in the name" of God the Son. God is against religion, and preeminently against worship, but God's opposition takes place, so to speak, from the inside out, reversing our gesture of departure into a gesture of return. The religious sword is conquered, to be sure, but not destroyed; the blade is preserved and remade into a plowshare.

And yet from this angle, too, liturgy is properly conceived as provisional and temporary, since Christians proclaim, in hope, that the work of reconciliation will one day give way to the play of redemption. Then the plowshares will also be left behind, for all the hungry "will be filled" (Luke 6:21). Vicarious participation in divine life will give way to bona fide participation in divine life. Thus, in the New Jerusalem, as John of Patmos puts it, there will be "no temple" (Rev. 21:22). Even as saving, reconciling work, liturgy in the end will come to its finale.

*   *   *

On his first Sunday morning as pastor of a small church in Safenwil, Switzerland, the young Karl Barth began a "series of sermons on the Lord's Prayer."[6] Fifty-seven years later, on the eve of his death, Barth was revising drafts for yet another chapter of his massive *Church Dogmatics,* a chapter on Christian life. Again, he turned to the Lord's Prayer as his topic and template. Thus it would seem that Barth brought his theological career to a close by returning once more to his opening theme.

But a formative turn to prayer, far from merely beginning and concluding Barth's theological work, in fact framed and founded it, provided a kind of skeleton on which that whole body of writing took shape. Barth thought through worship. And he argued, from both pulpit and lectern, that human beings live and die through worship, too. In this book I wish to engage Karl Barth — and later, John Calvin and Martin Luther — as a conversation partner, drawing out key features of his work. Sometimes this means bringing to the foreground aspects of Barth's case that he him-

---

6. See Eberhard Busch, *Karl Barth: His Life from Letters and Autobiographical Texts* (Philadelphia: Fortress, 1976), p. 61.

self leaves in the background; more often, though, it means emphasizing prominent aspects of his thought that other readers have de-emphasized or overlooked.

Barth's chief interpreters, rather than reading him as a fundamentally liturgical theologian, have instead focused on other aspects of his work, either passing by worship altogether[7] or assigning it a decidedly marginal role.[8] John Webster's fine book *Barth's Ethics of Reconciliation* is a rare exception to this rule, as is Eberhard Jüngel's essay entitled "Invocation of God as the ethical ground of Christian action."[9] These two commentators treat the posthumously published drafts of Chapter XVII of *Church Dogmatics,* where Barth develops at length the theme of "invocation," that is, calling on God in prayer, as the "general key" for properly conceiving of Christian life in light of the "Doctrine of Reconciliation."[10] They show how, in Barth's view, God's reconciliation of

7. For example, in *How to Read Karl Barth* (New York: Oxford University Press, 1991), George Hunsinger scarcely mentions worship at all and thus leaves the impression that reading Karl Barth can be done well without it. Of course, Hunsinger should not be expected to include everything in his fine book; the point is that in this respect he typifies the field.

8. In Bruce L. McCormack's magisterial *Karl Barth's Critically Realistic Dialectical Theology* (Oxford: Clarendon Press, 1995), liturgical life appears only here and there (usually as "baptism"; see, e.g., pp. 155, 286-87, 322, 392). The same is true of T. F. Torrance's *Karl Barth: An Introduction to His Early Theology, 1910-1931* (London: SCM Press, 1962), e.g., pp. 18, 41, 177, 186, 197, 214, 215; and John Webster's *Barth* (London: Continuum, 2000), e.g., pp. 157-60; as well as Hans Urs von Balthasar's influential overview, *The Theology of Karl Barth* (San Francisco: Ignatius Press, 1992), e.g., pp. 194, 381, 387. Von Balthasar, at least, explicitly acknowledges that he "narrows the focus" of his survey to "creation, Incarnation, and redemption," and that he largely leaves aside "the thematic cluster of Church, sacrament and Christian life." On his reading, Barth's "heart does not seem to be fully engaged" when it comes to these latter themes, and so, if Roman Catholics want more fruitful "ecumenical discussion" of these matters, von Balthasar avers (with unintentional comedy) that they "would do better to seek a Lutheran." These remarks indicate a considerable misreading of Karl Barth, first, insofar as they imply that Barth was less interested in worship than in "creation, Incarnation, and redemption," and second, insofar as they presuppose that Barth's ideas about "creation, Incarnation and redemption" can be so neatly cordoned off from "Church, sacrament and Christian life" in the first place (no doubt the Lutherans would know better!). See von Balthasar, p. 44.

9. John Webster, *Barth's Ethics of Reconciliation* (Cambridge, UK: Cambridge University Press, 1995); Eberhard Jüngel, "Invocation of God as the ethical ground of Christian action," in *Theological Essays,* trans. J. B. Webster (Edinburgh: T&T Clark, 1989), pp. 154-72.

10. Karl Barth, *The Christian Life* (Grand Rapids: Eerdmans, 1981), pp. 43, 9.

humanity in Jesus Christ has everything to do with prayer, with the "in-vocation of God," with "thanksgiving, praise, and petition," and thus with Christian liturgical life. But by treating this material squarely in the context of Barth's "ethics of reconciliation," Webster and Jüngel simultaneously suggest and yet leave unexplored how a turn to prayer — and to worship more generally — is formative for Barth's theology as a whole.[11]

In fact, Barth's fundamental turn to worship is by no means limited to these late drafts, or to his doctrine of reconciliation. In Volume I of *Church Dogmatics,* for example, Barth expressly characterizes his well-known starting point and continual refrain, "the Word of God," as a liturgical word, a divine "Word" that comes to human beings as "Church proclamation," and thus "in the form of preaching and sacrament."[12] That is, Barth argues that, for the Christian church, the Word of God always arrives as a proclaimed word, God's Word freely breaking through human liturgical "words,"[13] whether scriptural ("the Word of God written" and

---

11. For his part, Webster is clear that he means his close reading of Barth's unfinished "ethics of reconciliation" to be "a test case" for a much broader reconsideration of Barth's work. In this respect, then, Webster points to the wider significance of these drafts (as well as the published so-called "baptism fragment," *Church Dogmatics* IV.4) as windows through which we may fruitfully review the whole of Barth's thought. Webster's interests, broad as they are, are framed principally in terms of "ethics" and "moral ontology." See Webster, *Barth's Ethics of Reconciliation,* pp. 8-9.

12. Karl Barth, *Church Dogmatics* (Edinburgh: T&T Clark, 1975), I.1, pp. 47ff. For Barth, "God may speak to us through Russian Communism, a flute concerto, a blossoming shrub, or a dead dog," and we "do well to listen to Him if He really does"; but the only divine revelation that we, as Christians, are commissioned (and thus permitted) to proclaim to one another is the revelation attested by the biblical witness. If we proclaim on the basis of any other revelation, "we regard ourselves as the prophets and founders of a new Church." Short of this innovation, Barth contends, the only proper "Church proclamation" as such is proclamation of "the Word of God" as spoken in the biblical witness, that is, proclamation delivered in decidedly liturgical forms, in all their variety: "preaching and sacrament." See *Church Dogmatics,* I.1, pp. 55ff.

13. Ernst Troeltsch, Barth's older contemporary, opens his *Glaubenslehre* (1925) with an announcement that modern, critical Christian theology can only abandon two formerly held "presuppositions": first, in the new light shed by modern philosophy, Christian theologians must discard the "presupposition of a universal, rational knowledge of God"; and second, in the new light shed by modern historical studies of scriptural texts, we can only leave behind the "presupposition of the inspiration of the Bible." These judgments, of course, were starting points not only for Troeltsch but for a whole generation of theologians in the so-called "liberal" school, many of whom trained Karl Barth; by comparison and contrast,

read) or homiletical ("the Word of God preached" and heard).[14] Moreover, Barth goes on to argue that the only proper human posture for the
reception and interpretation of the Word in and through liturgical words
is likewise a definitively liturgical posture, the posture of prayer.[15] And to
complete this liturgical picture, he argues that the Word of God is in turn

---

they help illuminate Barth's distinctive case. Like Troeltsch, Barth affirms historical-critical
studies of Scripture, but for Barth this affirmation by no means requires the abandonment
of the "doctrine of inspiration," but rather its specification. That is, what we find in Barth is
an articulation of that doctrine in liturgical terms: the Christian Bible, Barth argues, is not
itself divine revelation, not itself "inspired" in the sense of having been dictated by God and
mechanically recorded by its original authors; rather, the biblical text, in all its complexity
and ambiguity as a human product, is now conceived as the principal potential occasion for
divine "inspiration" afresh in the liturgical context of "Church proclamation," i.e., in the
context of concrete interpretations of Scripture by concrete communities reading it,
preaching on it, and celebrating sacraments narrated in it. Accordingly, Barth describes
both Scripture and preaching as strictly human products always having to "ever and again
become proclamation" by the gift of God, a continual becoming that is never crassly guaranteed (as it is in the "mechanical" doctrine of inspiration), but in worship may be hoped for
and — in faith — expected. Thus for Barth, Scripture is inspired not in the sense that
Troeltsch rejects, but rather in the sense that in Christian liturgy, Scripture may "ever and
again become" inspired, may become a concrete occasion and raw material through which
God speaks to human beings. Here, then, is a signature example of what Hunsinger calls
Barth's "actualism"; but that label, for all that it helps to clarify, may obscure the fundamen-
tally liturgical orientation of Barth's thought in key cases like this one. By turning to liturgy,
Barth breaks new ground precisely where Troeltsch and others declare a dead end. See
Troeltsch, *The Christian Faith* (Minneapolis: Augsburg Fortress, 1991), pp. 12ff; and Barth,
Church Dogmatics, I.1, pp. 99ff. See also Hunsinger, *How to Read Karl Barth,* pp. 30-32, 67ff.

14. The other "form" of God's Word in Barth's account, of course, the primary form
on which Scripture and preaching/sacrament depend, is "the Word of God revealed" in Jesus Christ. But as we shall see, this primary form, too, may be understood as a liturgical
form, indeed as consummately liturgical, first because, according to the Gospel narratives,
Jesus continually undertakes Jewish liturgical life — from baptism to prayer to the Passover
meal; second, because according to key New Testament texts, Jesus is decisively both
"priest" and "sacrifice" (Heb. 10), "shepherd" and "lamb" (John 10; John 1); and third, because Christians confess that in their worship Jesus is present and active "among" and as
the liturgical assembly (Matt. 18:20). Indeed, insofar as Christians identify Jesus Christ
with the divine "Word" (John 1:1), Jesus himself is proclamation, a divine sermon and the
one true "sacrament," and for Christians, sermon and sacrament are the central,
consummately liturgical events. For Barth's discussion of "The Word of God in Its Threefold Form," see *Church Dogmatics,* I.1, pp. 88ff.

15. Barth, *Church Dogmatics,* I.2, p. 755: "[W]e have to be clear that both those who
speak and those who hear [church proclamation] necessarily rely on the free grace of God
and therefore on prayer."

properly "answered" by human beings in and through liturgical life. As Barth puts it, the fitting "answer to the proclamation heard" is none other than "the Church's prayer, praise, and confession."[16]

Barth opens *Church Dogmatics* by introducing the idea that God and humanity are properly pictured as engaged in an ongoing liturgical dialogue. On one side of this exchange, God's Word breaks in through Church proclamation in "the form of preaching and sacrament"; on the other, human words answer this proclamation in "prayer, praise, and confession." Thus, from the very first, Barth portrays in *Church Dogmatics* the relationship between God and humanity as a fundamentally liturgical dialogue. The same theologian who began his decade of preaching in Safenwil with a series of sermons on prayer also built his systematic theology along liturgical lines.

*   *   *

And so Barth's theological resort to worship — what might be called his liturgical turn — is basic to the architecture, substance, and choreography of his thought. Late in his career, he put it this way: "[I]t is imperative to recognize the essence of theology as lying in the liturgical action of adoration, thanksgiving, and petition. The old saying, *Lex orandi lex credendi* [the law of prayer is the law of belief], far from being a pious statement, is one of the most profound descriptions of the theological method."[17] Barth used his own version of this method throughout his work, in various ways and with various effects. And so his turn to invocation in his last drafts of *Church Dogmatics* was no innovation he came to late in life. On the contrary, it was an extension and development of a lifelong project.

Indeed, even the theme "invocation" is not unprecedented in Barth's writing prior to these late drafts: it also appears, crucially, in Volume III of *Church Dogmatics*, "The Doctrine of Creation."[18] There Barth sketches real humanity (that is, "the real and fulfilled human life") as "a being in responsibility before God," and thus as having "the character of an invocation of God."[19] In this context, the fundamental dialogue between God

---

16. Barth, *Church Dogmatics*, I.1, p. 50.
17. Karl Barth, *The Humanity of God* (Richmond, VA: John Knox, 1960), p. 90.
18. *Church Dogmatics*, III.2, pp. 166ff.
19. *Church Dogmatics*, III.2, p. 186.

and humanity is recapitulated in terms of God's work as Creator. Here the divine Word is a creative word, calling humanity into being; and here humanity itself has the character of an invocational response (a response-ability) to the divine summons.

Thus Barth's turn to invocation in the late drafts of Volume IV is yet a further recapitulation of the theme of covenantal dialogue, introduced in Volume I, specified in Volume III, and now keyed in Volume IV to God's work as "Reconciler." From this vantage point, we may describe Barth's theology as a theology of invocation, a detailed portrait, painted from various angles, of what is always a dialogue between God and humanity. And with respect to reconciliation, that dialogue takes shape as God speaks God's Word through liturgical forms, and humanity speaks genuinely human words through "the liturgical action of adoration, thanksgiving, and petition."

Barth planned but never began a fifth volume of *Church Dogmatics*, "The Doctrine of Redemption." If previous volumes are any guide, we may well speculate that Barth would have revisited and recast the covenantal dialogue in Volume V as well, this time in light of God's eschatological promises. But imagining this final movement of Barth's unfinished symphony, this last return to the invocational theme, raises an interesting possibility. For there are indications throughout Barth's work, both implicit and explicit, that picturing this dialogue eschatologically means picturing this dialogue's end. It means picturing the end of "invocation," the end of this mutual calling, the end of liturgy once and for all, and the beginning of an altogether new life with God, a redeemed life to which every excellent invocation, every call, every liturgy actually points. As early as Volume I, Barth intimates that the finally redeemed human being, "the man of eternal glory," will no longer require the covenantal dialogue: he or she "neither needs nor will need any special talk about God, and consequently any being addressed by God, and consequently any Church."[20] In this book I will trace and develop this idea, the groundwork for which is evident in not only *Church Dogmatics* but also Barth's earlier work, *The Epistle to the Romans*.

*   *   *

20. *Church Dogmatics*, I.1, p. 64.

As a brief systematic theology of invocation, this book proposes that Christian theology be thought through worship, that it be conceived, developed, and articulated in liturgical terms. And this is true, I contend, not only with respect to creation, reconciliation, and redemption, but also with respect to sin. That is, in what follows I argue that God's reconciliation of humankind is a radically liturgical solution to a radically liturgical problem: the problem, as Barth puts it, of "religion."

To demonstrate this point, I reconsider Barth's notorious critique, in both *The Epistle to the Romans* and *Church Dogmatics,* of "religion as the occasion of sin," the fatal alienation of humanity from God. I show how, in Barth's view, religion is at its heart the act of worship, so that sin is also best understood liturgically — indeed as occasioned by liturgy itself. From this angle, worship may be described as the venue for no less than humankind's original and continual "fall" away from God.

Barth was one of the first major twentieth-century theologians to grasp the importance of the modern category and criticisms of religion that were surfacing in various allegedly "nonreligious" precincts, not only among European socialists (as a young man, Barth was deeply involved in socialist politics) but also among those at work in two disciplines nascent in the early twentieth century, psychoanalytic theory and academic anthropology. In these quarters and others, new social-scientific ways of thinking about religion — often quite critically and polemically — had emerged and were continuing to develop. Marxists theorized religion in terms of class struggle; Freudians in terms of psychodynamics and neuroses; Durkheimians in terms of political power and social formation. For their part, Christian theologians had also begun to take up religion as an essential part of theology's subject matter. Schleiermacher's early lectures, for example, *On Religion: Speeches to Its Cultured Despisers* (1799), are an elaborate apologia for religion that he addresses to its critics. In his *Glaubenslehre* (1821), Schleiermacher begins with an analysis of "religion in general" and then proceeds by examining the Christian religion in particular.[21] Almost a century later,

21. See Friedrich Schleiermacher, *On Religion: Speeches to Its Cultured Despisers* (Cambridge, UK: Cambridge University Press, 1988) and *The Christian Faith* (Edinburgh: T&T Clark, 1989), "Introduction," esp. pp. 30ff. A version of this approach is also discernible in Calvin's *Institutes,* which begins with a general discussion of "knowledge of God," "knowledge of self," and the universality of incipient "religion": "God has sown a seed of religion in all men." Only against this background, then, does Calvin go on to discuss "the Christian religion." See Calvin, *Institutes of the Christian Religion,* pp. 35ff, esp. p. 47.

Ernst Troeltsch, Barth's older contemporary, took up the same mantle: "[S]ince the reorganization of modern theology that began with the work of Schleiermacher," he wrote, Christian theology can only begin with a "comprehensive treatment of the principal results of the philosophy of religion. . . a general investigation into the phenomena and essence of religion. . . [and an assessment of] the place of Christianity in the history of religions."[22]

Barth's view and critique of religion may be understood as both a variation on these trends and an attack on them. First, in the face of the modern criticisms of religion — and indeed of Christianity — by Marx, Feuerbach, and others, Barth not only simply agrees, but he appropriates versions of these criticisms as his own. He launches a trenchant, impassioned critique of religion and Christianity. And thus, second, in the face of Christian theological apologies for religion, and especially for Christianity, Barth objects in the strongest terms. He denies that religion is radically and basically a benign domain in human life arising out of, as Schleiermacher put it, a particular "feeling" or form of "piety."[23] Nor is religion fundamentally or potentially a civilizing influence (Locke), a solution to a perplexing human problem (Ritschl), or a comforting "component of human consciousness" without which, as Troeltsch puts it, human beings "would either succumb to an overwhelming sense of resignation, or else completely wither away."[24] Rather, Barth argues, religion is radically and basically nothing less than the occasion of sin, the "fulcrum" of human alienation from God.[25] Even conceived of as piety, civilization, solution, and comfort — precisely under all of these guises, Barth insists — religion carries out its disastrous work, and indeed carries it out all the more effectively because of this camouflage. In this way, Barth delivers one of the most interesting Christian theological responses to the charges brought by religion's modern critics: he appropriates the charges and intensifies them. And he applies them to religion in general, and especially to Christianity. As we shall see, by way of an account of religion that encompasses not only the world's so-called faith traditions, but also any serious program of "moral and legal ordering"

22. Troeltsch, *The Christian Faith*, p. 9.

23. Schleiermacher, *The Christian Faith*, pp. 5ff.

24. Troeltsch, *The Christian Faith*, p. 9; see also John Locke, *The Reasonableness of Christianity* (Bristol, UK: Thoemmes Press, 1997), and Albrecht Ritschl, *The Christian Doctrine of Justification and Reconciliation* (Edinburgh: T&T Clark, 1900).

25. Barth, *The Epistle to the Romans*, p. 248.

whatsoever, he effectively turns the critique on Christianity's modern critics as well.[26]

Barth takes cues here from the likes of Marx and Feuerbach, but also and particularly from a cluster of Christian thinkers he read closely as he prepared the second edition of *The Epistle to the Romans*: Søren Kierkegaard, Fyodor Dostoevsky, Franz Overbeck, Johann Christoph Blumhardt, and Christoph Blumhardt, among others.[27] In various ways, these thinkers put Christianity under the most stringent sort of theological criticism, and this kind of critique became a characteristic and indispensable habit of thought for Barth. In 1922, in the middle of a polemic against Schleiermacher, Barth put it this way:

> The very names Kierkegaard, Luther, Calvin, Paul, and Jeremiah suggest what Schleiermacher never possessed.... The negation and loneliness of the life of Jeremiah in contrast to that of the kings, princes, people, *priests,* and *prophets* of Judah — the keen and unremitting opposition of Paul to *religion* as it was exemplified in Judaism — Luther's break, not with the impiety, but with the *piety* of the Middle Ages — Kierkegaard's attack on *Christianity* — all are characteristic of a certain way of speaking of *God* which Schleiermacher never arrived at.[28]

For his part, Karl Barth explicitly thought of himself as standing in this "ancestral line," that is, as an heir to the tradition of Kierkegaard and Luther and Paul and Jeremiah.[29] Thus, throughout his theological career he sought repeatedly to arrive at this "certain way of speaking of God," this way of doing Christian theology in the Reformed tradition by speaking and writing against religion, piety, and especially "Christianity."[30]

26. *The Epistle to the Romans*, p. 232.

27. For a discussion of these influences, see Eberhard Jüngel, *Karl Barth, a Theological Legacy* (Philadelphia: The Westminster Press, 1986), pp. 54ff. See also Eberhard Busch, *Karl Barth: His Life from Letters and Autobiographical Texts*, pp. 115ff. Of the ideas that provoked and shaped Barth's thinking about religion, Christoph Blumhardt's remark is representative: "Nothing is more inimical to the progress of the Kingdom of God than a religion." See Jüngel, *Karl Barth*, p. 31.

28. Karl Barth, "The Word of God and the Task of the Ministry," in *The Word of God and Word of Man* (New York: The Pilgrim Press, 1928), pp. 196-97 (italics in original).

29. "The Word of God and the Task of the Ministry," p. 195.

30. Among Barth's interpreters, this critique of "religion" is often attributed primarily or even exclusively to his early work, particularly in *The Epistle to the Romans*. Bruce

I argue in this book that Barth's critique is, at its heart, a critique of worship. Precisely as the alleged height of piety, the most exalted religious activity, and the epitome of Christian good manners, worship is the principal target of Barth's attack and exposé. Moreover, I argue that this critique was not only a longstanding feature of his thinking,[31] but was also a

---

McCormack, for example, treats Barth's critique of religion as an important theme up to and in *The Epistle to the Romans;* thereafter, however, it all but disappears from view. See McCormack, *Karl Barth's Critically Realistic Dialectical Theology,* pp. 98ff., 130ff., 282ff. More explicitly, Hans Urs von Balthasar narrates Barth's theological development as if the critique of religion in its strongest form is found in *The Epistle to the Romans,* in a more moderate form during the 1920s, and then, von Balthasar implies, not at all (or at least not at all interestingly) in *Church Dogmatics.* By the time Barth wrote *Prolegomena* (1927), von Balthasar claims, he had moderated his critique of religion such that, as von Balthasar puts it, "religion can be saved in the precincts of faith" (p. 90). A more felicitous gloss of Barth's actual position would be: "Religion can be saved in the precincts of grace." This idea, far from being a moderation of Barth's case in *Romans,* is rather a version of it; moreover, the same idea can be found in significant detail in *Church Dogmatics.* As we shall see below, Barth's criticism of religion itself, like his criticism of sin and sinners (indeed of "religious men and women"), is always wholesale and uncompromising. At the same time, though, considered from the standpoint of God's promises, religion and its sinners can and (we pray) will be saved by God's graceful and merciful action — indeed saved precisely as "religion," in all its disgrace. Here Barth travels with Luther: God's salvation of humanity is always *iustificatio impii,* always the justification of sinners, and as such, always graceful. In short, von Balthasar mistakes one of Barth's affirmations of divine mercy toward religion for a moderation of his critique of religion; whereas, for Barth, affirming divine mercy toward religion only confirms and indeed heightens the account of religion as the actual and ongoing occasion of sin, i.e., the account of that about which God is forgiving and graceful. On this point, as on so many others, Barth's thinking takes this form: "For mortals it is impossible, but not for God; for God all things are possible" (Mark 10:27). And until the end of his career, Barth's critique of religion remained for him an essential theological theme. See von Balthasar, *The Theology of Karl Barth,* pp. 68ff., 90; see also Barth, *Church Dogmatics,* IV.1, p. 574; also I.2, pp. 298-337 (esp. p. 325). Barth's critique of "religion" can be found scattered throughout *Church Dogmatics,* but in its most elaborate and systematic form in § 17 of Volume I.2, the section entitled, "The Revelation of God as the Abolition of Religion"; see also *Church Dogmatics,* I.2, pp. 280ff.

31. Other interpreters have recognized that in *Church Dogmatics,* Barth by no means retracts or leaves behind his critique of religion. Both Garrett Green and J. A. Di Noia, for example, helpfully treat Barth's "theory of religion," one in the context of religious studies, and the other in connection with the question of "a theology of religions" and the prospects for interreligious dialogue. See Garrett Green, "Challenging the Religious Studies Canon: Karl Barth's Theory of Religion," *The Journal of Religion* (Oct. 1995), and J. A. Di Noia, "Religion and the Religions," in John Webster, ed., *The Cambridge Companion to Karl Barth* (Cambridge, UK: Cambridge University Press, 2000), pp. 243-57.

central and crucial one, a linchpin for holding together his accounts of sin, reconciliation, and redemption. Bearing in mind that, for Barth, as I shall argue, the heart of religion is worship, we can perceive the pattern in Barth's thinking: religion is the principal and ongoing occasion of sin; in God's work of reconciliation, religion is decisively transformed in Jesus Christ; and in God's play of redemption, religion is and will be brought to an end.[32]

But it is precisely here that an apparent tension, if not contradiction, opens up: how can worship be both (1) a reconciliation to the form of genuine Christian life, that is, to fully human dialogue with God, and (2) the heart of religion, which Barth describes as "the most radical dividing of

---

32. Perhaps the most significant thinker to both avowedly take up Barth's critique of religion and develop it at length in his own distinctive direction is Jacques Ellul, the late French sociologist and lay theologian. In Ellul's famous formulation, "religion goes up, revelation comes down" (*Living Faith,* p. 129), that is, religion is always a fruitless and destructive "effort to approach God" on our part, to "make our way to the heights where the god is enthroned" (*Living Faith,* p. 136), whereas revelation, in contrast to religion, is always a "coming down" on God's part, always a descent, a loving accommodation and renunciation of privilege and power culminating, Ellul contends, in the Incarnation of Jesus Christ, and finally in his crucifixion (Phil. 2:5-11). Ellul parts company with Barth, however, in at least two crucial respects: first, for all his criticism of religion as ineffectual and often harmful, Ellul stops short of describing religion as, in Barth's phrase, "the fulcrum of sin" itself, the very thing from which we require salvation; and second, though he is quite critical of Christianity as "institutional religion" (*Living Faith,* p. 154), at times Ellul writes as if there is nonetheless some pure, noninstitutional Christian way of being that is somehow exempt from religious difficulties, as when he contrasts "Christian faith" with "Christianity" (*Perspectives on Our Age,* p. 93), or when he writes, inexplicably, that on the basis of his own examination of Jewish, Christian, and other sacred scriptures, "I am practically certain that only Jewish and Christian revelation is radically contrary to religion" (*Living Faith,* p. 155). As we shall see, Barth explicitly rejects this kind of privileging of Christian faith or Christian revelation, and in fact argues that the critique of religion applies first and most damningly to Christianity — whether it be "institutional" or not! Indeed, this fundamental departure from (or misreading of) Barth can be traced back to Ellul's famous maxim: in effect, while Barth agrees religion indeed always "goes up," and revelation indeed always "comes down," for Barth these are not two separate arrows side by side, but rather a single track that, like Jacob's ladder, runs both ways. Thus in Barth's view, revelation always comes down through the utterly religious forms of "Church proclamation": "Scripture," "preaching," and "sacrament." See Barth, *Church Dogmatics,* I.1, pp. 47ff. For brief introductions to Ellul's treatment of these themes, see Jacques Ellul, *Living Faith* (San Francisco: Harper and Row, 1980), pp. 126-56; see also Ellul, *Perspectives on Our Age* (New York: Seabury, 1981), pp. 85-111.

men from God," a continual fall into "the realm of man's attempts to justify and to sanctify himself before a capricious and arbitrary picture of God"?[33] I will argue that these two views of worship — as reconciliation and as fall — stand in stark contrast, but not in contradiction. Taken together, like two sides of a hinge, they point to a fundamentally liturgical account of human salvation.

For just as God's reconciliation of humankind takes place in liturgical terms, the catastrophe of sin — the very situation, after all, that needs reconciling — occurs as worship in the first place. The cure, appropriately enough, applies directly to the disease, the forgiveness directly to the offense, the healing directly to the wound. And the fatal disease, offense, and wound of human life, in this view, arise not outside religion but rather at its very heart, in acts of worship. Thus Christian worship is simultaneously (1) an offense against God, a dividing sword, a fall into separation, and (2) the very act God transforms, a new plowshare, and thus the means by which God restores offenders to God, a reconciliation to friendship.

Understood in this way, the Christian Eucharist may be paradigmatic. For whenever it is celebrated, it is simultaneously a meal of consummate betrayal and desertion ("on the night of his arrest") and a meal of consummate joy and reconciliation ("for the forgiveness of sins"). In other words, it is a meal in which Christians at once play out the reality of our turning away from God and celebrate the reality of God's graceful reconciliation with us nonetheless — indeed precisely in the face of this ongoing turning away.

*   *   *

Finally, in Barth's descriptions of his own theological "ancestral line," the name of Martin Luther is prominent. Indeed, as George Hunsinger has pointed out, the longest entry for a theologian in the index volume of *Church Dogmatics* belongs to Luther.[34] Barth did not always agree with him, of course; but he often did. And no point of concord between them is more important in Barth's thought (and in Luther's, for that matter) than

---

33. Barth, *The Epistle to the Romans* p. 241; Barth, *Church Dogmatics*, I.2, p. 280.

34. George Hunsinger, "What Karl Barth Learned from Martin Luther," in *Disruptive Grace: Studies in the Theology of Karl Barth* (Grand Rapids: Eerdmans, 2000), p. 279.

the idea that human sinners are saved by God's gracious action in such a way that they remain thoroughgoing sinners: they are, in Luther's famous formulation, *simul iustus et peccator,* simultaneously righteous and sinners, "holy" and "profane."[35] In Chapter 4, I give a close reading of Luther's *simul* doctrine, and I argue that, for Luther, the *simul* is not just an idea to be thought but also a particular liturgical form of Christian life to be lived out, namely, the liturgical form of penitence, which is ultimately the form of baptism for Luther.[36] Thus I show how Luther's well-known

35. For a discussion of how Luther's *"simul"* doctrine likely influenced Barth, and how Barth developed it, see Hunsinger, "What Karl Barth Learned," pp. 295ff.

36. Like Barth, Luther is not often read as a fundamentally liturgical theologian; and yet, as in Barth's case, his work can be fruitfully read this way. Luther's chief interpreters tend to treat his well-known doctrine of justification, for example, as a polemic directed against the doctrinal alternatives of his day. And surely it was that. But as I will show, it was also a doctrinal polemic articulated and championed with a particular form of liturgical life in mind — namely, penitential, baptismal life — that (1) helped to provoke and drive the polemic in the first place, (2) substantively determined the doctrine as it was formulated, and thus (3) constituted the doctrine's end or goal, the way of life toward which the doctrine was supposed to direct Christian men and women. Like Barth, Luther thought through worship and conceived of Christian life as a life lived through worship. And thus, like Barth, Luther cannot be read well as long as his ideas about key doctrines such as justification are interpreted as if they stand apart from or beside his ideas about worship, especially since for Luther — as for Barth — these ideas so often come together. The point here is not merely to *connect* Luther's doctrinal work on justification, say, to his ideas about worship (for this his chief interpreters do well enough, typically arguing that this or that idea about worship follows from this or that theological position), but rather to show how, for Luther, such doctrinal work is constitutively and fundamentally liturgical from the very first. At bottom, the difficulty here may have to do with disciplinary lines in modern centers of theological education, i.e., with an institutional and conceptual division of labor whereby texts on Luther's theology end up on one shelf (or on one syllabus) and texts on Luther's ideas about worship end up on another. And this scholastic divide between theology and worship, far from being peculiar to Luther studies, in fact extends across most Western theological schooling. It is a radical problem, and scholars of Christian theology and liturgy alike would do well to uproot it. For representative overviews of Luther's theology, see, e.g., Heiko A. Oberman, *Luther: Man Between God and the Devil* (New Haven: Yale University Press, 1989); Paul Althaus, *The Theology of Martin Luther* (Philadelphia: Fortress, 1966); Alister E. McGrath, *Luther's Theology of the Cross: Martin Luther's Theological Breakthrough* (Oxford: Basil Blackwell, 1985); M. Brecht, *Martin Luther* (Philadelphia: Fortress, 1985); Karl Holl, *What Did Luther Understand by Religion?* (Philadelphia: Fortress, 1977); and B. Lohse, *Martin Luther's Theology* (Minneapolis: Fortress, 1999). For a treatment of Luther on worship, see Vilmos Vajta, *Luther on Worship* (Philadelphia: Fortress, 1958).

doctrine of justification by "faith alone" entails a distinct way of life for Christians, namely, an ongoing penitential pilgrimage, along which the Christian is "continually baptized anew."[37] Indeed, it is possible that Luther's penchant for thinking through liturgy contributed to Barth's. But, in any case, I argue that Luther's liturgical account of his *simul* doctrine is an interpretive key for understanding how Barth's seemingly conflicting construals of worship — as fall and as reconciliation — may be fruitfully held together.

My argument runs as follows. In Chapter 1, I sketch Barth's view of worship as fall, and I show how his critique of "religion" as the original and ongoing occasion of humanity's estrangement from God is, at its heart, a critique of worship. In Chapter 2, I turn to a close reading of Genesis 2–4, and I propose an interpretation of that passage that supports, clarifies, and extends Barth's case. That is, I argue that the opening biblical story of humankind's creation, fall, and exile east of Eden is also the story of the tragic rise of liturgy — *leitourgia* (literally "the work of people") — in human life. Thus Barth's critique of religion and worship effectively opens up a new reading of this key narrative, and the narrative, in turn, opens up ways to elaborate and build on Barth's critique.

In Chapter 3, I outline Barth's contrasting view of worship as God's work of reconciliation in Jesus Christ, the liturgical solution to the liturgical crisis outlined in Barth's critique and, by extension, in Genesis 2–4. To put it briefly, Barth argues that God the Son overcomes the catastrophe of worship by undertaking it, that is, by reworking its basis, direction, and purpose. God gracefully transforms worship from (1) a disastrous procedure carried out "over against" God "in the name" of allegedly independent human beings, into (2) a reconciling event carried out "in, with, and through" God "in the name of Jesus Christ." Thus *leitourgia,* as the work of people apart from God, is in Christ transformed into the work of people-with-God. Thus the ongoing Christian attempt to "make a name for ourselves" (Gen. 11:4) is in Christ transformed into a life in the name of Jesus Christ. Along the way, I bring into sharp relief the apparent contradiction between these two construals of worship — as fall and as reconciliation — and thus set the stage for Chapter 4.

There I turn to a close reading of Luther's doctrine of *simul iustus et*

---

37. Martin Luther, *The Babylonian Captivity of the Church,* in *Three Treatises* (Philadelphia: Fortress, 1970), p. 197.

peccator, arguing that Luther's liturgical account of that doctrine may provide an interpretive key for understanding Christian worship as simultaneously fall and reconciliation. The *simul* doctrine, I will show, crucially helps guard against two paradigmatically *religious* mistakes: first, the mistake of thinking that sin disqualifies sinners from God's saving work in Jesus Christ; and second, the mistake of thinking that God's saving work in Jesus Christ exempts Christianity from the critique of religion. Finally, in Chapter 5, I argue that conceiving of liturgy in this way, as both fall and reconciliation, entails an eschatological view of liturgy's end. For in God's promised play of redemption, of which humans are given a foretaste "already" but decisively "not yet," their alienation from God will no longer be possible. And likewise, in God's promised play of redemption, God's reconciliation of humanity will no longer be necessary. Christ's work of renovating human invocation will be complete, and humanity's vicarious participation in God will give way to bona fide participation in God. The work of people, and indeed the work of people-with-God, will give way to rest, Sabbath, celebration, *shalom.* Invocation will end. "Some sweet day" will dawn. The call, at the last, will give way to the kiss.

PART I

The Invention of God

An angry pope, the story goes, at last convinced Michelangelo to paint the vaulted ceiling of the Sistine Chapel. The artist protested that he was not a painter but a sculptor at his best, unfit for so difficult a task, and sure to fail. But Pope Julius II, temper flaring, insisted — and so Michelangelo began his work. He drew up designs, consulted theologians, and built his wooden scaffold to the chapel sky.[1]

Down the center of the ceiling, Michelangelo painted nine scenes from the book of Genesis: nearest the altar, three scenes from the story of creation in Genesis 1; three from the story of Adam and Eve in Genesis 2–3; and nearest the chapel entrance, three from the story of Noah in Genesis 6–9. Thus, at the heart of the ensemble, flanked on one side by pictures of God and on the other by pictures of wayward and vulnerable

---

1. For an account of the meeting between Pope Julius and Michelangelo, see Ascanio Condivi, *Vita di Michelangelo Buonarroti,* trans. A. S. Wohl, ed. H. Wohl (University Park, PA: Pennsylvania State University Press, 1999). Most critics agree that to produce such a complex and allusive work, Michelangelo probably consulted theologians in print and in person; but there is no surviving record of such a consultation. The artist himself wrote that Pope Julius simply permitted him to "make what I wanted, whatever would please me," and so the possibility remains that the theological vision reflected in the ceiling belongs to Michelangelo alone. See, e.g., Ross King, *Michelangelo and the Pope's Ceiling* (New York: Penguin, 2003), pp. 59ff.; Sydney J. Freedberg, "Michelangelo: The Sistine Ceiling," in Charles Seymour, Jr., ed., *Michelangelo: The Sistine Chapel Ceiling* (New York: Norton, 1972), p. 190; and Howard Hibbard, *Michelangelo* (New York: Harper and Row, 1974), p. 105.

humanity, are three pictures portraying the intimate life of God and humanity together: *The Creation of Adam, The Creation of Eve,* and *Temptation and Expulsion from Paradise.* The second of these, itself the fifth fresco in the ninefold sequence, is the central image of both this key trio and the entire work. At the apex and center of the papal chapel, the first man sleeps, as the first woman rises out of his side, stepping toward God with her hands clasped, raised, and pointed as if in prayer — the first human prayer — to her creator.

Some four centuries after Michelangelo painted it, this central image caught the attention of a young Swiss pastor from Safenwil.[2] If the painter put this image at the architectural center of his vision, the pastor put it at the heart of his first major theological work, though he did so via his own — perhaps surprising — interpretation. In *The Epistle to the Romans,* Karl Barth argues that humanity's fall away from intimacy with God is itself occasioned by none other than the act of worship. Thus the infamous alienation of humanity from God is, for Barth, best pictured not only as an illicit eating of fruit but also as the first human prayer. First, I will spell out Barth's argument in the contexts of *The Epistle to the Romans* and his later treatment of similar themes; second, I will argue that a close reading of Genesis 2–4 may support, clarify, and extend the case. In particular, I propose a reading of the Genesis text as both portraying and effecting a continual "invention of God," and thus as charting a "fall" that is at once a tragic "rise" — that is, the rise of liturgy itself.

In these first two chapters I argue that, by following Barth and the reading of Genesis his approach opens up, we may understand the basic human problem — the predicament from which human beings require salvation and redemption — as a fundamentally liturgical problem. In this view, the crisis of sin to which religion so urgently points arises within religion itself, and particularly arises within the pious choreography of its most exalted work.

And yet this critique is not Barth's final word on worship and religion. For, as he puts it, the liturgical problem in which humans are so embroiled is matched, accordingly, by a liturgical solution. To anticipate what Barth says later: he argues that the saving reconciliation to full humanity takes place as *leitourgia* — the "work of the people" — and is taken up, fulfilled,

---

2. Barth would not visit Rome in person until 1928, a decade later. See Eberhard Busch, *Karl Barth: His Life from Letters and Autobiographical Texts,* pp. 186ff.

and thus transformed in the work of Jesus Christ. Precisely as fully human and fully divine, this saving work overcomes the separation of sin, and thus it vicariously restores human beings to their proper and original humanity — with, in, and through Jesus Christ. I sketch this Christological solution in Part II. What follows here, in Part I, is a sketch of the human problem, first as Barth sees it and then as it may be read in Genesis 2–4.

CHAPTER 1

Karl Barth on Worship as "Fall"

1. The Work of "Religion"

Barth cites Michelangelo's *The Creation of Eve* in a comment on Romans 7:7-13, a passage in the thick of Paul's discussion of the relationship between the law and sin. "Apart from the law," Paul says, "sin lies dead. . . but when the commandment came, sin revived and I died" (Rom. 7:8-10). For Barth, "the commandment" in Romans is no archaic, cultic, or moral code, no narrow, strictly Jewish regulation from which Christians are simply exempt. Rather, Barth argues that the commandment is best understood as religious law in general, as *torah*, or "religious instruction," in the broadest terms — indeed, as religion itself. In this reading, not only Jews but every religious adult is *bar mitzvah* or *bat mitzvah*, a son or daughter of the commandment, and in that sense a son or daughter of religion. Accordingly, Barth's own heading for this section of his commentary is "The Meaning of Religion": reading Paul's "law" as "religion," Barth sets out what he takes to be religion's crucial relationship to sin, and here he makes his appeal to Michelangelo.[1]

As a preliminary thought, however, it is worth spelling out just what Barth means by "religion" in *The Epistle to the Romans*.[2] He begins his dis-

---

1. Karl Barth, *The Epistle to the Romans* (London: Oxford University Press, 1933), pp. 240ff.

2. For a general discussion of Barth's "theory of religion" in both *The Epistle to the Romans* and *Church Dogmatics*, see Garrett Green, "Challenging the Religious Studies

cussion by contending that, whatever else religion may be, it is always and everywhere strictly human work, its "frontier," or outer limit of competence, being "identical with the frontier by which all human possibility is bounded."[3] Men and women, and men and women alone, do "religious" labor, and thus the capacity and authority of religion, Barth argues, can only be human capacity and authority. Thus the identification of the frontier of religion with the frontier of "all human possibility" means, first of all, that religion goes as far as human work can go — and no further.

But the situation can also be described conversely: if religion and all human possibility share the same frontier, then human work can go as far as religion goes — and no further. Here Barth refers to religion as "the last human possibility," the outer limit of human achievement. In this way — by identifying the two frontiers — Barth also points to the finally religious character of human undertaking in general, to the idea that human striving does and will eventuate — if it is taken as far as human striving can go — as "the possibility of religion." In this view, religion is not only a strictly human possibility, it is "the last and most inevitable human possibility," the upper rung on the human ladder of endeavor to which every other rung, if climbed and surpassed, finally leads (*Romans,* p. 230). Religious conduct is not strictly inevitable for Barth — a human being "may or may not act religiously" — but it is, as the furthest reach of human grasping, the "most inevitable" among humanity's alternatives (*Romans,* p. 236). Religion, in short, is both the limit and the consummation of human labor. Yet this only sharpens the question: What is this limit and consummation? What is this "religion"?

Barth reads Paul's "law" as religion, and thus Barth's "religion" in *The Epistle to the Romans* fundamentally concerns "moral and legal ordering" (p. 232). For Barth, "the possibility of religion" is the possibility not of any particular set of beliefs, practices, or regulations, but rather of believing, practicing, and regulating at all, of moral and legal ordering per se. Its varieties are abundant, and we may and do move between them. We may, as

Canon: Karl Barth's Theory of Religion," *The Journal of Religion* (Oct. 1995). See also Bruce McCormack, *Karl Barth's Critically Realistic Dialectical Theology* (Oxford: Clarendon Press, 1995), pp. 98ff., 130ff., 282ff.; and J. A. Di Noia, "Religion and the Religions," in John Webster, ed., *The Cambridge Companion to Karl Barth* (Cambridge: Cambridge University Press, 2000), pp. 243-57.

3. Barth, *The Epistle to the Romans,* p. 231 (hereafter *Romans,* page references cited in parentheses in the text).

Barth pictures it, occupy one and then another "shelf in the emporium of religion," alternately "ticketed and labeled with this or that philosophy of life." Indeed, such change is a characteristic mark of both the religious marketplace and the religious person, who typically "changes color like a film of oil on the top of water." But while we can and do move between departments in the "emporium of religion," in Barth's view, as long as we work along human labor's maximal frontier, "we cannot escape the store." We may trade one platform for another, but we cannot reside "in the air." Barth puts it this way: "living in the world, and being what we are, we cannot hope to escape the possibility of religion." The flower of the law, of religion, of moral and legal ordering will variously but assuredly bloom. The Jew, the Christian, the humanist, the vendor of any "philosophy of life" whatever — each goes about his or her peculiar business inside the religious horizon. "Moving within the frontier of human possibility," says Barth, "I have no alternative but to appear as, and actually to be — a religious man" (*Romans,* pp. 230-32).

As we shall see, at key points in the argument, the Reformed roots of Barth's case can be traced at least as far back as John Calvin's *Institutes of the Christian Religion.* Here, for example, Barth's claim that full-blown human work has "no alternative" than to be in some form religious is both an echo and a development of Calvin's idea that "the knowledge of God has been naturally implanted in the minds of men. . . from which the inclination toward religion springs as from a seed."[4] For Calvin, even the "reprobate" unwittingly demonstrate their "sense of divinity" when they fear God in distress, or seek God in despair. "Actual godlessness," Calvin concludes, "is impossible."[5] And so for Calvin, what we might call "actual religionlessness" is impossible, too, precisely because "God has sown a seed of religion in all men" such that "from the beginning of the world there has been no region, no city, in short, no household that could do without religion."[6] Barth's development of this claim — and indeed his reckoning with the fact that many "households," in his day as well as ours, ostensibly "do without religion" quite nicely — is to define religion as by no means limited to its so-called traditional forms (churchgoing, for ex-

---

4. John Calvin, *Institutes of the Christian Religion,* ed. John T. McNeill (Philadelphia: The Westminster Press, 1960), pp. 43, 45.

5. *Institutes,* pp. 51, 45.

6. *Institutes,* pp. 47, 44.

ample, or explicit references to God). That is, while echoing Calvin's claim about the universality of religion, he develops the claim by defining religion as "moral and legal ordering." And again, though Barth does not mention it, the roots of even this development may be discernible in Calvin's argument that the "reprobate" have their own sense of divinity from which "religion springs as a seed." Indeed, in Calvin's eyes, who would be more reprobate than those who neglect traditionally religious forms and practices? In other words, for Calvin, even the "irreligious" nevertheless manifest the basic "inclination toward religion," and Barth develops this line of thought in his own distinctive way.[7]

Thus, whatever the term *religion* may indicate elsewhere, in Barth's *The Epistle to the Romans* it points to that fundamental, widespread human procedure whereby we carry out moral and legal ordering, take and issue instructions, compose and live out philosophies of life, are subject to and subject others to decrees, prohibitions, advice, and applause. For Barth, therefore, religion is the procedure whereby we endeavor to stand aright. Precisely as law, religion presents a program — *torah,* law, instructions, rules — for this good standing. Along "the frontier of human possibility," wherever human beings strive, achieve, and seek to stand, there is law, and thus there is religion — in both implicit and explicit varieties.

The term is generic: as Barth's image of the emporium suggests, the genre of *religion* includes any number of forms (lists of commandments, codes of conduct, manifestos, practical manuals), and only some of these will make clear reference to "God," "gods," or "the spiritual plane." Such references are not requirements for admission to the emporium. Rather, the retailer must only be peddling a program for standing aright, for moral and legal ordering, for implementing a philosophy of life; and for this purpose, explicit reference to divine things is incidental. Over the emporium entrance, so to speak, hangs the question: *What then must I do?* To do right, to work well, to be in the most elemental and far-reaching sense a law-abiding citizen, and to receive whatever benefits or rewards await such people — here, for Barth, is the fundamental "religious" project.

In this view, then, religion is by no means restricted to what most modern interpreters have taken it to be, namely, purported dealings be-

---

7. Whether or not Barth consciously borrows from Calvin here is, for my purposes, beside the point. Rather, my interest is to call attention to the similar framework and "Reformed resonance" between the two positions.

tween human beings and divine ones. Some religious programs may well claim to include such dealings, but others may not, and for Barth these others are no less religious. Wherever people carry out moral and legal ordering, specifying requirements and enforcing regulations, there is religion. Nonetheless, from Barth's point of view, the human being's actual situation is always in relationship — even if it is only a broken relationship — with God, and this starting point has at least two consequences for Barth's discussion of religion. First, he contends that every program of moral and legal ordering will include, if only implicitly or negatively by virtue of its vehement denials, the trace of its theological character. Hanging like a smoke screen over every human program, Barth insists, no matter how avowedly secular, the "memory of that lost direct relationship with God is everywhere retained" (*Romans,* p. 230).[8] Thus, while many varieties of religion make no overt mention of divine things, and while some explicitly disown them, for Barth they nonetheless attempt to address a fundamentally theological problem. The emporium's question (What then must I do?) is, for Barth, always posed and answered in the shadow of "that lost direct relationship with God," and thus is ultimately a theological question.

The second consequence follows from the first. For Barth, the human attempt to stand aright is correctly understood by more fully explicit varieties of religion as an attempt to stand aright before God, that is, before an ultimate tribunal transcendent and superior to all merely human tribunals. In this view, in their moral and legal ordering, the most fully articulated species of religion turn overtly and in earnest to "the relationship between men and God" (*Romans,* p. 240). In this ultimate or maximally explicit form, religion is nothing less than "the loftiest pinnacle of human

8. Barth presupposes a Christian theological account of human being and "that lost direct relationship with God"; he does not argue for that account, claim to prove it, or attempt to derive it by discovering theological traces in every program of "moral and legal ordering." For Barth, such discovery is only possible, to the extent that it is possible, by presupposing "the lost direct relationship" at the outset; but this is precisely the presupposition that a non-Christian may lack or reject. Thus Barth's case here is not intended, on its own, to prove or even argue that Christian presuppositions are necessary; rather, it is an investigation taken up from a Christian standpoint in the first place, and so in that sense is "faith seeking understanding." If it compels a non-Christian, it does so not because it has shown her or him that Christian presuppositions are necessary or unavoidable, but rather because it has shown them to allow for considerable insight and explanatory power.

achievement," the gesture in which humanity reaches and confronts its own limit. It clearly identifies the human problem and task (to stand aright before God), and it sets about this mission with matchless vigor and imagination. Here is human accomplishment at full stretch: "In religion," Barth says, "the supreme competence of human possibility attains its consummation and final realization." Thus full-blown religion — the human work of striving to stand aright before God — is for Barth the ultimate, noblest, preeminent human work.

Precisely here, however, with this evocation of the prevailing positive view of religion — or at least of Christianity — among most Christian theologians, clergy, and laypeople of his day, Barth begins his notorious critique of religion. For as he reports it, the news regarding the exploits of the human "supreme competence" finally realized in full-blown religion is by no means good news. With Marx, Barth indicts religion as an ingenious narcotic: far from helpfully transforming human beings and communities, religion "acts upon them like a drug which has been extremely skillfully administered. Instead of counteracting human illusions, it does no more than introduce an alternative condition of pleasurable emotion." Moreover, religion's failure to "counteract human illusions" is equaled by its success in propagating them. Barth indicts religion for presenting itself as not only opposed to sin and death but also as standing over against them, that is, as standing on a specious "holy ground." Assured by this misleading presentation, with "earnest and vigorous acts of piety," religious men and women "cling to religion with a bourgeois tenacity, supposing it to be that final thing of soul and sense which is deathless and unshattered" — when in fact all human labor, and preeminently all religion, can only be shattered work carried out squarely "under the shadow of death" (*Romans,* pp. 236, 238).

Finally, with Feuerbach, Barth charges that "by the consciousness of religion we make human thought and will and act to be the thought and will and act of God," effectively rendering "human behavior" as "supremely impressive, significant, necessary, and inevitable" (*Romans,* p. 236). Religion thus performs an excellent and insidious sleight of hand. When a person acts "religiously . . . it is widely supposed that he does well, and is thereby justified and established and secure. In fact, however, he merely establishes himself, rests upon his own competence, and treats his own ambitions as adequate and satisfactory" (*Romans,* p. 236). Thus Barth contends that religion, as the "supreme competence of human possibility," is not that competent after all; or better, it is all too competent as it carries out its treacherous work. Masked as an enemy of sin, religion invites us to imagine ourselves, as religious men and women, to be pious, sanctified, and free. In the guise of humility and the service of God, religion furtively extends sincere congratulations — to itself.

Here again, the fundamentals of Barth's position may be traced back not only to Marx and Feuerbach but also to Calvin and, as we shall see, to Luther. In the *Institutes,* for example, Calvin begins by asserting religion's universality, but then quickly turns to religion's universal corruption: there may be a "seed of religion in all men," he says, but there is "none in whom it ripens — much less shows fruit in season. . . . And so it happens that no real piety remains in the world."[9] This is not to say, of course, that there is no *alleged* piety in the world; on the contrary, says Calvin, alleged piety abounds. But it is counterfeit; it is "superstition."[10] It is, as Calvin puts it, some three centuries before Feuerbach, human work by which "in seeking God, miserable men . . . are worshiping not God but a figment and a dream of their own hearts."[11] Therefore, they "set up their own false rites to God," but in fact only "worship and adore their own ravings."[12] They "perform some semblance of religion," but in fact carry out "a vain and false shadow of religion, scarcely even worth being called a shadow."[13] And in Calvin's view, from the perspective of our own resources, "all" who supposedly seek God are precisely thus "miserable," "vain," and "false."[14]

The early Reformers, we must recall, were nothing if not critics of re-

---

9. Calvin, *Institutes of the Christian Religion,* p. 47.

10. *Institutes,* p. 47.

11. *Institutes,* pp. 47-48.

12. *Institutes,* p. 49.

13. *Institutes,* p. 50.

14. *Institutes,* p. 47. For Calvin, of course, the saving, sanctifying activity and fellowship of Jesus Christ and the Holy Spirit make "real piety" possible for human beings. But this only sharpens Calvin's point in this passage: namely, that for real piety to be realized in human life, we can in no way rely decisively on our own religious resources, for these resources alone are not only inadequate to the task, they are, in practice, profoundly counterproductive. When it comes to "real piety," Calvin goes on to contend, we can only rely in the first place on divine mercy, generosity, and deliverance. This basic theological choreography — a critique of religion, a consequent insistence on human incapacity to save ourselves, and then a proclamation of divine rescue — is precisely the one Barth adopts, as we shall see, in his own distinctive way.

ligion intent on reforming it.[15] The "protest" from which Protestants take the name is, at bottom, a protest against the prevailing religion of the day, a theological critique of religious practices as "miserable," "vain," and "false." But in sixteenth-century Europe, we may ask, was this critique actually leveled against religion as such, as it is in Barth's *The Epistle to the Romans*? Or was it instead always an assertion of one religious form (say, a Calvinist form) against others, and thus ultimately an affirmation of (say, Calvinist) religion? Indeed, doesn't the very idea of "reform," as distinct from "prohibition" or "demolition," imply such affirmation? Therefore, we may ask: Does Barth's radical criticism of religion stand within the Reformed theological tradition — or against it?

To be sure, early Reformed critiques of religion were always to some degree bound up with polemics against aspects of Roman Catholicism or other Reformed sects, and were often completely overtaken by such polemics. In the early pages of the *Institutes*, for example, Calvin's attack on "superstition" and "false rites" may certainly be read as a thinly veiled attack on his theological opponents. But, on the other hand, it is all the more striking, for just that reason, that Calvin does not say, "Real piety is found only among Reformers," or "No real piety remains in Rome." Rather, he says, "No real piety remains in the world." The critique is categorical. And note that it is categorical not only because Calvin takes sin's corrupting influence to be categorical, as if all extant religion comes under the critique simply because everything else does as well. Rather, the critique of religion is categorical because, for Calvin in the early chapters of the *Institutes*, sin itself is first, foremost, and fundamentally a corruption of religiosity.

In fact, Calvin, in no less important a place than his opening discussion of sin in the *Institutes*, strikingly portrays sin as a fundamentally religious disaster, issuing in both a corrupted "semblance of religion" (by which sinners hypocritically "seem to approach the God from whom they

15. The modern category of "religion," as it is used today, was of course unavailable to the early Reformers. On the other hand, Luther, Calvin, et al. were transitional figures into the modern period in the West, and their use of the term "religion" (e.g., Calvin's claim for the universality of "religion" across peoples and places, and indeed his chosen title, *Institutes of the Christian Religion*) at times bears ancestral, prototypical resemblance to how the term commonly figures today. In any case, to say that both Karl Barth and the early Reformers were critics of religion is to speak, if not quite anachronistically, then certainly analogically, across a considerable historical distance.

flee") and, as he later puts it, a religiously degenerate human nature: "[M]an's nature, so to speak, is a perpetual factory of idols."[16] For Calvin, corrupt religiosity is a primary and fundamental effect of humanity's fall away from God. Accordingly, Calvin begins Chapter IV of Book I of the *Institutes,* his inaugural treatment of sin in the text, with the idea that there is "a seed of religion in all men." And he concludes the chapter with the claim that "this seed is so corrupted that by itself it produces only the worst fruits": "superstition," "idolatry," and "hypocrisy," each one of which he casts as a differently distorted form of religiosity.[17]

Moreover, precisely because Calvin grounds this critique anthropologically — that is, at the level of human "nature" east of Eden — he ensures that it cannot properly be taken to apply only to Roman Catholics, say, or only to any other subset of humanity. It must apply across the board. After the exile from the garden, not only non-Calvinists, but also Calvinists, are by *nature* "perpetual factories of idols." Thus Calvin argues: "In all ages, this irreligious affectation of religion, because it is rooted in man's nature, has manifested itself and still manifests itself; for men always delight in contriving some way of acquiring righteousness apart from God's Word."[18] Thus our "works righteousness," that great critical theme in Reformed theology, is itself, for Calvin, an "irreligious" distortion of our proper religiosity, a good thing gone terribly, and universally, wrong.

In other words, however frequently Calvin's followers (and indeed Calvin himself) may apply his critique of religion to non-Calvinists, the basic critique itself is wholesale. It applies to human nature east of Eden, and thus it applies to every form of piety, bar none, that "remains in the world."[19] In *The Epistle to the Romans,* Barth builds up from just this kind of groundwork. In brief, we may put it this way: in the *Institutes,* Calvin sets up a contrast between the "real religion" for which human beings are created by God and the "irreligious affectation of religion" that humans actually and invariably practice on their own. Then, by way of an account of the pervasive, religious character of human "depravity," Calvin denies that such real religion is possible for human beings without divine rescue.

16. *Institutes,* pp. 50, 108.
17. *Institutes,* p. 51.
18. *Institutes,* p. 371.
19. *Institutes,* p. 47.

In *The Epistle to the Romans,* Barth picks up on this Reformed critique and denial; and then he intensifies them, in effect insisting that an "irreligious affectation" is all religion is and can ever be.

Therefore, for Barth there is no "real religion" above or beyond the degenerate religion we actually and universally find in practice. He thus breaks with Calvin decisively, but only by developing and extending aspects of Calvin's case. It is as if Barth, brandishing a theological version of Ockham's razor,[20] cuts away and discards the category of "real religion," since, even in Calvin's view, no such thing "remains in the world" after Eden. Apart from God, all we actually have is degenerate religion, and thus, practically speaking, degeneracy ("superstition," "idolatry," and "hypocrisy") is what religion actually is. Barth thus radicalizes the Reformed critique of religion (or, one could argue, makes more explicit its inner implications) by conceiving of extant religion not as a "vain and false shadow" of something salutary, but rather as merely vain and false, indeed as the ingenious hypocrisy by which human beings only "seem to approach the God from whom they flee."

In the end, then, Barth's view of religion — as "the last and most inevitable human possibility" and "the loftiest pinnacle of human achievement" — amounts to a thoroughgoing critique, a trenchant development of the Reformed tradition. Even as the last human possibility, religion is nonetheless a strictly human possibility, "flesh" and not "spirit," and as such "stands within the bracket which is defined by the all-embracing word *sin*" (*Romans,* pp. 238, 235-36). Accordingly, the "loftiest pinnacle of human achievement" turns out to be no less than "the loftiest summit in the land of sin" (*Romans,* p. 242).

But the critique cuts still deeper. Barth argues that the human work of religion is not only subject to sin, not only infected by it, but is in fact its principal occasion, the original and continual circumstance for the human fall away from primordial intimacy with God.[21] As the "last and

---

20. "Ockham's razor" was named for the English logician and Franciscan friar, William of Ockham (c. 1285-1349), who maintained that explanatory theories should be as simple as possible, i.e., all unnecessary assumptions should be cut away and discarded.

21. Here we must part company with Bruce McCormack. First, he describes Barth's "critique of religion" in *The Epistle to the Romans* as "not directed against religion as such but against *Religion an sich* — religion for its own sake." To put it briefly, there is no other kind for Karl Barth. If we flee "religion for its own sake," there is no "religion as such" or any other kind of religion, for that matter, where we may take up a new position. There is only

most inevitable human possibility," religion is the consummation of human labor, the highest rung on the human ladder of endeavor. But standing on this top rung, as any housepainter knows, is the most precarious position of all; and it is by attempting to take up just this position, Barth argues, that humanity tumbles to ruin. Barth charges religion with being nothing less than "the most radical dividing of men from God" (*Romans*, p. 241). That is, the human being's fundamental alienation takes place just when he dares, "as a religious man," to ascend and take up the religious position and posture, "to leave the region of mere worldliness and press forward" (*Romans*, p. 245).

For Barth, this fatal "leaving" and "pressing forward" can be located more exactly, even *within* the religious sphere. It has coordinates. It has a name. It is, predictably enough, the very gesture that presents itself within religious life as most laudable, blameless, devout — and thus beyond critique. In this way, it hides in plain sight. As the pressing forward that is also "fall," it occurs in the last place the religious person would expect to find it: at the very heart of religion and piety, not outside but inside the "holy of holies," not peripheral but central to the sanctuary. Its name is *worship*. To illustrate how this is so, Barth turns to Michelangelo and the central image on the Sistine Chapel ceiling.

2. *The Creation of Eve*

To return to Paul: "Apart from the law sin lies dead. I was once alive apart from the law" (Rom. 7:8-9), which is to say, in Barth's reading of it, "I was once alive apart from religion." Barth locates this "once," this human situation prior to religion, in the book of Genesis and the story of humanity's original life in the garden of Eden. There sin, the movement away from

---

religion for its own sake. Though religion may repeatedly claim to "point beyond itself" (indeed this is religion's characteristic mark), it is always, Barth contends, precisely "for its own sake" — thus Barth's critique. Second, McCormack maintains that, for Barth, "the Church is the *locus* of divine judgment." And so it is. But, as we shall see, Barth's critique of religion, and indeed of the church, strikes deeper. Most fundamentally, McCormack's language of *locus* misses or elides Barth's case that religion is not only the "arena" in which the disaster under judgment comes into view; it is also the perpetrator of that disaster in the first place. Relative to divine judgment, the church is less *locus* and more "offender." See McCormack, *Karl Barth's Critically Realistic Dialectical Theology*, pp. 282ff.

God, existed only in its "primal form," only as "the possibility that the union between men and God may be broken," and only, as Barth puts it, "in the secret of God" — that is, hidden and unknown to God's creatures. The original man and woman did not know about "the possibility of rebellion," of breaking from intimacy and "dependence upon God," the very intimacy and dependence that makes for genuine human being. They did not know about the possibility of taking up a posture of alleged independence and self-sufficiency, of doing exactly what they ought not do, namely, "as creatures, to be some second thing by the side of the Creator" (*Romans,* pp. 246-47).

This position "by the side" of God is prohibited, in Barth's view, because human beings in their original and intended state are not "some second thing": "Originally, there was no separation. . . . The world was originally one with the Creator, and men were one with God." Thus, according to Barth's interpretation of Romans 7 and Genesis 1–3, there were not two things in the first place, or many things, but one. God was all in all. The rebellion of sin was only a possibility, "God's secret" withheld from human knowledge. The "once" before law, before religion, was characterized first of all by the union of God with God's creation (*Romans,* pp. 246-47).

This union, however, was not the union of identity, since, even in Eden, human beings were human beings, and God was God. Humanity — 'adam[22] — lived and acted in the garden with genuine human freedom, but this freedom was always with, in, and through God. For Barth, the garden originally was not void of difference — only "separation." Therefore, the original union was the union of intimate fellowship, communion, and above all "the equality of friendship" (*Romans,* p. 247). Human beings were free to live and act, but only in this communion, only "in dependence upon God" as Creator, sustainer, partner, and friend. In this original partnership, God always occupied the position of priority and

22. Hebrew 'adam, "humanity," "the human being." At least some of the controversy and confusion, especially among readers unfamiliar with Hebrew, over whether Genesis 1–3 should be read as "history" or "myth" might be clarified if this term's meanings were more widely known. The English terms "Adam" (KJV, RSV) and "the man" (NRSV), for example, give no indication of the comparatively broad semantic range of the Hebrew word, and so they effectively present 'adam as an apparently specific historical individual. Fewer readers in English, however, would be tempted to read this way if the story of 'adam were rendered as the story of a person named "Humanity."

power, and *'adam* was always properly "dependent." But precisely as "upon God," this human dependence was neither restriction nor forfeiture; instead, it was constitutive of full humanity. In the garden, to be fully and freely human was to be "in dependence upon God." Human beings were not created to be some second thing, but rather to be in union with God, partners in the equality of friendship.

And yet, in light of this "dependence," this "equality" could only be apparent: in Barth's view, God and creatures as such were not, are not, and can never be equals. Nonetheless, the intimate friendship of equals, and decidedly not the mere friendliness and good manners possible between superiors and inferiors, is what God wants with humanity. Here, then, is the meaning and purpose of "God's secret": the radical inequality or "infinite qualitative distinction"[23] between God and human beings was as real in Eden as it is outside it, but originally the fact of this distinction was mercifully withheld, lovingly hidden from humanity. And this concealment in effect made possible Eden's apparent "equality of friendship." If human beings were made aware of this distinction, their dependence discovered and their apparent equality revealed as merely apparent, then for them — precisely as creatures — the idea of any equality of friendship with God could only appear as preposterous and impossible.

Aristotle defines "perfect friendship" as "the friendship of men who are good, and alike in excellence"; but for Barth, with respect to "excellence," God and humanity are in no way alike. As the philosopher puts it, since "the gods . . . surpass us most decisively in all good things," they are far "removed" from us; and "when one party is removed to a great distance, as God is, the possibility of friendship ceases."[24] Once the secret discrepancy of excellence between God and creatures becomes known to human beings, once their utter dependence on God is unveiled, then for them the equality of friendship with God, the genuinely intimate posture of true fellowship, becomes inconceivable.

But God desires just this fellowship, and thus withholds this knowledge. Amid all the gifts of the garden, an entire landscape of permission and enjoyment — there is this one exception, this single secret. God pro-

---

23. The phrase is Kierkegaard's; see *Romans,* p. 10.

24. Aristotle, *Nicomachean Ethics,* 1156b 7; 1159a, 4; see also 1158b, 33-35: "If there is a great interval in respect of virtue or vice or wealth or anything else between the parties . . . then they are no longer friends, and do not even expect to be so."

hibits the eating of the fruit of one tree, "the tree of the knowledge of good and evil," which Barth glosses as the tree of "the knowledge of the contrast between the primal state [i.e., good] and its contradiction [i.e., evil]" — that is, the contrast between the union of friendship and the separation of sin. As long as human beings were ignorant of the radical inequality between them and God, friendship with God was possible; and as long as separation, the contradiction of this friendship, was likewise unknown, it could not and would not arise.

Thus, in Barth's view, the divine discretion amounts to nothing less than the gift of life with God. With respect to the infinite distinction and radical dependence between creator and creature, so long as creaturely "ignorance prevailed, the Lord walked freely in the garden in the cool of the day, as though in the equality of friendship." Everything hangs on the phrase "as though." To allow for a fellowship of apparent equals, the radical inequality and dependence between God and humanity could only remain "God's secret," hidden because God desires this fellowship with human beings, this intimate friendship, this walking together in the cool of the day (*Romans,* p. 247).[25]

But the idea that a divine secret is an indispensable condition of the original, intended intimacy between humanity and God may appear counterintuitive at first glance, even troubling. For does secrecy not undermine intimacy? Does not a secret imply shadows and mischief, distance and deception, while friendship, by contrast, implies openness, disclosure, and plenty of light? Barth might first respond to this challenge by referring to Genesis 2: there the famous divine prohibition, after all, is against eating the fruit of the tree of the knowledge of good and evil; and so in any case, however this "tree" is to be interpreted, some kind of knowledge, some "knowing" and "not knowing," is fundamentally at stake (Gen. 2:17). There is something knowable in the garden that is nev-

---

25. Though Barth does not mention it, Kierkegaard may be influential here as well. For Barth's theme of divine secrecy as a condition of divine-human friendship recalls Kierkegaard's "poetic" treatment of the Incarnation: "The king could have appeared before the lowly maiden in all his splendor . . . and let her forget herself in adoring admiration. This perhaps would have satisfied the girl, but it could not satisfy the king, for he did not want his own glorification but the girl's." Thus, "[i]n order for unity [of love] to be effected, the god must become like this one. He will appear, therefore, as the equal of the lowliest of persons . . . consequently, the god will appear in the form of a *servant.*" See Kierkegaard, *Philosophical Fragments* (Princeton, NJ: Princeton University Press, 1985), p. 31.

ertheless better left unknown to human beings, that is, better left as "God's secret," and the fact that it does not remain so leads directly to humanity's exile. From a strictly exegetical point of view, then, the interpretive question is not *whether* a divine secret is a key condition of humanity's original situation with God in Eden, but *what* that secret is, and exactly how it conditions the original divine-human friendship. For Barth, that secret is the possibility of sin, of separation and estrangement from God. Thus we may note in passing the ironic ambiguity of theological work in this view: the assiduous examination of sin, so fundamental to Christian theology, turns out to be an examination of exactly what never should have been examined in the first place!

But the plausibility of this strange coupling — secrecy as a condition of intimacy — goes well beyond interpretive fidelity to Genesis. For even in the most familiar and intimate relationships between human beings, neither knowledge nor disclosure is ever total. Healthy, flourishing intimacies between friends, lovers, and family members are invariably attended, and indeed partly constituted, by a thousand loving secrets, that is, discreet withholdings of what should not be disclosed. Or, to flip the coin over, intimacy's openness is always structured, shaped, and made possible by intimacy's discretions. There are always things we do not know, as well as things we should not know. Genuine intimacy involves secrecy, not secrecy that covers up what should be uncovered, but secrecy that — out of love and wisdom — refrains from uncovering what should remain covered. This is especially clear, of course, wherever there is significant inequality between the parties, as between, say, parents and children.

Think of the care mothers and fathers use in managing their children's knowledge: knowledge of their parents, certainly, but also knowledge of the world (in all its unspeakable "good and evil"), and, in some instances, knowledge of themselves. In each of these spheres it is always possible to "know too much"; and caring parents, well aware of this danger, actively guard against it. In love and wisdom, they keep secrets. They withhold what should be withheld. For the beloved child is not able or ready to know everything the parent knows (indeed, how much more so in the case of a beloved child of God!). Therefore, the caring parent, human or divine, does not only lovingly reveal reality to her children; in key instances she also lovingly conceals it. For example, a mother may conceal from her young child the real possibility that their profoundly interdepen-

dent relationship is vulnerable to rupture, that there is a conceivable scenario in which the child could become radically and unnaturally separated
and estranged from her parents. In love and wisdom, as her baby plays and
sleeps at her breast, the child's mother keeps this secret to herself.[26]

In Barth's reading of Genesis, humanity was originally protected by
precisely this divine love and discretion, by God's secret about the possibility of humanity's separation from God. But this intimate "once," like
every mythological "once," was and is disrupted by a disastrous "and
then." The original man and woman do take up the fatal position as some
second thing by the side of the Creator: they do discover the "as though,"
they do realize "the possibility of rebellion," and they embark on a course
of alleged independence and self-sufficiency. They do, in a word, *fall* —
away from intimate union with God and into the disunion and separation
of sin. In an important sentence, Barth glosses the original divine secret
this way: "Men ought not to know that they are merely — men" (*Romans,*
p. 247). And yet this is just what the first man and woman come to know,
not only that they are "merely" man and woman, but also that God is
"merely" God.

For humanity, the departure from union and friendship with God is
also an arrival at an entirely new vantage point. Once the radical distinction between God and humanity is laid bare, human beings for the first
time appear to themselves as "merely" human beings, that is, human beings conceived as mere creatures apart from intimate union with God.
Thus we might say that "mere humanity" is, in this sense, an idea invented
in Eden. And likewise, "mere God" comes into human view at precisely
this point, that is, God conceived as apart from intimate union with human beings. So the story of the break from divine-human friendship is
also the story, from the human point of view, of the invention of God. In
this way, the possibility of rebellion becomes a reality. Just as the Latin
invenire ("to find out, to come upon") is the root of the English word "invention," the first couple's discovery of God's secret is, in Barth's account, the root of twin conceptual inventions: 'adam-alone and God-
alone. Intimate friendship is broken. In their rebellion, human beings

26. Think, too, of the damaging ways in which children and adults come to "know too
much" in times of war, strife, disaster, abuse, or other trauma, and likewise, the ways in
which loving caregivers appropriately withhold certain facts or shield certain situations
(i.e., "keep secrets") in these contexts.

strive to be "some second thing"; likewise God, once an intimate friend, now, for the first time, becomes in their eyes merely . . . God. The "once" gives way to the "and then." The original situation, which was prior to religion, gives way to religion. For this rebellion, Barth argues, this invention, this fall takes place as religion.

"Look how Michelangelo has depicted the 'Creation of Eve,'" Barth writes, turning to the heart of his case:

> [I]n the fullness of her charm and beauty she rises slowly, posing herself in the fatal attitude of — worship. Notice the Creator's warning arm and careworn, saddened eyes, as He replies to Eve's gesture of adoration. She is manifestly behaving as she ought not. Eve — and we must honor her as the first "religious personality" — was the first to set herself over against God, the first to worship Him; but, inasmuch as *she* worshipped *Him,* she was separated from Him in a manner at once terrible and presumptuous (*Romans,* p. 247).

Religion breaks onto the scene, not as dogma, or creed, or charity, but precisely as "the gesture of adoration," precisely as worship. Here is "the fatal attitude," the model performance of the "ought not": for here, Barth argues, the first woman sets herself "over against God" and is thereby separated from God and from all possibility, as far as she is concerned, of intimate friendship with God. Worship, with its characteristic adoration and reverence and confession and praise, effectively excludes all equality of friendship from the relationship of humanity to God. Indeed, Barth charges that worship is in fact the reversal of this friendship, testifying as it does — in prayers and hymns and sermons and ceremonies — to the most drastic inequality between Creator and creatures that human beings can imagine. At every turn, worship reminds and insists that "God is in heaven, and thou art on earth" (Eccles. 5:2); at every turn, *leitourgia,* the proper "work of people," is understood and carried out as the work of adoration. And yet, for Barth, this liturgy is exactly the work that God originally did not intend for human beings: "Notice the Creator's warning arm and careworn, saddened eyes." Insofar as worship adores and reveres and sets God apart, it is "the fatal attitude," the gesture that in effect sets human beings apart from the union and intimate friendship with God for which they were created. Humankind's fall, we might say, is a fall to our knees, a "terrible and presumptuous" fall — into prayer.

41

The Creation of Eve, from the ceiling of the Sistine Chapel, by Michelangelo Buonarroti

Photo credit: Erich Lessing/Art Resource, NY

This fall is terrible, according to Barth, insofar as it disrupts and breaks off the intimacy of the garden. As the "gesture of adoration," worship is also a withdrawal from the original face-to-face encounter with God. Bowing their heads and closing their eyes, liturgists retreat from divine intimacy and instead take up the work of obeisance, praise, and supplication. Moreover, for Barth, this work amounts to injurious gossip: carried out in the knowledge of the radical distinction between God and human beings that is properly only God's secret, worship also lays bare that distinction, broadcasts it, makes it just what no divine secret should be — that is, manifest. Thus it takes place as a consummate breach of confidence, a preeminent talking out of turn. In this way, the practice of worship arises as a continual disclosure of precisely what should not have been disclosed.

Furthermore, Barth argues, worship not only proceeds from the knowledge of the secret, not only discloses it, but realizes it, transforming the possibility of sin into its "terrible and presumptuous" actuality. Worship takes place over against God, that is, it takes *a* place over against God, beside God, as "some second thing." What thing? The thing that presents God with offerings, makes sacrifices, delivers and dedicates goods and services: it is the thing that presents God with, in a word, *works* — or better, *leitourgia*. And here, above all, Barth says, this whole procedure emerges as not only terrible but also presumptuous.

Engaged in the original partnership, human beings were fully intimate and dependent on God for life and act and freedom. For them, God was all in all, and so human beings, as God's intimate friends, undertook every aspect of their work in the garden with God. To pick out any particular task or activity from this original work as strictly human labor, accomplished apart from God, would be to presume a fantastic and audacious brand of human sovereignty. It would require the creature to claim for himself exactly what he cannot rightly claim: a base of operations beside or beyond God. Once the "and then" arises, however, and the infinite distinction — in terms of both divine excellence and human dependence — is unveiled to human beings, intimacy and friendship with God appears impossible for them, and a brand-new task appears to be altogether fitting and compulsory. The new task is this: in order to stand aright before God, mere humanity, as utterly dependent and less excellent in every respect than (mere) God Almighty, shall present to this God earnest and suitable "offerings."

And yet this new procedure could take place only under a new presumption. Instead of intimacy and friendship with God, a clear separation must supposedly emerge between the partners, a stepping back from the original embrace in order to make room both for the formal presentation of gifts and its alleged corollary, the act of standing aright before God. That is, as a strictly human performance of offering, this new task demands clear positions, distance, and roles: a position from which to offer (presenter or donor), a position to which to offer (recipient), and thus a separation, a distance across which an offering, in all its earnest sincerity, can be conspicuously delivered. "Notice the Creator's warning arm and careworn, saddened eyes." Union is forgotten; one becomes two, and human beings — precisely as merely human — busy themselves with *leitourgia*.

To put it another way, in worship *'adam* for the first time carries out "independent action," and this, according to Barth, is expressly prohibited: "Men ought not to be independently what they are in dependence upon God," for "when their direct relation with Him gives birth to independent action, then all direct relationship is broken off" (*Romans*, p. 247). The human "offering" of worship is only possible by way of a stepping back, a bowing out, and an attempt to stand aright — in short, a setting over against God and thus a grasping at a specious and illicit independence on the human side. Withdrawing from the original posture of graceful dependence and recline, now human beings stagger to their own feet, raising holy hands in prayer. Insofar as worship undertakes this retreat and this offensive, insofar as it recoils from God and lunges for autonomy, then its "terrible" fall is also "presumptuous" for Barth. *Leitourgia,* the work of people as opposed to the original work of people-with-God, is the particular work that people "ought not" do. Only dependent action, human action "in dependence upon God," is genuinely and properly human, undertaken within the bounds of the original friendship between creature and Creator. Pressing beyond these bounds, humanity fashions itself as that "second thing"; under the sign of devotion, *'adam* secures a supposed sovereignty, and thus the primal communion dissolves.

But there is also a second problem embedded in human offering, not explicit in Barth's case, but nonetheless possible to build up from it. In recent decades an array of anthropological and critical-theoretical thinkers, including Marcel Mauss, Pierre Bourdieu, Jacques Derrida, and Jean-Luc

Marion, among others, have variously explored the ways in which gift-giving is implicated in economies of exchange and obligation. Bourdieu, for example, argues that every gift, precisely in order to appear as a gift, requires a "misrecognition" of this economic implication: that is, while both donor and recipient are "not entirely unaware" of the ways in which the gift in question functions as a quid pro quo, at the same time "they must refuse to know and above all to recognize it" as such.[27] In other words, your gift to me in some sense puts me in your debt (think of the complicated feelings and dynamics that occur among friends and families at gift-giving occasions); but if we shine too bright a light on this fact, then your "gift" appears to be no gift at all, but a mere mechanism of obligation, one side of an exchange, a bargain, a deal. And so we keep the light dim. In gift-giving and -receiving, Bourdieu argues, we strategically recognize and misrecognize the economic implications of our actions. On the surface we act as though the gift is entirely "free," and we may quite sincerely believe it to be, even as we simultaneously recognize — behind our own backs, so to speak — its economic consequences.

Developing and radicalizing this critique, Jacques Derrida argues that this kind of economic implication extends even to situations where the recipient is as yet unaware of the donor and gift. For the moment the donor identifies her gift as "a gift" (and so herself as "a donor"); at that very moment, Derrida insists, "the gift is annulled," because for the donor such an identification means that the gift "falls within the ambit of an economy." "For there to be a gift," Derrida says, "there must be no reciprocity, return, exchange, countergift, or debt," because such things transform the "gift" into a "trade" of goods whose values cancel each other out. But as soon as someone even "intends to give," identifying an object as a gift to be given, he immediately begins "to pay himself with a symbolic recognition, to praise himself, to approve of himself, to gratify himself, to congratulate himself, to give back to himself symbolically the value of what he thinks he has given or what he is preparing to give."[28] And this is no less true, Derrida continues as he turns to the New Testament, if in our calculations we replace earthly economies with a heavenly

27. Pierre Bourdieu, *Outline of a Theory of Practice* (Cambridge, UK: Cambridge University Press, 1977), pp. 5-6.

28. Jacques Derrida, *Given Time: I. Counterfeit Money* (Chicago: The University of Chicago Press, 1992), pp. 12-15.

one: as long as our giving takes place as an attempt to "lay up treasures in heaven" (Matt. 6:20), then our giving is actually a mode of (postponed) taking. Our giving is, in Derrida's terms, fundamentally "mercenary and mercantile" (from the Latin *merces,* "reward").[29]

Borrowing from these lines of thought, we may develop Barth's critique of worship by pointing to the ways in which liturgical offerings — our various "sacrifices to God" of goods, services, praise, thanks, adoration, and so on — are likewise implicated, wittingly or unwittingly, in economies of exchange and obligation. According to this line of critique, liturgists give in order to receive. We give, that is, in order to be rewarded in turn, to gain material or spiritual benefits (salvation, forgiveness, divine favor), some form of honor or prestige (righteousness, holiness, piety, "spiritual depth"), or indeed some combination of these goods. Religious people may deny all of this, of course, and we often do, which demonstrates nicely our own "misrecognition" of our religious work. In fact, as I will argue in Chapter 2, a devastating version of this economic critique of "offering" runs through Genesis 2–4: there we read the story of the rise of *leitourgia,* culminating in humanity's original (and thus continual) gift to God, Cain's "offering," which was nothing so much as a "mercenary and mercantile" bid for divine regard and acceptance (Gen. 4:3, 5, 7).

Finally, to fill out his account, Barth turns from *The Creation of Eve* to its well-known counterpart:

> In the fresco of *The Creation of Adam,* Michelangelo depicts God and Adam looking one another straight in the face, their hands stretched out toward one another in a delicious freedom of intercourse. The air is charged with the deep, triumphant, moving peace of the eternal 'Moment' of creation. And yet, the scene is heavy with tragedy; for it portrays the direct relation as not yet lost; it portrays the relation in which religion plays no part (*Romans,* p. 249).

With gestures contrasting sharply from the deference and distance of adoration and warning, here creature and Creator look each other "straight in the face," not touching — their difference is intact — but nonetheless engaged, reaching toward each other, intimately joined "in a delicious

29. Derrida, *The Gift of Death* (Chicago: The University of Chicago Press, 1995), pp. 109ff.

The Creation of Adam, **from the ceiling of the Sistine Chapel, by Michelangelo Buonarroti**

freedom of intercourse." Here, then, is a portrait of the "once," of the very dependence and direct relationship that is disrupted and broken in worship. Here, Barth says, "religion plays no part": that is, *worship* plays no part, the human liturgy of adoration, reverence, and awe plays no part. Adam is the picture of repose. God's face, far from any dark concern, is luminous and clear.

"So it is," Barth says, "that religion becomes the occasion of sin." The first fresco gives way to the second; "peace" and "delicious freedom" give way, tragically, to worship and religion.[30] Far from the graceful calm of the prior image, now *'adam* strikes awkward, desperate postures: the first man lies twisted and asleep, his body a contorted parody of the original reclining pose; and the first woman stumbles forward, hands anxiously raised, mouth agape in the first human prayer. Seeing with Barth, we may interpret the scene as the invention of mere humanity, *'adam* apart from the original intimacy with God, distorted now into the awkward, wretched arrangements of religion: stupor (Adam) and supplication (Eve). And along with this invention, on the opposite side of the fresco, comes its counterpart: here God stands earthbound, the great cloak — originally flowing open in a gesture at once majestic and intimate — now wrapping and concealing the divine body. This is no friend but a master, with "warning arm" and "saddened eyes," expressions that exhibit scarcely a trace of invitation to fellowship.

Here, then, as the corollary and complement for mere humanity, is the human invention of God. In both frescoes, God and the human being are spatially separated by hardly an inch; but in the prior scene, the sliver

---

30. To illustrate (1) the original divine-human friendship, and (2) the emergence of religion and thus the occasion of sin, Barth chooses (1) a picture apparently depicting the creation of male humanity, and (2) a picture depicting the creation of female humanity, respectively. This arrangement maps all too neatly onto one of the most lamentable and injurious ideas in Christian history, namely, that male humanity is associated more intimately with God and that female humanity is associated more intimately with sin. This neat correspondence alone is problematic. More troubling is the fact that, in his discussion, Barth does little to qualify or explicitly advise against this kind of association. But that he actually goes some distance toward encouraging it — claiming, inexplicably, that religion emerges as a woman's work because "women are more acutely disturbed than men are by the riddle of direct relationship" — is simply intolerable. See Barth, *Romans,* p. 248. As we shall see below, Michelangelo's frescoes can readily be interpreted in more complicated ways; more decisively, there are good grounds in Genesis 2–4 to reject any special connection between women per se (or men per se) and either religion or sin.

of sky appears overcome by the intimate gaze, "as though in the equality of friendship." In the second scene, the same distance now appears unfathomable. The cloak is pulled tight. Human beings, as merely human beings, for the first time confront God as "merely" God. A new creaturely posture is invented — "opposition to God" — and just as this posture comes into being, mere God is invented, too (*Romans,* p. 248).

This stance of opposition takes place as religion, but that does not imply, says Barth, that "religion" and "sin" are simply equivalent terms. Rather, religion is sin's principal "occasion," the circumstance within which the possibility of separation, once God's secret, is unveiled and realized in human life:

> The commandment [i.e., law, religion] is therefore the lever or *occasion* of sin: clothing time with eternity, it presents piety as a human achievement, evokes worship which knows not how to be silent before God, and names such worship "religion"; concealing from the worshipper, not merely how questionable the world is, but how utterly questionable religion is, it compels him to lift up hands in prayer, then lets them drop back wearily, and in this weariness spurs him unto prayer again (*Romans,* p. 253).

Draped in the dazzling promise of holiness — that is, the promise of "piety as a human achievement," of "standing aright before God" as a human possibility — religion conceals how "utterly questionable" it actually is. Its impressive regalia, these garments of alleged eternity, may be opulent or austere, extravagant or modest, high church or low church, since in any case the pretense is the same. For all its incessant talk of "piety" and "prayer" and "relationship to God" — and indeed by way of this talk — religion emerges as the "occasion of sin," the tragic "means of separation." Elsewhere Barth puts it this way: "Religion is the working capital of sin; its fulcrum; the means by which men are removed from direct union with God and thrust into disunion, that is, into the recognition of their — creatureliness" (*Romans,* p. 248). The infinite distinction between 'adam and YHWH is unveiled, realized, and proclaimed in religion. Appearing on the "very brink of human possibility," religion presents human beings as merely human, God as merely God, and so itself as "a final human capacity — the capacity of knowing God to be unknowable and wholly Other; of knowing man to be a creature contrasted with the Creator, and, above all, of offering to the Unknown God gestures of adoration" (*Romans*, p. 250). Thus religion is "above all," for Barth, the *leitourgia* of "offering." And thus Michelangelo's *The Creation of Eve* portrays not only the first human prayer but also the invention of religion and its tragic choreography of weariness and zealotry, withdrawal and offensive — even, we might say, "secular" and "sacred." The work of "offering to the Unknown God gestures of adoration" both inaugurates and epitomizes the whole religious project over against this God, once an intimate friend, now invented as unknown.

In Barth's telling of it, then, human beings fall precisely when and where they seek to stand aright. The crisis of sin, of separation, of being away and apart from God, takes place as the human attempt to carry out — apart from God — the "work of people." The original walking *with* God in the cool of the day could only be disrupted and displaced by an attempt to walk — indeed, to stand — *before* God. This attempt is exactly what Barth points to with his use of the term "religion." Following this argument through, we might expect Barth to advise an immediate end to all such attempts, a boycott on all such "religion." If the crisis of sin is a crisis of division from divine friendship, and if religion is indeed "the most radical dividing of men from God," then should we not make haste to reject and dispose of religion? Might salvation from sin consist in just this disposal? Thereafter, should we not be constantly vigilant and on guard, keeping everything religious strictly at bay? In short, as Barth puts it, "Should we not embark on a war against religion?" (*Romans*, p. 241).

To return to Paul: "What then shall we say? That the law is sin? By no means!" (Rom. 7:7). Reading "the law" as religion, Barth argues that, while religion is sin's "occasion," the two terms should not be thought of as merely identical. Indeed, no single human possibility — including the possibility of religion, the very occasion in which sin "comes into being" — should be understood as identical with sin, "for sin is not one possibility in the midst of others." That is, Barth argues, sin is not an alternative among other alternatives for us, one course of action on a menu of many. On the contrary, the departure from divine friendship casts its shadow over every strictly human course of action, and hence our separation from God cannot simply be erased or evaded by our more prudent selection of a more pious or radical or intellectually radiant human possibility.

Therefore, says Barth, when men and women imagine themselves to forsake religion in favor of some "superior thing," they are doubly forgetful. First, they forget that religion is the "supreme possibility of all human possibilities," that to abandon one religious form can only involve either a demotion to an inferior position or a lateral step to another religious form in the emporium of religion. The second oversight follows from the first: those who would wage a "war against religion" forget that "a like resentment must be applied to the totality of that new thing which they erect upon the ruins of the old." Pieties, Barth argues, may only be replaced by other pieties. The human attempt to stand aright — that is, religion in its implicit and explicit varieties — cannot itself be abandoned without paradoxically undertaking that very attempt. As the "last and most inevitable human possibility," religion may and should be critiqued, reproved, and reformed; but it may not be discarded: "There can be no question of our escaping from this final thing, ridding ourselves of it, or putting something else in its place" (*Romans*, pp. 241-42).

But can we not surely rid ourselves of worship? Even if Barth's idea of religion, defined as the basic human attempt to stand aright, is understood as finally inescapable, are we not surely able to escape the temple, refrain from holy offerings, and shun the work of praise and prayer and supplication? Barth's answer here, via Paul, is again: "By no means!" Any particular liturgical form, of course, any given object, gesture, or design may be incidentally taken up or left behind; but as long as human beings carry out their work within the horizon of moral and legal ordering — that is, within the horizon of religion — that work will be "above all" *leitourgia.* If we cannot quit religion without at the same time settling for an inferior position, then it follows that we cannot quit worship — the gesture that "above all" constitutes religion for Barth — without incurring the same demotion.

How is this so? As we have seen, from Barth's point of view, the explicit, full-blown forms of religion correctly perceive human attempts to stand aright to be in fact human attempts to stand aright before God, and within these religious forms, gestures of worship (i.e., acts of offering to God in order to secure good standing) are numerous and clear. Whether these donations consist of goods, oaths, or acts of charity, whether they take place inside or outside any specific sanctuary, they are all *leitourgia,* the work of people undertaken in order to stand aright before God. On the other hand, those forms of religion that make no mention of God or divine things are, for Barth, no less religious, and hence fundamentally no less liturgical. They may not be accompanied by incense or hymn-singing or solemn routines, but they are nonetheless *leitourgia,* nonetheless *works* carried out in order to stand aright. These labors may not be explicitly put forward as offerings to God or any divine tribunal, but they are put forward just the same, presented before an authoritative standard, registered as evidence of good legal standing and propriety.

In other words, for Barth, *leitourgia* is in no way restricted to Christian, sacred, or even "ceremonial" practices. Rather, as the work of people to stand aright before God, liturgy in this sense spans the whole range of human programs for "moral and legal ordering." At the heart of any such program, whether or not it explicitly refers to God or divine things, lies an ideal posture of obedience to a particular law, *torah,* or set of instructions, and thus a posture of deference and duty to a particular authority. That is, every endeavor to stand aright involves both a standard of righteousness and a program for meeting it; and whether I conceive of this standard as divinely instituted, cosmologically intrinsic, or arbitrarily decreed by a concrete human community, I nonetheless effectively present my efforts before this authority in my attempts to stand aright. To put it another way, any act of moral and legal ordering entails a moral rule, a legal order, and a regulative program for playing by this rule and maintaining this order, that is, a program for standing aright before a particular moral and legal tribunal. Again, this tribunal may be conceived of as human or divine, anthropomorphic, impersonal, or some complex combination. The crucial issue is that, in any attempt to stand aright, human beings carry out this presentation for judgment, this offering that may or may not take the full-blown form of adoration, but in any case always takes the form of human achievement, of feats of excellence — in short, of *works.* Barth's emporium of religion, then, turns out to be an emporium of *leitourgia,* stocked with the varied work of people carried out in answer to the emporium's defining question: What then must I do?

Barth thus argues that religion and worship are "by no means" to be identified with sin itself; rather, sin "takes occasion" (Rom. 7:8) by way of religion. In *leitourgia,* sin "comes into being." And yet precisely here, in Barth's view, lies the indispensable utility of religion, the sense in which it is nonetheless "holy" (Rom. 7:12) — and hence his explanation for why religion is, after all, "the supreme possibility of all human possibilities." For Barth, *leitourgia* is not only ultimately unavoidable, it is also obligatory, not because of its effectiveness but because of its "ineffectiveness," not for what it does, but for what it cannot do:

> The veritable KRISIS under which religion stands consists first in the impossibility of escape from it *as long as* a man *liveth* [Rom. 7:1]; and then in the stupidity of any attempt to be rid of it, since it is precisely in religion that men perceive themselves to be bounded as men of the world by that which is divine. Religion compels us to the perception that God is not to be found in religion. Religion makes us to know that we are competent to advance no single step. Religion, as the final human possibility, commands us to a halt. Religion brings us to the place where we must wait, in order that God may confront us — on the other side of the frontier of religion (*Romans,* p. 242; italics in original).

Understood correctly, Barth argues, the proclamations and choreographies of religion, and above all of worship, decisively disclose the impotence of *leitourgia.* They demonstrate the emptiness of offerings delivered in order to stand aright, the catastrophe of sin and separation from divine friendship — in short, the tragedy of the human situation apart from God. And for this very reason, religion is indispensable. Without it, the true circumstances of human life would go unrecognized. Without it, the very misperceptions and maneuvers to which religion itself so easily gives rise, and which in turn work to conceal religion's actual character, would have the final word.

Barth argues that religion reaches its "highest and purest peak in the Law of Israel, that is, in the assault made upon men by the Prophets," an assault with many features, to be sure, but which continually takes aim at liturgical life.[31] The prophets, as religious men, nonetheless deliver a blistering critique of Israel's *leitourgia,* and this self-critical disclosure, Barth says, is the height of religion's historical development. Indeed, as "the loft-

---

31. Amos 5:21ff. is representative: YHWH declares to Israel, "I hate, I despise your festivals, and I take no delight in your solemn assemblies. Even though you offer me your burnt offerings and grain offerings, I will not accept them; and the offerings of well-being of your fatted animals I will not look upon. Take away from me the noise of your songs; I will not listen to the melody of your harps. But let justice roll down like waters, and righteousness like an ever-flowing stream." In light of Barth's turn to Michelangelo's scenes from Genesis, and anticipating my close reading of Genesis 2–4 below, it is worth noting that the polemics against Israel's liturgy in both Amos and Micah are roughly contemporary with J's narrative in Genesis 2–4. Dating J is a controversial business, but Amos and Micah were both written in the eighth century B.C.E.; scholars date J's text anywhere from the ninth to the seventh centuries B.C.E.

iest summit in the land of sin," religion is no departure from sinful territory, but it allows us to survey the entire ground. That is, religion is, for
Barth, "the point at which sin becomes an observable fact of experience"
(*Romans,* p. 242). It is "the place where men are most evidently men,
where they are most completely removed from direct union with God,
and where human existence is most heavily burdened with its own questionableness" (*Romans,* p. 252).

And this is, says Barth, "our place." Alienated from divine friendship,
surrounded on all sides by the religious emporium, our proper posture is
to confess our disorientation: "There is for us no honorable alternative
but to be religious men, repenting in dust and ashes, wrestling in fear and
trembling, that we may be blessed; and, since we must take up a position,
adopting the attitude of adoration" (*Romans,* p. 252). The very moment we
take up another position, and another "attitude," implicitly or explicitly
declaring ourselves to be free of "the ambiguity of religion" (*Romans,*
p. 254), to have escaped the disaster of *leitourgia* — at that very moment
we replay the disaster once again, unwittingly setting out on another liturgical procession. Thus, for Barth, the only "honorable alternative" is to
both admit and enact the tragedy of adoration, to take up the stance of repentance, and to adore and repent as one who knows that her gestures
themselves by no means reverse but rather only maintain her predicament. Separated from divine friendship, mere humanity can only carry
out the work of people, and wherever this work is undertaken in clear view
of its own desolation, "heavily burdened with its own questionableness,"
and in such a way that it both "makes us to know that we are competent to
advance no single step" and thus "commands us to a halt" — there, Barth
says, religion emerges as "the supreme possibility of all human possibilities."

As the work that most fully discloses the tragic picture of our situation, religion is necessary work: "Let us be convincedly nothing but religious men; let us adore and tarry and hurry with all the energy we possess;
let us cultivate, nurse, and stir up religion; and above all, let us reform it;
nay more, revolutionize it" (*Romans,* pp. 254-55). That is, from Barth's
perspective, the more clearly and powerfully religion lays bare human
alienation from God, the more it approximates the prophetic "assault"
and disclosure, the more it makes the often veiled or disregarded separation of sin "an observable fact of experience" — the better. Thus, without
withdrawing his critique of religion, Barth situates *leitourgia* as both

tragic and indispensable, disastrous and necessary, deceptive and disclosive. Insofar as it proclaims the truth of human trouble, it may correctly be called "holy and just and good" (Rom. 7:12). But no matter how vivid and compelling this proclamation, religion does not and cannot provide deliverance from its own snares: "Religion possesses no solution of the problem of life; rather it makes of the problem a wholly insoluble enigma" (*Romans*, p. 258). As the chief witness to this enigma, and the principal example of its insolubility, religion carries out its wholly ambiguous work.

To return, finally, to Michelangelo: Barth takes *The Creation of Adam* to be a picture of that "once" that is prior to religion; yet, for just this reason, he says, "the scene is heavy with tragedy." Here in this fresco and finally in our own viewing of it, we might say, is "the ambiguity of religion." In this "eternal 'Moment' of creation," the human being and God are face to face, "as though in the equality of friendship." And yet bystanders cannot miss the "as though." If the gaze is face to face, God is obviously the superior figure, hovering with his entourage above Adam and the earth. If both hands, Adam's and God's, approach each other on the same plane, "as though" in mirrored equality, God's hand is plainly figured as the hand of creative power, while Adam's rests in a languid posture of dependence.

To gaze at this scene, then, this "delicious freedom of intercourse," is to be a voyeur. We witness the tender union, but we witness it, so to speak, from the outside. And so we are able to see what Adam, whose eyes are fixed on the eyes of God, does not see, namely, God's secret, the infinite distinction, with mere humanity on one side, mere God on the other.

In short, we see the "as though," and by taking up this vantage point, we ourselves parabolically reenact the scene in Genesis: "Remembering [our] direct relation to Him, its loss becomes an event, and there breaks out a sickness unto death" (*Romans*, p. 244).[32] For Adam above, the distinction is here still unguessed; for us below, the voyeurs, the distinction is clear. In a masterstroke of staging, Michelangelo has effectively painted us into the picture: even as we behold the original intimacy for which we are intended, we also behold the infinite distinction — and thus we cut ourselves off from that intimacy. In an unwitting, enacted parable of the orig-

---

32. Again, the phrase "sickness unto death" is Kierkegaard's; see also John 11:4.

inal fall, we are also caught up again in *invenire,* the discovery that is also invention, the "finding out" that is also "falling out." We recognize the infinite distinction that Adam does not yet recognize, and thus we reinvent for ourselves the disastrous ideas of *'adam*-alone and God-alone. The divine secret is again unveiled: precisely by surveying the scene, we come to know too much. As in all voyeurism, we look on; but we can only look, because we are separated from the situation by our own surveillance and by our own illicit knowledge.

In Barth's *The Epistle to the Romans,* this is "religion." Disclosing the truth of our loss and separation, religion at the same time renders that loss "an event" once more. Proclamation and alienation, witness and withdrawal, coincide. Barth says that "the scene is heavy with tragedy," and in the end, the scene and the tragedy include us as well, standing below, looking up from the chapel floor.

3. Revelation and Idolatry

In his later work, Barth develops these ideas, setting and reorienting them principally in the first volume of *Church Dogmatics,* "The Doctrine of the Word of God." In part three of the chapter entitled "The Revelation of God," Barth turns to "The Outpouring of the Holy Spirit," and he once again takes up the theme of religion and its place in human life. The Holy Spirit, he says, confronts human beings "in the world of human religion, that is, in the realm of man's attempts to justify and to sanctify himself before a capricious and arbitrary picture of God."[33] Barth calls this section "The Revelation of God as the Abolition of Religion,"[34] and he reprises

---

33. Barth, *Church Dogmatics* (Edinburgh: T&T Clark Ltd., 1956), I.2, p. 280 (hereafter *CD,* page references cited in parentheses in the text).

34. While "abolition" is surely a serviceable translation of Barth's "*Aufhebung,*" the German term's Hegelian pedigree suggests that Barth intends not merely cancellation but also, in some sense, both preservation and transcendence. Garrett Green, e.g., suggests "sublation" as an analogous term in English, since it may be understood at once as cancellation and transformed preservation. See Green, "Challenging the Religious Studies Canon: Karl Barth's Theory of Religion," *The Journal of Religion* (Oct. 1995): 477. As we shall see below, the more familiar English verb "to lift" may also help here, if only analogously, since "lift" can refer both to elevation ("to lift a glass") and to cancellation ("to lift a ban"). The English "to hold up" can mean elevation ("to hold up a hand") or cessation ("to hold up traffic"). Preservation, the third resonance in the German term, is not prominent in common usage of either of these En-

and elaborates the main themes that he outlined in *The Epistle to the Romans,* though now in a new context with new ends in view: religion as (1) the strictly human attempt to stand aright before God, (2) entailing the disastrous inventions of mere God and mere humanity, and (3) nonetheless indispensable. In what follows I will highlight three key shifts and developments in Barth's case: new emphases on divine revelation, on *leitourgia* as idolatry, and on the prevenient role of the Holy Spirit.

In *The Epistle to the Romans,* Barth's treatment of religion takes place as commentary on Paul's discussion of the law and sin; in *Church Dogmatics,* he sets that treatment within a chapter on how God is known through divine revelation. He still casts religion as attempted human opposition to divine work, but the change of setting makes for a change in emphasis. If, in the earlier text, religious attempts at self-justification work to oppose justification by divine grace, in the later text Barth adds that religious attempts to grasp and secure "the knowledge of God" work to oppose divine revelation. That is, while the accent in *Romans* is on moral and legal ordering and standing aright, the emphasis in *Church Dogmatics* is on knowing God, and thus a new feature of religious work comes to the fore.

In religion, Barth says, we not only work to stand aright before God — and here he uses the classic theological terms for such standing, "justification" and "sanctification" — we also "attempt to know God from our standpoint," that is, on our own terms, as we see fit (*CD,* I.2, p. 301). For Barth, however, God can only be known from the divine "standpoint," on divine terms, and as God sees fit. So the strictly religious endeavor to know God can only exclude the proper human posture for such knowledge, namely, the posture of reception, acceptance, and belief in divine revelation. Thus Barth, in *Church Dogmatics,* sums up the root failure of religion in the phrase "religion is unbelief" (*CD,* I.2, p. 299). As the ungrateful rejection of "God's self-offering and self-manifestation," religion emerges as nothing less than the contradiction of divine revelation, the human refusal to "trust," "obey," and "listen" — in short, the refusal to take up the posture of faith in the revelation of God. Barth puts it this way:

> [The religious man] does not do what he has to do when the truth comes to him. He does not believe. If he did, he would listen; but in reli-

glish alternatives, though it is interesting to note that both "to lift" and "to hold up" can also refer to theft, and thus to commandeering something into one's own safekeeping.

gion he talks. If he did, he would accept a gift; but in religion he takes something for himself. If he did, he would let God Himself intercede for God: but in religion he ventures to grasp at God (*CD*, I.2, pp. 302-3).

As presumptuous chatter, religion disrupts the proper work of listening to God; as a "venture to grasp" and to "take," religion disrupts the proper work of receiving the gift of divine revelation. Rather than accepting God's self-offering in a posture of faith and radical dependence, the religious person "steps out in a bold bid for truth, creating the Deity according to his own image" (*CD*, I.2, p. 315). In other words, for Barth, religion amounts to the human attempt not only to self-justify, but also to contrive and erect a counterfeit divine image, and in that sense a counterfeit God. Thus theology itself — to the extent that it takes up the religious task — is a sham, a fraudulent if sometimes spectacular exercise in the human invention of God.

In *Church Dogmatics,* then, religion is both an attempt at self-justification and "the attempted replacement of the divine work [i.e., revelation] by a human manufacture. The divine reality offered and manifested to us in revelation is replaced by a concept of God arbitrarily and willfully evolved by man" (*CD*, I.2, p. 302). The invented God replaces God, and thus "the knowledge of truth" is not only overlooked, it is refused and ruled out: "In religion man bolts and bars himself against revelation by providing a substitute, by taking away in advance the very thing which has to be given by God" (*CD*, I.2, p. 303).

With this shift in emphasis, Barth fills out his account of religion. If religion is primarily the human attempt to offer works in order to stand aright before God in *The Epistle to the Romans,* in *Church Dogmatics* it is also the rejection of God's "self-offering and self-manifestation." The religious person's labor is still conceived of as "undertaking to justify and sanctify himself in conformity with what he holds to be the law"; but now it is also understood as the unbelieving refusal of the divine gift. Thus Barth's critique of worship is broadened and specified in a new way. Not only does human offering make actual the separation of sin, it also forestalls the divine self-offering, setting up a religious "human manufacture" in its stead. Where religion emerges, the divine work of generosity is displaced by the preemptive and presumptuous work of people. Hands full of their own precious gifts, liturgists leave aside the gift of God. Talking rather than listening, taking rather than receiving, and, most significantly, making their own "bold bid for truth," liturgists refuse truth itself.

Accordingly, in *Church Dogmatics,* Barth frames his discussion of worship principally in terms of idolatry. Here the idea of the invention of God, which was nascent in *Romans,* Barth develops and makes fully explicit: religion and worship, he says, always entail an invention of mere God, an image of God that is of "human manufacture" presented before the assembly with a solemn liturgical declaration: "This is your God" (Exod. 32:4; *CD,* I.2, p. 302). Indeed, Barth points out that in the book of Exodus, the "golden calf" episode at Sinai does not take place in some ad hoc ceremony, but precisely as "a festival to YHWH" (Exod. 32:5): that is, not on the margins but precisely at the heart of Israel's most exalted *leitourgia.* In other words, in Exodus the golden calf is presented as YHWH himself, not a divine rival, and this presentation is made at the very height of Israelite history and liturgy, in a sacred festival at the foot of the holy mountain. In *Church Dogmatics,* Barth observes that, even in its most illustrious forms, human worship is idolatry and thus violates the first — and, for Barth, the fundamental — commandment: "You shall have no other gods before me" (Exod. 20:3). Barth considers this commandment fundamental because, as he puts it, the "transgression of the first commandment inevitably involves that of the others," that is, the idolatrous work of *leitourgia* inevitably involves "all ungodliness and unrighteousness" (Rom. 1:18):

> [U]ngodliness and unrighteousness . . . does not mean a profane and secular attitude orientated away from the divine. It is rather the worship offered by man in a fine loyalty to what he regards as the divine. . . . It is this supposedly very best that men do, this worship of theirs, which is "ungodliness" and "unrighteousness." . . . [I]n the very best that they have done they are guilty of apostasy from God (*CD,* I.2, pp. 304-5).

In "this worship of theirs," this "very best that they have done," human beings turn away from God and toward the mere God of human manufacture. Both reprising and developing the argument he had made in *Romans,* Barth says that "where we want what is wanted in religion, i.e., justification and sanctification as our own work . . . we lock the door against God, we alienate ourselves from Him, we come into direct opposition to Him" (*CD,* I.2, p. 309). In *Romans,* Barth emphasizes how "the gesture of adoration" involves a new stance of "opposition to God"; in *Church Dogmatics,* his emphasis is on how this adoration is disastrously misdirected, how, in their alleged attempts to make offerings to God, human beings effectively invent an idol, a dazzling image of God modeled by religious men and women meticulously after their own. Indeed, though Barth does not mention them here, the Sistine frescoes themselves may be interpreted from this vantage point. In *The Creation of Adam,* for example, God appears in human form as a bearded, European patriarch, as if the scene depicts not only God's creation of humanity in the *imago dei,* but also humanity's invention of God — via the brush of Michelangelo — in an *imago homini.*

Moreover, as the worship of the liturgist's own image, *leitourgia* amounts to self-adoration, and hence to humans setting themselves up as no less than God. For Barth, this desire to be as God is exactly "what is wanted in religion" (*CD,* I.2, p. 309). This emphasis governs Barth's interpretation of Genesis 3 in *Church Dogmatics:* in this reading, the serpent's promise — "you will be like God" (Gen. 3:5) — is the promise of religion, an all-too-compelling appeal to the "spiritual or pseudo-spiritual desire . . . to become as God, and to know good and evil." Likewise, in a passage recalling his argument in *Romans* that religion involves an illicit lunge for autonomy over against God, Barth suggests that religious work issues from the desire to become a "being as subject," to possess "self-determination outside the divine predetermination," and that "all other desires are rooted in this desire." He thus sharpens and develops his critique of religion as a tragic withdrawal from divine intimacy to a specious independence: "Unbelief," he says, "is always man's faith in himself." In idolatry and self-justification, in liturgy's offerings and refusals, human beings take up and live out this faith as their own. And "this faith," says Barth, "is religion" (*CD,* I.2, p. 314).

Finally, in *Church Dogmatics,* Barth amends his case by emphasizing and extending the prevenient role of the Holy Spirit in any critique of religion. As we have seen, Barth argues in *Romans* that "the evolution of religion reaches its highest and purest peak in the Law of Israel, that is, in the assault made upon men by the Prophets" (*Romans,* p. 243). Here he sees the "prophetic KRISIS" as arising out of "the evolution of religion" itself, in effect as an intramural criticism issued by religious people against religious people — in short, as religious self-critique. Within the religious sphere, he says, while it is by no means possible to move beyond the failure of religion, it is nonetheless possible to recognize the failure and spell it out.

In *Church Dogmatics,* however, Barth rejects this view: now any critique of religion, and preeminently the critique delivered by the biblical prophets, is only possible in the light of divine revelation, that is, via the event named in Barth's heading for this third part of Chapter 2: "The Outpouring of the Holy Spirit." On its own terms, religion can still be "called into question from within" as strangely "self-contradictory," "unsettling," profoundly "uncertain," or even as "idolatry and self-righteousness." But this critique, delivered apart from the light of divine revelation, "does not show religion to be unbelief. For [the critique] falls under the same judgment. Even at the supposedly higher level where it tries to overcome idolatry and self-righteousness in its own strength and its own way, religion is still idolatry and self-righteousness." In other words, apart from God the Spirit, human beings are enclosed within their own house of idols. They are, as Barth puts it, "still alone" (*CD*, I.2, p. 313). Though they may energetically resist idolatry and self-righteousness, as long as they act with their own "strength" in their own "way," even their resistance can only be "still thoroughly self-centered"; therefore, even their self-critique can only emerge as itself a liturgy, itself a proud, lonely attempt to name the truth and stand aright (*CD*, I.2, p. 315).

As in *The Epistle to the Romans*, Barth's critique in *Church Dogmatics* by no means entails or recommends an outright rejection of worship, for there is no position available to human beings beyond or above the liturgical position. No advance is possible; we have come to a dead end. From the point of view of human beings and their strictly human competence, worship is "the very best that they have done" and can do (*CD*, I.2, p. 305). And precisely here, says Barth, in this "very best" that is nonetheless "unrighteousness," in this realm where the liturgist "attempts to justify and to sanctify himself before a capricious and arbitrary picture of God," precisely here, at the end of the blind alley that is "the world of human religion," the Holy Spirit confronts human beings. Liturgists can no more effect this confrontation than the earth can effect sunlight; but in Barth's view, this confrontation can and does occur. The sun does shine on earth. By way of this encounter, human beings recognize the desolate and critical character of the religious situation, the loneliness and self-entrapment of *leitourgia*. And by way of this encounter, religion may meet its abolition, though here, too, Barth's term *Aufhebung*, with its Hegelian pedigree, points not to mere annihilation but rather to an act both subsuming and transcending religion, a divine mission "not to abolish, but to fulfill" (Matt. 5:17).

Thus, for the later Barth, in religion something still "makes us to know that we are competent to advance no single step," something still "commands us to a halt," something still "brings us to the place where we must wait, in order that God may confront us" (*Romans,* p. 242). But now this making, commanding, and bringing to a halt are no longer conceived as the work of religion; rather, they are conceived as the prevenient work of the Holy Spirit through and against religion. As strictly human striving to stand aright before God, religion is still, in a newly qualified sense, the "supreme possibility of human possibilities." But when it comes to recognizing the fundamental human predicament, the "loftiest summit in the land of sin" is as shrouded in clouds as are the valleys below.

In other words, while in *Romans,* religion at its best proclaims its own dilemma with tragic accuracy, in *Church Dogmatics,* such a proclamation is possible only by the light of divine revelation. Thus religion itself, shorn of even this advantage, amounts to no more than the bare attempt to do precisely what we cannot do alone. No cause is nobler, and no alternative is better, and in this sense, religion is still the "very best" humanity can muster. But religion itself, no matter how exalted by its adherents, is a picture of defeat. Here Barth sounds the long-standing Reformed theological theme that was so clear in Calvin and, as we shall see, in Luther: apart from God, even the most excellent human resources are utterly incapable of providing either remedy or rescue from the separation of sin. Apart from God, Barth says, the "very best" we can do is take up the hollow labor of religion and thus maintain and fortify that very separation.

The actual abolition of this labor and this separation, deliverance from the loneliness and self-enclosure of strictly human liturgical life, means a return to divine intimacy, to the friendship and liberating dependence in which human beings are centered not in themselves, not in religion, and preeminently not in *leitourgia* — but in God. This return, and Barth's liturgical solution to this fundamentally liturgical crisis, is the subject of Part 2 of this book. First, however, I turn to Genesis 2–4, both to clarify and extend Barth's case, and then to argue that his striking account of worship as "fall" opens up a fruitful reading of not only the central images on the Sistine Chapel ceiling but also the tale they portray: the inaugural biblical story of human life with God.

CHAPTER 2

Rereading Genesis 2–4

At first glance, Barth's account of worship as "fall" seems at best to follow from his interpretation of the Sistine frescoes, not from any reading of Genesis itself. After all, while *The Creation of Eve* may portray the first human prayer, where is there a mention of any such thing in Genesis 2? Or for that matter, where in Eden is there any mention of "religion"? And if there is none, can Barth's indictment of religion and worship as "fall" be said to have any grounds in Genesis at all? To close Part 1, I argue that there are such grounds, and that rereading Genesis 2–4 may support, clarify, and extend Barth's case. In short, I propose a reading of the Genesis text as both portraying and effecting an "invention of God," and thus as charting a fall that is at the same time a tragic "rise" — that is, the rise of liturgical worship itself.[1]

---

1. In this chapter I will undertake a so-called theological-literary reading of Genesis 2–4, the sort of narrative reading Barth himself frequently undertook. Indeed, Hans Frei points to Barth as a virtuoso and exemplar of this approach. In Frei's terms, this kind of reading takes seriously the "realistic," or historylike, character of biblical narratives, without "falling into the trap of instantly making history the test of the *meaning* of the realistic form of the stories." See Frei, *The Eclipse of Biblical Narrative* (New Haven: Yale University Press, 1974), p. viii. Moreover, while this way of reading by no means ignores source criticism and other historical-critical approaches — on the contrary, has frequent recourse to them — the premium is finally on the received text as we have it, regarded, in all its redacted, historical complexity, as a theological-literary whole. For variations on this general approach, see, e.g., Stephen Geller, *Sacred Enigmas: Literary Religion in the Hebrew Bible* (New York: Routledge, 1996); Paul Ricoeur and André LaCocque, *Thinking Biblically* (Chicago:

1. Eden and Intimacy

To worship God is arguably the most highly regarded activity among most Christians and many other religious people today. Therefore, any critique of worship, to say nothing of an account of worship as fall, may well be met with considerable skepticism in many religious quarters. And yet this high view of liturgical life may itself provide a starting point for rereading Genesis 2–4. If religion and worship are, in fact, as unequivocally fitting and commendable as many take them to be; if the worship of God is, in fact, no less than a chief purpose for which human beings were originally created[2] — then the story of creation in Genesis 2 seems to contain a rather glaring omission. In short, we may ask: Where is the temple in Eden? If God created human beings to offer God thanks and praise, then how is it that the first man and woman receive no such instruction, nor offer any such thing? In Genesis 2 the author J describes the garden in some detail, and yet we find in this description neither sanctuary nor altar, neither psalm nor sacrifice.[3] If these things emerge — and they do emerge

---

The University of Chicago Press, 1997); Christopher Seitz and Kathryn Greene-McCreight, eds., *Theological Exegesis* (Grand Rapids: Eerdmans, 1999); Stephen E. Fowl, ed., *The Theological Interpretation of Scripture* (Malden, MA: Blackwell, 1997); Mary Kathleen Cunningham, *What Is Theological Exegesis? Interpretation and Use of Scripture in Barth's Doctrine of Election* (Valley Forge, PA: Trinity Press International, 1995). Finally, in the following interpretation I pay special attention to the fact that Genesis 2–4, as a Christian Old Testament text, is often read in liturgical assembly. That is, in a kind of liturgical version of reader-response criticism, I seek to take account of the facts that (1) the readers of these texts often read them aloud to others in worship, i.e., they deliver them in a particular scenario; and (2) the responders for these texts are often hearers, not readers, embroiled already in ceremonial work. As we shall see, this kind of reading situation can and should make a difference in how a text is understood; thus, with respect to biblical texts, some version of "liturgical criticism" is appropriate and promising. See, e.g., my essay, "Forsaking God: A Theological Argument for Christian Lamentation," *Scottish Journal of Theology* (Jan. 2002).

2. For a theological claim typically interpreted in this way, see the Westminster Catechism's opening exchange: Q: "What is the chief end of man?" A: "To glorify God, and to enjoy Him forever." As I shall argue, this "glorifying" and "enjoying" need not be identified strictly or even primarily with worship, as they often are.

3. Among modern critical readers of Genesis, the author of Genesis 2–4 is conventionally dubbed J. The letter abbreviates the German word for "Yahwist," which itself derives from the name of God — *YHWH elohim* — that is used in this narrative but not, e.g., in Gen. 1:1–2:4a.

later in J's narrative — they emerge only subsequent to the original creation, only outside the garden, and thus only after and apart from the original friendship between human beings and God. There is no temple in paradise, and, in that sense, no liturgy. Understood in this way, the conspicuous absence of worship and religion in Eden is the first indication that the narrative may plausibly be read in light of Barth's account. Genesis 2–4 charts the rise of *leitourgia,* but the very lack of liturgy at the outset points toward the possibility that the story of this rise is also the story of humanity's fall away from God.

A second indication is in J's description of God's purpose and instructions when God initially places *'adam* "in the garden of Eden" (Gen. 2:15-17).[4] As J tells it, the earth that God created originally was not a garden of delight — many commentators link the Hebrew word *'eden* to "delight" — but rather a barren landscape. J reports that a stream watered "the whole face of the ground," but no plant or herb grew there yet, because "there was no one [*'adam*] to till the ground" (Gen. 2:5-6). Here is J's first mention of *'adam;* thus humans are introduced, even before they are created, precisely as the ones who "till" (*'avad*). Therefore, once *'adam* is formed by way of an intimate communion between the barren "dust of the ground (*'adamah*)"[5] and the divine "breath of life," God places this new "living being" in the newly planted garden of Eden "to till it and keep it" (Gen. 2:15). For J, then, *'adam* is not only the first living being in creation but also the custodian of life on earth, the caretaker created to both till and keep the garden of delight. God alone "planted" the garden (Gen. 2:8), but human beings cultivate, preserve, and enjoy it.

This third aspect of human life, enjoying the garden's fruit, becomes clear in God's command immediately on placing humanity in Eden. Indeed, the well-known prohibition against eating from the tree of the knowledge of good and evil, the "you shall not" that has so captivated many readers of the story, is preceded and made possible by an equally important, if not more important, "you may": the declaration of God's permission to "freely eat of every tree of the garden" (Gen. 2:15). In other words, in the compact narrative of Genesis 2, J sets out a suggestive an-

---

4. Hebrew: *'adam,* "humanity," "the human being." See Ch. 1, note 22.

5. A version of the apparent connection in Hebrew between the terms for humanity (*'adam*) and ground or earth (*'adamah*) may also be discerned in English, since "human" likely derives from the Latin *humus* ("soil").

thropology: human beings are the ones who till, keep, and enjoy God's garden. To care for the world, to protect the world, and to enjoy the world — this, according to J, is the original human vocation.

But what does any of this have to do with an account of worship as a fall away from God? In the first place, and in keeping with the previous point, there is a conspicuous omission, especially striking for religious readers, in this anthropology and vocation: tilling, keeping, and enjoying the garden, as a pattern of practices, lacks any reference to liturgical works of adoration, praise, or offering to God. In fact, this pattern lacks any reference to "God" at all.

The point is crucial. According to J, human beings are originally neither called nor commanded to any practice that would take "God" as its object or end. Humanity is created and commanded to till, keep, and enjoy the garden, but not to till, keep, enjoy, or otherwise confront God per se. This by no means entails the idea that human beings were originally to have nothing to do with God; on the contrary, J narrates a host of elaborate interactions between 'adam and YHWH elohim, from caring for the divine garden to creating and naming "every animal of the field and every bird of the air" (Gen. 2:8-9, 18ff.). Indeed, in J's account, originally the human being simply is that handful of 'adamah in communion with the divine "breath of life."[6] Thus J's story suggests that God and humanity were originally on radically intimate terms; but the original human vocation, the purpose for which humanity was and is created and the work humanity was and is given to do, is nevertheless to care for the world, not for God, and to enjoy the world, not God apart from the world. To put it simply, originally human beings were radically *with* God in the garden, but never set *over against* God in their work.

This reading, then, is in agreement with Barth's account of genuine human being as constituted by divine-human intimacy, so that human life and act and freedom find their place in God, but never beside or over against God, never taking God as object or end. In properly human action, God is never object but always subject: that is, God is always inter-

6. See also Gen. 6:3: "The LORD said, 'My spirit shall not abide in mortals forever, for they are flesh; their days shall be one hundred twenty years.'" That is, according to J's anthropology, living human beings are constituted by communion between divine spirit and "flesh," or 'adamah. Thus, for J, God's intimate animation of 'adam in Gen. 2:7 is no one-time event, but the beginning of a continuous condition of each human life over its entire span.

subject or open subject with whom ʾadam may live and work. Genuine human action, in this view, is always carried out in communion with *YHWH elohim,* or, as Barth puts it, in "dependence upon God." Allegedly unilateral human works, feats carried out for or before or otherwise independent from God, are only possible by way of dissolving this communion and thus dissolving the possibility of genuine human act and life.

Further, J's account of human vocation gives this act and life a particular form and program: the original and genuine human being-with-God and work-in-God is expressly to cultivate and care for barren ʾadamah, so that it might bear the fruit of delight — including the barren ʾadamah from which all living creatures are formed (Gen. 2:19) and from which ʾadam was and is made (Gen. 2:7). Thus caring for ʾadamah involves caring for all creatures, including humankind. Here, then, are the proper bounds of human work for J: in a situation of radical intimacy with God, human creatures are to enjoy, to keep, and above all to till the dust of the earth.

The verb "till" (ʿavad) is central to J's narrative and anthropology. As we have seen, it introduces ʾadam and defines God's purpose in creating humankind; moreover, God eventually expels ʾadam from Eden "to till the ground from which he was taken." The first couple's eldest son, Cain, is explicitly called "a tiller of the ground"; and the consequence of Cain's crime is that "when you till the ground, it will no longer yield to you its strength" (Gen. 3:23; 4:2, 12). At every turn — creation, expulsion, human procreation, crime — the verb ʿavad is pivotal, and thus it merits close attention.

While the English term "till" is certainly one legitimate translation, the Hebrew ʿavad admits of other primary meanings that are not evoked by the English "till." First, ʿavad commonly means "to work" or "to serve"; in most dictionaries of biblical Hebrew, this is the first definition given for ʿavad. Thus we may understand J's narrative anthropology as portraying human beings as those who not only till but work or serve the dust of the earth. This aspect or resonance of the Hebrew word, obscure in the English "till," brings into sharper focus the conspicuous lack of liturgical practices in J's report of the original human vocation: remembering that *leitourgia* is the work of people and the "service of God," we find it all the more striking that, in J's account, God commands ʾadam to work and serve not God but ʾadamah, creation's barren land.

This contrast, however, is most poignant — and in this reading, most decisive — when a third primary meaning of the Hebrew verb comes into view: *'avad* also commonly means "to worship."[7] It turns out that J does mention "worship" in Genesis 2, or at least a common word for it, but only by way of indicating that such activity is properly carried out with regard to the garden, not to God: *YHWH elohim* puts *'adam* in Eden expressly "to till [*'avad*] it and keep it" (Gen. 2:15). In this particular sense, then, the divine purpose is indeed for humankind to worship (i.e., *'avad*) but only with respect to "the ground," the garden, the *'adamah.* Therefore, the conspicuous absence of "worship" in the story of Eden is not quite an absence after all; or rather, its absence is made all the more conspicuous by the frequent and pivotal presence of its verbal sign. In other words, the term does appear, repeatedly and at key turns in the narrative, but only in such a way as to deny its ceremonial, religious sense, maintaining instead that the only fitting way for humans to *'avad* is to work and serve and till the garden, the dust, creation itself — indeed, all things great and small — but by no means *YHWH elohim.*

Moreover, as if to underscore the point, J sets alongside *'avad* another — arguably *the* other — patently liturgical verb in Hebrew Scripture: *shamar* ("to keep"). The range of primary meanings for this term include "to have charge of," "to guard," "to tend" — but also "to observe" or "to celebrate" a religious festival, for example, the Passover liturgy ("You shall keep the festival of unleavened bread" [Exod. 34:18]) or the sabbath day ("Observe the sabbath day and keep it holy" [Deut. 5:12]). Humankind, created to be *shomrey 'adamah,* keepers of earth, only later become *shomrey shabbat.*

If we read it this way, we can see that J simultaneously critiques liturgy and foreshadows its emergence. On the one hand, J excludes the "worship" of God and the "keeping" of religious liturgy from the original human vocation by invoking the terms themselves in explicit connection with the ground and the garden, not with God. On the other hand, J uses these terms to point to just what is at stake in the story, namely, the proper human vocation to "*'avad* and *shamar,*" and the improper human distortion of these practices and that vocation. That is, in this reading, J features the words *'avad* and *shamar,* in all their semantic ambiguity, to coordinate the original human vocation in Genesis 2 and the disastrous events in Genesis 3 and 4. If the divine purpose and instructions to *'adam* are origi-

7. For example, see the same verb in Isa. 19:21: "Worship [*'avad*] with sacrifice and burnt offering." See also Exod. 3:12; 4:23; Deut. 5:9; and Ps. 100:2, among others.

nally to *'avad* creation and not *YHWH elohim,* that is, to work with God and never over against God, then the story's subsequent events chart a fall from this purpose and these instructions. And this fall is at once the rise of *leitourgia,* the emergence of a new, religious set of instructions to *'avad YHWH elohim,* not creation. Thus these terms, like two hinges, sit at the center of the account. Made to *'avad* and *shamar* creation, human creatures turn — semantically, practically, and tragically — to *'avad* their Creator, and *shamar* the work of people.

2. *Leitourgia* and Separation

In Genesis 3, of course, this turning begins. As we have seen, the conspicuous offerings of *leitourgia* involve a stepping back, a bowing out, and thus a spurious taking up of a position beside and apart from God as "some second thing." Originally as radically intimate with God as the original human body's *'adamah* is with the divine breath of life (Gen. 2:7), human beings fall into the tragic separation of prayer and holy offering in Genesis 3 and 4. But the inauguration of this fall, the innovation that makes full-blown liturgy possible, is the introduction of alleged distance into the divine-human relationship — that is, distance across which human liturgists may proclaim and deliver their gifts. This distancing, then, this retreat from intimacy, is nothing less than the condition of the possibility of worship. If human beings are to carry out acts that take "God" as their object or end, they must first attempt to disengage themselves from the divine embrace, from the genuinely human situation in which every human act is undertaken in and through God. In short, the human being must move to take up the position of a subject not with God but beside God, not reclining in friendship but standing alone.

In this reading, this is where the fall begins. The hairline marks of fracture appear, and communion gives way to separation. The intimacy of "I," "thou," and "we" shifts into an entirely new situation and vantage point: a third-person point of view in which "God" may be understood to be not here but elsewhere, not as close as our own breath of life but at some distinct remove, and thus as someone we may approach and abandon, and who may approach and abandon us in turn. In the original and intended "intercourse" between *YHWH elohim* and *'adam,* between "I" and "thou," there is indeed the difference that makes for intimacy; but precisely in this intimacy there is no separation, no distance, no breach or seclusion. In the first and fatal step toward *leitourgia,* however, the intimate "with" of creation gives way to a "beside" and an "over against," and also the possibility of a "without." In Genesis 3, J narrates this fatal step as an encounter between *'adam* and an "animal of the field." Now the serpent insinuates himself into the story.

The serpent does so with a question: "Did God say, 'You shall not eat from any tree in the garden'?" (Gen. 3:1). As a question, this locution initially appears not to provide information but merely to seek it; but, in fact, it accomplishes a great deal more than that. The serpent's arrival on the scene signals a key break in the text, and his apparently simple query — the world's first question, in J's account — carries with it a set of presumptions, not only about the speech situation itself, but also about the relationship between Creator and creation.

J begins this episode: "Now the serpent . . ." (Gen. 3:1). With this single word in Hebrew — *wehanahash* — the narrative shifts markedly, and this shift itself points toward the oncoming break between *'adam* and *YHWH elohim.* With this word, a third presence, neither human nor divine, makes its entrance onto the stage. And with this word, the viewer's — that is, the reader's or listener's — gaze pivots away from God for the first time in the story, a "turning away" that itself prefigures the imminent human departure from divine intimacy. In the language of film and television, we may say that the word *wehanahash* signals a "cut," an entirely new scene and situation. The story's soundtrack changes, and a new character appears within a whole new frame.

Moreover, J marks this textual break by placing in the mouth of this new character a new form of speech: the question. In particular, the serpent's query is catechetical, a question about God, ostensibly seeking to clarify the divine instruction and thus the genuine human vocation as well. And yet, like all catechisms, this very act of asking indicates twin vulnerabilities: the vulnerability of God's reputation and the vulnerability of human knowledge. First, by evoking an unprecedented, starkly inaccurate picture of God, the question introduces the possibility of slander. Regardless of whether the serpent asks out of malice or mere confusion, his version of the divine instructions perfectly contradicts them: he replaces "you may freely eat of every tree" with "you shall not eat from any tree." The divine reputation, it turns out, may be impugned. And by gesturing toward this vulnerability, the serpent effectively invites the man and woman to take up God's defense. "Is God a miser?" he asks implicitly. "Has God prohibited the very food you need to live?" In short: "Has God denied you life?"

For the man and woman, this invitation proves irresistible; at least they do not resist it. The catechetical opening, with its implied threat to the divine reputation, calls the man and woman to complete the form, to answer, to set the record straight, to proclaim God's generosity against any suggestion to the contrary. Along the way, they may demonstrate their own excellent grasp of God's intentions. Creation's first question, then, gives rise to the first possibility of orthodoxy. The prospect of wrong doctrine calls for the right one. That is, the query "Did God say . . . ?" amounts to a summons to interpretation and testimony, an opportunity for human beings to display their expertise in elucidating the divine command — *torah,* instructions, law. The serpent makes the humans an offer, provides them with a chance to speak well and do well, and thus to stand aright before God. By way of his question, the serpent recruits the first couple into the rabbinical, pastoral, and theological role, and they are only too eager to oblige.

Second, if the serpent's catechism invites the man and woman to defend God's vulnerable reputation, it also presses them to admit the vulnerability of human knowledge. Posing the query as a request for clarification — "Did God say . . . ?" — implies a lack of clarity in the first place, and thus it introduces the idea that God may be misunderstood, by humans as well as "animals of the field." Indeed, the question's phrasing is so close to the original divine command that the first couple may well infer that the serpent overheard it incorrectly. But this small difference in words, and its great difference in meaning, implicitly raise the issue of whether the first couple themselves have heard God correctly, and thus whether their understanding is sound after all: *Have you misunderstood God? Are you sure you know your own vocation?* The serpent's question makes explicit a permanent hazard of creaturely life in general, and human life in particular: the ubiquitous possibility of misunderstanding and mistake. The very fact of a catechetical question at all, of questions and answers and differing opinions, signals the perpetual, indelible human need for interpretation, even with respect to such fundamental matters as divine instruction and human vocation — perhaps especially then. *What exactly did God say?* As we have seen, up to this point in the narrative, J has featured several kinds of speech, both divine and human: permission, command, reflection, declaration; but so far there have been no questions, no discussion, no direct address aimed at eliciting a spoken answer. The serpent introduces this new form of talk, and thus his query founds not only theological conversation — the preeminent "crafty conversation"! — but also conversation itself, unveiling the perpetual human needs for interpretive discussion, corroboration, reassessment, and doubt.

The serpent thus points to the idea that human knowledge, even at its most fundamental, is uncertain, open to question and challenge, and in that sense is vulnerable, exposed, and "naked." This last term — 'arom ("naked") — is crucial for J: the serpent appears on the scene immediately after the first man and woman are described as "naked ['arummim] and not ashamed"; by way of a conspicuous pun, J links this feature of the human situation explicitly to the serpent by describing him as "crafty" ('arum) (Gen. 2:25, 3:1).[8] That is, J punningly connects the serpent's "crafty" ('arum) actions with the "naked" ('arummim) vulnerability of humankind. And as 'arum sets its sights on 'arummim, human beings scramble not only to God's defense but to their own as well. Faced with the prospects of these twin vulnerabilities, human beings speak up; they take their stand. The serpent stops short of heresy, but he unveils its possibility in the form of a question. For the first couple, this new possibility goes neither unnoticed nor unanswered.

The woman, with her husband standing "with her" in mute approval (Gen. 3:6),[9] first attempts to vindicate God's benevolence: "We may eat of the fruit of the trees in the garden" (Gen. 3:2). For the first time inhabiting the rabbinical, pastoral role, the woman and man paraphrase and clarify the divine command with precision, effectively correcting the errant version nested in the serpent's question. But they do not stop there. The

8. While the English word "crafty" is often used pejoratively, the Hebrew term is more ambivalent: in its negative sense, as "crafty" or "cunning," it appears, for example, in Job 5:12-13; in its positive sense, as "sensible," "clever," or "prudent," it appears in Prov. 8:5, 14:15, and 22:3. The term's ambiguity, then, enhances the serpent's ambiguous role in the narrative: he can neither be solely saddled with blame, as the woman tries to do (Gen. 3:13), nor solely exempted from it.

9. A further indication that the woman answers not only for herself but also on behalf of her husband is obscured in English: in the Hebrew, the serpent's question is in the second-person plural, and so might be translated: "Did God say, 'You two shall not eat . . . ?'" — or better, taking the readers of the narrative into account, "Did God say, 'You all shall not eat . . . ?'" (Gen. 2:1).

woman next delivers the first sermon, the first human words explicating the divine Word, and like so many of her progeny, she preaches for too long! She has already answered the serpent's question, but she goes further, anticipating a question the serpent has not asked, recounting God's prohibition as she and her husband understand it. That is, the woman and man sense an implicit indictment in the serpent's question: the idea that they, misunderstanding and thus frustrating the divine intention, have not done well before God. Accordingly, they rise to refute the phantom charge. Now they will show that they are not only well aware of God's generosity but also of the actual prohibition, and that they have obeyed it conscientiously and commendably. Now their sermon will vindicate not only God's name but their own as well.

And so the woman quotes the original directive. Rather, she misquotes it, adding the gratuitous clause "nor shall you touch it" (Gen. 3:3) to God's command that they not eat of the tree of the knowledge of good and evil (Gen. 2:17). As if to certify and make a show of their own impeccable orthodoxy and obedience, humans overstate the divine prohibition. They manufacture an amendment. They lie — a somewhat well-intentioned lie perhaps, but a lie nonetheless — anxiously aiming to preempt the potential charge that they have mistaken God's instructions, that they have been disobedient, that their creaturely vulnerabilities have led to disaster.[10] With this lie they have added merely human words to the divine Word, and thus the first concrete "work of people," a merely human prohibition against touching the tree, is born.[11] By announcing this liturgical design, human

10. Some commentators have suggested that the woman's amendment is not dishonest: rather, they argue, since she was not present at the time of the original command, her husband must have misinformed her. In the first place, however, this view ignores the plausible reading that both man (*'ish*) and woman (*'ishah*) are created after the command is given (2:21ff.) — separated, we might say, out of the original *'adam,* or "human being" — and thus that the woman was privy to the original instruction just as well as the man was. Further, since her husband is silently "with her" (3:6), they have told a lie in any case: either the woman lies and the man joins her in silence, or the man lies by allowing the untruth to stand.

11. It is worth remembering that, for J, *'adam*'s original vocation was to till or serve the ground so that every plant may grow, including the tree of the knowledge of good and evil. God places *'adam* in Eden when it is still a wasteland; the garden is planted, but it has not yet appeared "out of the ground" (Gen. 2:8-9). In other words, *'adam* cares for the garden's trees from the seed stage on, and since caring well for saplings and trees frequently involves touching them, the woman's amendment, far from simply an addendum, may be under-

beings confidently declare (a little too loudly) that they are beyond re-
proach, that they have been unimpeachably careful (indeed, more careful
than God has instructed them to be), and thus that they do stand aright before God. With this apparently confident declaration, then, they betray
their anxiety, deny their vulnerabilities, and thus deny their creatureliness.
The hairline fissures grow wider. Now religion insinuates itself into the
story.

In *The Epistle to the Romans,* Barth calls the woman "the first 'religious personality.'"[12] We may add, however, that if she is indeed the first
rabbi and preacher, appending merely human words to the divine Word,
and thus anxiously exaggerating God's command, then her husband is simultaneously the first religious congregant, no less anxious and responsible in his silent, all-too-agreeable piety and discipleship. He, too, takes up
the religious vocation. Originally not ashamed of their earthy vulnerability, now human beings stammer to insist on both divine generosity and
their own admirable compliance. Confronted with the risks of creaturely
life — that is, with the fact that they are naked and vulnerable creatures —
human beings rush to declare safety, establish a sanctuary, and demonstrate their good standing. In this way, under the guise of good doctrine
and adamant devotion, religion appears on the human horizon.

By now, in this reading, the serpent's chief work is done. Or better,
the disastrous human work of separation — of which the serpent's remarks are only the catalytic occasion — is already set in motion. With
their gratuitous amendment, the first couple makes this work of separation manifest, but the decisive, inaugural maneuver is even earlier in the
narrative. Indeed, as soon as the woman and man respond to the serpent's
question with their own answer, they take the fatal step. They engage him
on his own terms, and from his point of view. That is, when the serpent
appears, a third person arrives on the scene, coming between *'adam* and
YHWH elohim by way of a question about one posed to the other.

With this interpolation comes a new vantage point, a new third-person
perspective on the interpersonal arrangements of creation. Genesis 2's narrative of intimacy, gift, and collaboration, in which the second-person
"you" or "thou" and the first-person "I" and "we" frame the interactions be-

stood to contradict the original instruction: it completely cuts off human beings from a part
of creation for which they are called to care.

12. Barth, *Romans* (London: Oxford University Press, 1933), p. 247.

tween *'adam* and *YHWH elohim,* is now disrupted by a new point of view, a perspective from which it is deemed possible, for the first time, to speak *about* God at a distance, as if God were not privy to the conversation: "Did God say . . . ?" If God is at hand, then obviously the question is better put to God; the very act of putting the question to the woman implies that God is not at hand but is elsewhere, distant, out of range. In this new scenario, and on this new footing, a new thing is possible: hearsay, rumor, and gossip about God.

This picture of the relationship between Creator and creation is only implicit, hidden away in presupposition and implication; but it is nonetheless formative for what follows. With his question, and particularly with his subsequent discourse — "You will not die; for God knows . . ." (Gen. 3:4-5) — the serpent conjures up a world in which such talk is possible, a frame within which creaturely action takes its place, an account of God's relationship to creation, and thus an account of God. That is, the serpent's remarks imply that God is not privy to the conversation, that God is somewhere else. Therefore, they presuppose a picture of God as someone who comes and goes, and with whom intimacy may come and go accordingly. In short, for the serpent, God may be absent, remote, secluded, out of sight and out of mind. J's account of intimacy and friendship — human beings with God, and God with human beings, as close as their own breath of life — now gives way to the serpent's third-person account, where humans are some second thing beside God, not in and with but set over against their Creator. To return to Michelangelo, the intimate gaze between *'adam* and *YHWH elohim* is now interrupted and opposed by another, serpentine perspective, looking up from below: this third vantage point invents God as a distant, alien power. At the same time, as the woman and man take up the serpent's vantage point, and as we do from the Sistine Chapel floor, they reinvent themselves as mere voyeurs. Looking in on friendship from the outside, *'adam* becomes an outsider.

To put it differently, in the serpent's view, God may be now with us, now without us; humankind may, in turn, approach or retreat from God, drawing near or hiding out, whispering gossip, speaking not with but about their Creator. The world is thus construed as a place where merely human activity — *leitourgia* — is possible, where man and woman may live and labor on their own, beside and apart from God, and where the divine presence and activity move like a searchlight over the outer grounds of a prison, or a lantern among the rooms of a house. Its range may be comprehensive, but there are always places to hide. In short, in this view it is possible to be without and away from God. Indeed, when the man and woman eventually attempt to "hide themselves" from *YHWH elohim* after their transgression (Gen. 3:8), they merely act according to the framework already presupposed well before the illicit meal, already implied by the serpent's catechism. By asking and speaking about God as if God were remote and out of earshot, the serpent presents *'adam* with the possibility of separation; by engaging the serpent in conversation on these terms, the woman and man make separation a reality.

They, too, talk *about* God. They, too, cite God incorrectly, with their own words, though they do so not in the form of a question but in the form of an answer. In contrast to the serpent, they take their stand; and, adopting the serpent's perspective on God and creation, they now conceive themselves to stand alone, set over against and apart from God. Distance, the chief condition for the possibility of *leitourgia,* opens up between *'adam* and *YHWH elohim,* and the work of separation takes up its concluding choreography. In the very midst of the Garden of Eden, the inaugural liturgy, complete with word and sacrament, begins: *'adam* intones the sermon's opening words, interpreting the divine command; now the serpent ascends the pulpit and delivers his invitation to the meal.

In *The Epistle to the Romans,* Barth calls the serpent "the first shepherd of the souls of men," that is, the first rabbi and pastor, expounding the divine instruction by way of "the archetype of all sermons," the first "advice concerning the commandments of God."[13] As we have seen, however, it is not the serpent but the woman and man who offer the earliest such advice, spelling out the divine word and inventing the original liturgical injunction: "You shall not touch it." In the beginning, we might say, there were not ten commandments but two, a divine command and a merely human one. But the latter is by no means presented as such; instead, it is placed by *'adam* in the mouth of *YHWH elohim,* passed off as divine and thus as beyond question. Here J, narrating the original homily, points to one of the ineradicable features of not only preaching but also the whole range of verbal practices in religious life, namely, the permanent possibility, realized even in Eden, of attributing merely human words to God. Therefore, even at the mythic outset, the quintessentially religious claim for J, "thus says the Lord," is an ambiguous, interested,

13. Barth, *Romans,* p. 247.

questionable claim. Subsequently, in the serpent's discourse, J points to another possibility: that human religious congregants, naked and vulnerable, will give a fair hearing not only to divine promises but to other promises as well. The woman and man commence liturgical life with speech; now they settle down to listen, to attend to and consider what even this "animal of the field" has to say.

Wasting no time, the serpent proclaims his gospel promise: "You will not die" (Gen. 3:4). It is a remarkable statement because it is both contrary to God's own words ("you shall surely die" [Gen. 2:17]) and in one sense true: for as the story goes on to make clear, the humans do not biologically die after eating the fruit. Rather, it is to their genuine, original life-with-God that they "die" by way of their transgression and expulsion. Here the term "die" is ambivalent, signaling two different phenomena in two different contexts. Trading on this ambiguity, the serpent begins his homily with the idea that God may be untrustworthy and that 'adam may be misled. "God said that you will die? You will not die." The remark could only compound whatever disquiet the initial question had already introduced; moreover, following up on these anxieties, the serpent promises not only that the woman and man "will not die" if they eat the prohibited fruit, but also that they "will be like God, knowing good and evil" (Gen. 3:5). That is, having evoked with his opening query the vulnerability of human knowledge, the serpent now presents the perfect remedy: "Your knowledge may be vulnerable now," he implicitly suggests, "but it needn't be for long. Eat from this tree, and your eyes will be opened; you will know good and evil; you will be like God — invulnerable, informed, secure." He has delivered the invitation; the preacher rests. Now the word gives way to sacrament, and the meal begins.

The first gesture of this sacramental liturgy, according to J, is the gesture of taking: "She took of its fruit and ate" (Gen. 3:6). She does not receive the fruit from the serpent, nor does she merely submit to some direct command or instruction from him. She takes. She eats. With her husband looking on in full and approving complicity, she acts on their behalf, making a merely human bid for security, for protection, for bona fide membership among the garden's intelligentsia. In the face of God's generosity, they might have been grateful; but in the face of their own vulnerabilities, they are instead distracted, unsettled and afraid. And thus, in a perfect reversal of gratitude, they move to shore up their position, to take refuge in a sanctuary of strictly human design. It is revealing that they can only violate the divine injunction by way of first violating their own: in "taking" the fruit, the woman first defies her own added commandment, "You shall not touch it," and only subsequently God's commandment, "You shall not eat it" (Gen. 3:3, 2:17). J suggests that the human beings explicitly break with their own integrity on the way to explicitly breaking with God. In this liturgy of alienation and ingratitude, the woman and man turn against themselves first of all.

Only after the woman has taken and eaten does her gesture of giving arise; note that, in J's account, even after she has taken and eaten, her eyes are not yet opened. The rite is still incomplete. Now the first sacramental priest turns to the first sacramental parishioner, and she gives some of the fruit to him: "And she also gave some to her husband, who was with her" (Gen. 3:6). He receives. He eats. No less responsible for being chronologically in second place, and certainly no less anxious and engrossed in the proceedings, the man seizes his share of the spoils. Now, with his wife looking on in full and approving complicity, he acts on their behalf: like the woman, he takes the fruit, but he takes it out of human hands. Originally created and placed in Eden expressly to receive the gifts of God, the man seeks out in this entire landscape of grace the one thing that is not granted, the one that rests, so to speak, not in divine hands but in the palm of a merely human hand, presented with a merely human generosity.

Having found this one thing, the man receives it as a gift. He accepts and enjoys it, not from God, nor from a creature-with-God, but from a creature attempting to act without and against God. In other words, he puts a fellow human being in the place of the principal, ultimate giver, that is, in God's place. In this way, the woman and man collaborate in a mutual society of ruin: if the woman inaugurates the ungrateful bid for illicit knowledge and security, the man inaugurates idolatry and betrayal. As priest, 'adam becomes an apostate, "standing away" from her creator;[14] as parishioner, 'adam becomes an idolater, displacing his Creator with a creaturely substitute. Originally fashioned to be "one flesh" (Gen. 2:24), the woman and man now join in one sacramental body, a ruinous body of desperate maneuver and misplaced trust. She takes. He takes. In humanity's first act of gift-giving, she gives exactly what should not be given, and he receives as a gift what is no gift at all, but instead plunder, and treats as God one who is not God at all, but rather a fellow creature, acting as if alone.

---

14. "Apostasy": from *apo-,* away from, + *histanai,* to stand.

Only then, J reports, only once the whole ceremony of taking, giving, receiving, and eating is complete, do the promised consequences emerge: "Then the eyes of both were opened, and they knew that they were naked" (Gen. 3:7). That is, only after all the sacramental roles are played out — celebrant and congregant, priest and parishioner — does 'adam's new knowledge arise. Thus J's story does not point to the tree or its fruit as magical objects that provide knowledge simply on the basis of being consumed; if that were the case, then the woman's eyes would have opened before the man's. Rather, by narrating both the man's and the woman's epiphany as occurring simultaneously at the close of the rite, J points to the whole liturgical pattern as eye-opening: taking, eating, giving, receiving, and eating. What transforms the human situation in this narrative is not the ingestion of some occult substance but the carrying out of a particular procedure, namely, the procedure of cooperatively attempting to establish a base of operations in which human beings are beside and opposed to God.

As we have seen, this work begins with words: a human homily engaging the serpent on his terms and from within his presupposed picture of God and creation, followed by a human hearing given over to the serpent's gospel. Now words and hearing culminate in decision and choreography, a wholly collaborative undertaking in which woman and man take, eat, give, and receive precisely what should not be taken, eaten, given, or received. Anxious about the possibility that they are vulnerable, and thus fascinated by the serpent's gospel promise — not only "you will not die" but preeminently "you will be like God" — the man and woman lunge for alleged independence and self-sufficiency, for a supposed chance to stand on their own two feet, to take up a position beside God as gods in their own right. The procedure begun in the conversation with the serpent culminates in the original sacramental meal, the first attempt to take an invisible good by means of a visible, material operation, and the first attempt by creatures to give and receive that good on their own, and thus to usurp the divine role. Here, in the gestures of this dark Mass, 'adam presides over, gives, and receives not the gifts of God but rather the gifts — that is, the spoils — of mere humanity.

Accomplishing this procedure does indeed open their eyes, but their new knowledge affords insecurity rather than security. Maneuvering against the possibility that they are naked and vulnerable — a possibility obliquely but effectively suggested by the serpent's catechism — they come to "know" the very thing they hoped to guard against: "that they were naked" (Gen. 3:7). Far from quelling their fears, the first couple's evasions only confirm those fears. They are naked. They are vulnerable, fallible creatures, formed from dust, bound by limitations, by no means gods, however like God they may have become. Their supposed safeguard, the choreography of disobeying and abandoning God, only brings the reality of these conditions into the cool light of human knowledge. In *The Epistle to the Romans,* Barth argues that, at its best, religion plays just such a revealing function: it is "the point at which sin becomes an observable fact of experience,"[15] the site "where men are most evidently men, where they are most completely removed from direct union with God, and where human existence is most heavily burdened with its own questionableness."[16] In other words, religion makes known the mere humanity of mere humankind, 'adam's desperate and disoriented condition apart from God. In this sense, J's "tree of the knowledge of good and evil" is in effect "the tree of religion," or, as Barth glosses it, the tree of the "knowledge of the contrast between the primal state and its contradiction."[17] That is, in this original, disastrous religious liturgy of word and sacrament, sin — the break from union with God — becomes for 'adam not only an event but also "an observable fact of experience." By the time the rite is over and hindsight is possible, this observable fact may indeed be observed, and in that sense becomes retrospectively "known" to humankind.

To put it differently, by carrying out this procedure, the man and woman break from intimate friendship with God: having carried it out, they retrospectively come to know that such rupture is possible, that they are capable of effecting it, and that they have in fact effected it. Now the full range of their moral possibilities unfolds before them, and their eyes are opened. By acting out their capacity for misunderstanding and miscalculation, they come to know the truth of the serpent's suggestion that human knowledge and judgment are vulnerable, fallible things. By acting out their capacity for fear, ingratitude, distrust, and infidelity, they come to know that their efforts to do well before God are likewise vulnerable efforts. In the original instance of "learning by doing," human beings learn

15. *Romans,* p. 242.
16. *Romans,* p. 252.
17. *Romans,* p. 247.

firsthand that they are capable of both good and evil.[18] A dull horror sets in. In their bid to shield their suspected vulnerabilities, the man and woman have come to know just how vulnerable they really are.

Here, then, is the knowledge that dawns on them once the liturgy is complete, the reality to which "the eyes of both were opened" (Gen. 3:7): in brief, they come to know their earthy vulnerability. J puts it this way: "They knew that they were naked." And for the first time, they decide that this condition is both something to hide (Gen. 3:7) and a cause for fear (Gen. 3:10). In Barth's terms, the new liturgical procedure and the knowledge it makes possible give rise to a new thing: at this point "mere humanity" emerges on the scene. Now the man and woman stand alone, dismayed, self-consciously fragile and anxious, oriented away from God (that is, *dis*-oriented), and thus apart from the proper dependence on God that makes for genuine human life. Therefore, they scramble to cover their vulnerabilities in other ways: sewing leaves, making clothes to wear, and finally, as night falls in Eden, veiling themselves in the garden's shadows, hiding out at the sound of God's approach.

In Barth's view, the invention of "mere humanity" entails the invention of "mere God." Likewise, in J's narrative, the portrait of *YHWH elohim* undergoes a key shift in the wake of that first liturgy: now God again comes on the narrative stage — rather, the "sound" of God drawing near enters the narrative from offstage. For the first time, J pictures *YHWH elohim* as one who can be heard approaching when not yet seen, that is, as a localized presence who can be remote, retreating or advancing from afar off. Accordingly, this distant, noisy God is described for the first time as earthbound, walking in a particular time ("the time of the evening breeze") and a particular place ("in the garden," out of sight [Gen. 3:8]). While J certainly includes anthropomorphic hints in the portrait of God earlier in the story — for example, when God "formed *'adam* from the dust of the ground" (Gen. 2:7) — God has not been located with such specific coordi-

---

18. In a kind of reversal of Immanuel Kant's well-known formula, "ought implies can," here the man and woman undergo a process of discovery closer to "can implies ought": by learning that they are capable of transgression and infidelity, of "good and evil," they learn that their merely human decisions, vulnerable as they are apart from union with God, must take place under the sign of moral life, under the sign of "ought," that is, under the sign of religion. Apart from God, the "oughts" of religion — in Barth's terms in *Romans,* "moral and legal ordering" — are necessary precisely because, apart from God, both "good and evil" are possible.

nates in space and time up to this point in the narrative. Indeed, in Genesis 2, God is only located in relationship to 'adam's location and corporeality, for example, when God breathed into 'adam's nostrils, or "took 'adam and put him in the garden of Eden" (Gen. 2:7, 15). But in Genesis 3, for the first time, God is specifically located apart from 'adam, walking alone, off at a distance. Thus, immediately after the rite's completion, J strikingly portrays YHWH elohim in the image of humankind: an earthbound presence who comes and goes — now here, now there — and from whom the man and woman attempt to hide themselves (Gen. 3:8).

Like Michelangelo, J paints two portraits of God in this story. In Genesis 2, God is a creator who is as present and intimate with human beings as their own breath of life, neither strictly incorporeal nor limited to any particular time or space, analogous to the divine figure in *The Creation of Adam*. In Genesis 3, God is an earthbound, local presence, distant and disapproving, analogous to the divine figure in *The Creation of Eve*. In the first portrait, God fills the narrative frame: the picture does not exclude the stuff of creation, from trees to 'adam, but God is always in radical intimacy with them, making them grow, breathing into them the breath of life, and collaborating with them to name the world and find companionship (Gen. 2:7, 9, 18ff.). In the second portrait, God is one figure among others within the larger narrative frame, absent initially, and later returning like one player amongst a larger cast. It is as though the author J, in Genesis 3, also takes up the serpent's-eye view; or it is as though the reader of Genesis 3, by way of J's narrative mastery, also undergoes a parabolic version of the transformation and fall undergone by the story's protagonists. Mere humanity and mere God are not merely invented for the first man and woman; they may also be invented and reinvented for any men and women who read this narrative with care. Whereas humans and God were once intimate friends, now God walks alone on earth, and human beings run for the trees. Now we get creation's second question: it is God's call (Gen. 3:9), "Where are you?" Mere God and mere humanity confront each other for the first time.

On the one hand, the question involves a return to second-person address, a counterpoint to the serpent's third-person perspective; on the other hand, precisely as a calling out, the question is an acknowledgment that a distance has opened up between 'adam and YHWH elohim. Most Jewish and Christian interpreters have read this query not as a request for information — for that would contradict doctrines of divine omniscience

— but rather as an invitation and provocation for the man and woman to reorient themselves, to reflect on their position and correct their course. In this sense, God's question may be understood as a call to repentance and *metanoia*.[19] Therefore, the first couple's responses may be understood as the first acts of human prayer and confession. Despite their new knowledge, however, or perhaps in part because of the new worries it has engendered, the humans do not find their balance, but continue to stumble. To be sure, they do confess, saying, ". . . and I ate." But they both preface this single word in Hebrew, this single term of confession and responsibility, with several other words of explanation, excuse, blame, and, finally, outright dishonesty. Like the serpent's homily, the words they speak — "the woman gave me fruit" and "the serpent tricked me" — may be technically true; but in context they amount to denials of responsibility, attempts at deception, and hence refusals to repent. Here J points to another permanent temptation and risk in religious life, namely, that words spoken under the sign of confession may in fact deny accountability, that in the flurry of realization and defense, even technically true words may serve to make false accusations. Finally, by way of his accusation, the man turns against his companion for the first time and thus inaugurates yet another temptation in religious life: the seductive tendency to clamor for divine favor at the expense of other human beings, pointing to another's deficiencies as a way of denying our own.

The first couple's disorientation, and thus their fall into ruin, continues apace. Evasions compound evasions, with no end in sight. Indeed, just as their descent began well before the occasion of their infamous meal, it ends well after it, after their eyes are opened, after they refuse repentance, even after their exile from the garden altogether. It is with the story of Cain, in Genesis 4, that the narrative begun in Genesis 2 reaches its nadir and culmination.

3. Religion and Murder

It is customary in Christian theology and biblical commentary to conceive of the fall of humankind as taking place in the midst of the garden,

---

19. *Metanoia* is the biblical Greek term commonly translated as "repentance" (literally, "change of mind").

with the illegal eating of fruit being the decisive event, and the exile from Eden being that event's outcome and the story's dénouement. Many fine biblical commentaries, both premodern and contemporary, locate the key account of humanity's fall in Genesis 3; therefore, in Christian thought and art there are countless representations of the original human tragedy as having to do with that tree, that serpent, a tempting red apple, and so on. On this familiar reading, the story of Cain and Abel is understood as an ensuing episode that is consequent to the fall but not constitutive of it, the opening chapter of human life, now fallen, outside the garden's precincts.

But I will argue that there are good reasons to locate J's account of human ruin not only in Genesis 2 and 3 but also in Genesis 4. In the first place, the received text's form suggests that we should read these three chapters together, as a kind of trilogy. The extended genealogies from Genesis 4:17 to 5:32 provide a conspicuous narrative break; moreover, J has arranged the story of 'adam and the story of Cain in conspicuously parallel sequence, as though they are to be read together:[20] creation/birth, liturgy, transgression, divine question, human evasion, divine curse, divine care, and, finally, human dislocation east of Eden.[21] In the second place, key themes and story lines in Genesis 3 are reprised, developed, and brought to provisional conclusion in Genesis 4. If we keep these formal and thematic continuities in mind, I argue that the story of humanity's fall is best conceived as the whole course of Genesis 2–4, culminating not merely in an illicit eating of fruit but also in the original act of violence and murder. In this reading of the drama, the curtain does fall after the exile from Eden, but it rises again for a third and final act.

Driven from the garden, the man and woman conceive and bear a son, the first-born heir to their vocation, expressly "a tiller ['avad] of the ground" (Gen. 4:2). J points to a cluster of ideas with the name Cain (qayin). The word's Hebrew root, qyn, is linked to both metallurgy and music, and J reports that Cain's descendents would pioneer in these arts in human history (Gen. 4:21-22). J also reports that Cain himself would build the

---

20. Most contemporary scholars of Genesis agree that the story of 'adam and the story of Cain derive from different traditions; but this only makes all the more striking the fact that J has redacted them into parallel sequences.

21. For a Jewish treatment of some of these parallels, see Michael Fishbane, *Biblical Text and Texture* (Oxford: Oneworld Publications, 1998), pp. 23-27.

first city (Gen. 4:17). Cain is thus the name of the first human artisan, the first builder, smith, and maker, the founder of human ingenuity. Moreover, J punningly links the name to the word *qanah* ("gain," "acquire," or "possess"). Of Eve it is said: "She conceived and bore Cain [*qayin*], saying, 'I have acquired [*qanah*] a man with the help of the LORD'" (Gen. 4:1). Thus J associates Cain not only with invention but also with acquisition and possession. Finally, these two terms — *qayin* and *qanah* — morphologically, phonetically, and thematically evoke a third: *qana'*, which means both "to be jealous" and "to be zealous." J thus verbally foreshadows the oncoming catastrophe: the first human maker, acquirer, and possessor of things also brings jealousy, outright zealotry, and murder into the world.

As we have seen, there is no temple or altar in Eden, no sacred offering or sacrifice, and therefore no worship, no "gestures of adoration" performed toward God. Certainly, the work of people, undertaken apart and away from God — *leitourgia* at its most rudimentary — does emerge in the garden, as do the quintessentially religious forms of catechism, sermon, and sacrament. We might say that the groundwork for holy piety is laid in Eden. But full-blown worship, the familiar business of adoration, the prayer and praise and invocation of God that is the height and hallmark of full-blown religion, does not arise until after the exile, after the intimate friendship with God has been broken. This conspicuously late appearance alone lends support to the idea that humanity's fall amounts to a descent into religious worship; but it is all the more striking that, at the very outset of Genesis 4, human life outside the garden opens with the story of the first worship service. As if to underscore the liturgical character of the trouble begun in conversation with the serpent, J begins exilic history with human "gestures of adoration," precious offerings presented to God by the first human generation born east of Eden.

Thus the religious attempt at atonement, we might say, begins immediately. His parents were banished for attempting to acquire security by taking, eating, and offering prohibited "fruit" to one another, and now Cain attempts to acquire security by presenting a gift, *minchah* ("gift" or "offering") of "fruit" to God (Gen. 4:3). The original transgression, according to this logic, will be reversed and atoned for by a show of adoration and gift-giving. Stolen fruit will be restored by given fruit. But this form of donation, notwithstanding its guise of generosity and gratitude, is actually an attempt at acquisition (true to Cain's name): the original human maker and acquirer of things, Cain puts his ingenuity to work in a bid to obtain divine favor, to stand secure and aright before God. His parents' strategy of naked grasping, the fiasco that led to disgrace and exile in the first place, is now left behind; rather, Cain contrives an ingenious sleight of hand, an attempt at gain that takes place under the sign of giving. Thus full-blown "worship," that is, full-blown "religion," is born. Cain invents the *minchah,* the gift, for the first time (Gen. 4:3).[22] Liturgy's basic gestures were already invented in Eden, but now Cain, the original human maker, designs and enacts his allegedly new-and-improved *leitourgia* — the original religious "reformation"! Now the brazen grab, his parents' initial gesture of taking, is disguised as a form of offering (Gen. 4:3). The merely human lunge for security, very much intact, is now cloaked in devotion.

But this veil, which may conceal things from Cain himself, as well as from others, is all too thin, and God, by way of an elegant exposé, lays bare Cain's — and *leitourgia's* — true intentions. Indeed, in this culminating narrative in humanity's fall, J makes explicit the fundamentally interested and tragic character of worship and religion. For in this original service of offering and adoration, things go awry; rather, things that have already gone awry now come to the surface with devastating ferocity. Here, precisely in the scenario of worship, a corpse appears in creation for the first time.

The trouble begins when God has "no regard" for Cain's offering of fruit, but does have regard for Cain's brother Abel's offering of "fat portions" from his flock (Gen. 4:3-5). J does not give a reason for the difference in God's "regard," and thus provokes in the reader the very confusion that drives Cain to indignation: "So Cain was very angry, and his countenance fell" (Gen. 4:5). That is, by leaving the difference in God's judgment of acceptance and rejection unexplained, J invites the reader into Cain's consternation; this makes God's response to Cain a response to the reader as well: "Why are you angry, and why has your countenance fallen?" (Gen. 4:6). It is a worthy question, both for Cain and his inter-

22. The term here — *minchah* — appears twice more in Genesis, and each time it applies to a gift given expressly in order to appease and atone, and thus as part of an exchange (Gen. 32:13ff.; 43:11ff.). In Genesis 32, for example, Jacob sends a *minchah* of livestock to his approaching brother, Esau, from whom Jacob has stolen the birthright, and whom Jacob now fears will kill him (32:11). And Jacob offers this *minchah* with explicit intentions that may as well be Cain's: "For he thought, 'I may appease him with the present [*minchah*] that goes before me, and afterwards I shall see his face; perhaps he will accept me'" (32:20).

preters. Like God's earlier question of *'adam* ("Where are you?" [Gen. 3:9]), God asks this question not to seek information but to provoke reflection: What gives rise to this anger? What presuppositions? What view of creature and Creator? Cain is no doubt angry because he believes that something crucial is at stake in God's reception or rejection of human offerings, and so he believes that he has been denied a precious thing that his brother Abel has now acquired.[23]

What precious thing? God's response provides a clue, though a precise translation of that response has been controversial. The NRSV puts it this way: "If you do well, will you not be accepted?" (Gen. 4:7). The JPS translation is: "Surely, if you do right,/There is uplift."[24] Thus, according to God's response, Cain is angry because he believes that he has not been "accepted" (NRSV), that there has not been "uplift" (JPS). At issue here is the Hebrew word *se'et,* a term that admits of a range of meanings, principally "to lift up," "to bear," and "to take away" or "to forgive." In fact, J uses the word in each one of those senses elsewhere in Genesis.[25] Thus we may literally translate the verse as follows: "If you do well, there is lifting of/bearing of/forgiving of."[26] But Cain is angry because he believes that he has not been "uplifted," "accepted," or "forgiven"; this belief, in turn, sheds light on the true motivations behind his liturgy in the first place.[27] In the face of his parents' transgression and exile, Cain believes that by worshiping God he will gain divine favor, that what is at stake for him in worship is not only his gift's "acceptance" but his own as well. Cain may present his fruit as an offering, but this gift has strings attached, so to

23. In this reading, Gen. 4:1-16 is the story of Cain, with Abel functioning as merely a supporting character, a kind of placeholder. Indeed, J's choice of the name "Abel" (Hebrew *hevel,* "nothingness," "vapor," "breath") may further support this interpretation.

24. *TANAKH* (Philadelphia: The Jewish Publication Society, 1985), p. 8.

25. For "to lift up," see, e.g., Gen. 7:17: "the waters increased, and lifted up the ark"; for "to bear" or "support," see Gen. 13:6: "the land could not support both of them"; and for "to bear punishment," see Gen. 4:13: "my punishment is greater than I can bear!"; finally, for "to take away [guilt]" or "forgive," see Gen. 18:26: "I will forgive the whole place for their sake."

26. This odd construction in English is also odd in Hebrew: *se'et* is a construct infinitive without pronominal object.

27. Alternately, if we read the object of *se'et* as having to do not with Cain but with the divine countenance (cf. the same verb in the well-known benediction in Num. 6:26: "The LORD *lift up* his countenance upon you, and give you peace"), then we may understand Cain to be attempting to acquire divine blessing and "peace," and God to be assuring him that, as long as he "does well," he is already so blessed.

speak, and hence is actually no gift at all. Rather, it is a tactic, a resourceful attempt to secure a reward of uplift, acceptance, forgiveness, and reconciliation.

As we saw in Chapter 1, recent theoretical work on gift-giving is consonant with J's critical portrait of humanity's original *minchah*. [28] That is, Cain's solemn bestowal to God is nothing if not "mercenary and mercantile" (Derrida),[29] strategic work carried out in order to acquire remuneration. And note that this work may or may not be explicitly conscious and calculated on Cain's part. He may well "misrecognize" it (Bourdieu); in any case, its strategic status is not immediately obvious on its face.[30] But God's response to this original worship service amounts to an elegant exposé: by having "regard," or respect, for Abel's offering and then "no regard" for Cain's with no explanation, God provokes the elder brother to involuntarily confess — to God and to himself — the interested, economic character of his offering. If the presentation of fruit were truly and merely an expression of generosity or gratitude, given with no expectation of exchange, that is, if it were a true gift, then no precious good would be at stake for Cain in how God receives it. Whether there was divine regard or no regard, there would be cause for neither satisfaction nor anger. But Cain does get angry because, for him, there is indeed something at stake in how it is received: to be lifted up again from what he takes to be his low position, to be forgiven what he takes to be his sin, to be accepted from the midst of what he takes to be his exile. Thus his offering is not a gift; rather, it is a quid pro quo. It is bound up in a supposed economy of obligation and exchange. And when God does not deliver on the divine side of this imagined bargain, human ingenuity ignites into human rage.

To put it another way, in his actions and anger Cain presupposes a particular vocation for human beings, namely, to win divine favor by way of dutiful worship. But God, neither approving this vocation nor allowing it to go uncorrected, confronts Cain first with a question and then with a discourse: "If you do well, will you not be accepted? And if you do not do well, sin is lurking at the door; its desire is for you, but you must master it" (Gen. 4:7). In other words, God again provides human beings with an op-

28. See above, pp. 43ff.

29. Derrida, *The Gift of Death* (Chicago: University of Chicago Press), pp. 109ff.

30. Pierre Bourdieu, *Outline of a Theory of Practice* (Cambridge, UK: Cambridge University Press), pp. 5-6.

portunity for reorientation: Why are you angry and crestfallen? Your true vocation is to do well (NRSV), to do the work of righteousness (JPS). Like the polemics against liturgy in Amos and Micah, documents that are roughly contemporaneous with J's text, God spells out in this passage the original human vocation in terms of right livelihood, a matter not of proper offerings presented in worship but of "doing well" and "doing right."[31] As we have seen, in J's account, for human beings to do well and do right means to carry out their true vocation with God, to care for creation and enjoy its fruit (Gen. 2:15-16).[32] Insofar as Cain has lived out this call, God assures him that he is already "accepted" (NRSV) and that there is already "uplift" (JPS). Therefore, there is no need for his reverent attempts at negotiation, his fundamentally proud efforts to appear perfectly humble.

But Cain is not satisfied. Perhaps doubtful of his ability to do well; perhaps afraid to forsake the alleged independence his parents invented and bequeathed to him; perhaps offended by God's suggestion that he has misunderstood his own vocation, embarrassed and ashamed that his fine offering of fruit is not at all what God desires — perhaps for all these reasons his anger does not subside but rises to fury. And God lays bare the violence at the heart of *leitourgia*. In the garden, 'adam's retreat from divine intimacy and lunge for autonomy apart from God appear to be a bid for self-protection, an all-too-understandable attempt by human beings to shield their vulnerabilities and shore up their position. Its real consequence, however, is a devastating attack on genuine humanity, a tragic act of self-sacrifice for the sake of a specious self-preservation. In the original and founding act of "misrecognition" in human work and life, the man and woman mistake losing themselves for saving themselves, and in the name of self-interest, they commit the original suicide.[33] It is not, of

---

31. Cf., e.g., Micah 6:6-8: "'With what shall I come before the LORD, and bow myself before God on high? Shall I come before him with burnt offerings, with calves a year old? Will the LORD be pleased with thousands of rams, with ten thousands of rivers of oil? Shall I give my firstborn for my transgression, the fruit of the body for the sin of my soul?' He has told you, O mortal, what is good; and what does the LORD require of you but to do justice, and to love kindness, and to walk humbly with your God?" See also Amos 5:21-24, cited in Ch. 1, note 31.

32. See above, pp. 63ff.

33. For an argument that all human practices involve such "misrecognition," see Bourdieu, *Outline of a Theory of Practice*, e.g., pp. 5ff.; see also Catherine Bell, *Ritual Theory,*

course, a biological suicide: as the serpent quite correctly informs them, they will not die as a result of eating the prohibited fruit (Gen. 3:4). Rather, their act is suicidal only with respect to their genuine life-with-God, the life for which they were and are created, that is, the life constituted by radically intimate friendship with their Creator. To this life, as God quite correctly informs them, they "shall die" and do "die" as a result of their transgression (Gen. 2:17). They violate not only the divine command and trust but also their own genuine life and work; and this violation is, in a word, violent. Human beings take the fruit, and in so doing they take their own lives. The work of the first *leitourgia,* then, is violent work, a personal disorientation so profound that it amounts to suicide, precisely as *YHWH elohim* had warned,

And yet, despite this loss of life — or, perhaps, precisely because of it — the violent heart of *leitourgia* is not clearly understood by either the first couple or their children. Their misrecognition continues: they scramble for cover, refuse responsibility, and, in the liturgies of Cain and Abel, repeat the original rupture in a different guise. Human beings set themselves over against God in worship. They act alone — apart and away from God. Like so many consecutive human generations, the younger sets out to depart from the work of the older, but ends up performing that work all the same. In distinction from their parents, the second generation seeks to acquire divine favor — that is, to assuage the divine disfavor they believe the first generation incurred for humankind — by way of presenting God with solemn gifts. In solidarity with their parents, they take up the work of merely human self-assertion, the "work of people," to shore up their position beside God as some second thing, independent subjects

---

Ritual Practice (New York: Oxford University Press, 1992), e.g., pp. 82ff. By narrating the original human practice as including misrecognition, J would seem to sketch a similar picture of human practice in general. However, what neither Bourdieu nor Bell seems to fully confront is the fact that the theory that all human practices involve misrecognition by their practitioners, if true, must also extend to the practices of theorizing that Bourdieu and Bell themselves undertake. That is, no less than the observed practitioner, the academic observer cannot stand in a privileged position somehow outside "practice" and thus evaluate "objectively" (Bourdieu). Rather, the observer, too, must practice and misrecognize; thus the theory outlines a situation in which every human practice, including observing, theorizing, and book-writing, is likewise suspect, likewise disguised to itself. And this confounding and confounded situation — disguises amid disguises — is in keeping with the one J portrays in Genesis 3–4: a mire from which human beings alone cannot deliver themselves, that is, a thoroughly "fallen" situation.

in their own right and on their own feet. The risks of genuine love, intimacy, and partnership, to say nothing of the radical dependence of creature on Creator, seem to them too fearsome, too insecure. Thus the only "friendship" they seek with their Creator is strictly collegial, the distant, approving nod of respect, recognition, and reward.

Cain desires to stand aright before God, to be lifted up, forgiven, and accepted. That is, Cain desires the full-blown religious desire. And the sheer intensity of this desire, an intensity toward violence, is unveiled once and for all by the divine exposé. The hidden suicide in the garden has left humankind gasping for genuine breath, desperate for new life — indeed, desperate enough to take life if necessary. Suicide begets homicide, and the violence at the heart of *leitourgia* is now laid bare in all its brutality: Cain, consumed with anger, turns his gaze on his own brother. Abel's gift has been accepted. Now Cain's other near-namesake — *qana*' ("jealousy," "zealotry") — surfaces in human society, and creation's original suicide makes way for creation's original murder. Now death takes its unmistakable form, the form of a corpse.

As if to eliminate his rival for God's acceptance and benediction, and thus to acquire and possess these things for himself, Cain murders his brother: social violence is born, and the story of humanity's fall descends to its abysmal conclusion. God confronts humanity with the world's third question: "Where is your brother Abel?" (Gen. 4:9). As an echo and counterpart to the first divine question of *'adam* ("Where are you?" [Gen. 3:9]), this question provides Cain with a final opportunity for reorientation and confession, a last chance to tell the truth and return to God. But Cain, refusing this opportunity, instead gives an answer that seals human ruin once and for all. As we have seen, humans are originally placed in Eden "to till [*'avad*] and to keep [*shamar*]" the ground and garden (Gen. 2:15). At the beginning of Genesis 4, Cain and Abel unhinge the first of these verbs from its proper role: twisting their capacity to till and to serve from creation to their Creator, they enact for the first time that term's other principal meaning in Hebrew: to worship. The service of *'adamah* gives way to the exclusive service of God; cultivation gives way to cult. Now, as the story comes to a close, the second vocational verb, *shamar* ("to keep"), is likewise undone. Cain responds to God's question with a lie, and then his own question: "I do not know; am I my brother's keeper [*shamar*]?" (Gen. 4:9).

Of course, that is exactly what he is; rather, that is exactly what he is originally created and called to be, the keeper of not only his brother but *'adamah* as a whole. And he forfeits this vocation by his brutal act and by this denial. Keeping gives way to killing. The reversal is complete: called to till and serve creation, humanity turns to worship and serve mere God Almighty. Called to keep *'adamah,* humanity takes up the work of killing it. Abel's broken body has fallen, and so has humankind. With his crass, deceitful question — according to J's account, the first *human* question — Cain unwittingly names his true identity, and loses it.

We can see from this reading of Genesis 2–4 that the story of humanity's fall and of liturgy's rise is the same story. In conversation with the serpent, human beings invent *leitourgia,* and they also invent mere humanity and mere God along with it. East of Eden, people disguise and develop their work into full-blown worship, and the personal disorientation of the garden ("Where are you?") is matched by the social disorientation of the field ("Where is your brother?"). Thus doubly lost, humans settle in "the land of Nod" (Hebrew *nod:* "wandering"), that is, in a rootless place where no true settlement is possible at all. They build a city, human ingenuity and arts flourish, but so does the violence and zealotry at the heart of *leitourgia* — suicidal at first, homicidal at last. Indeed, the very last verse of Genesis 4, as though to finally confirm that the story of humanity's defeat is also the story of liturgy's victory, records without fanfare the triumph of religion: "At that time," J writes, "people began to invoke the name of LORD" (Gen. 4:26).

J narrates the "in the beginning" of such an invocation, liturgy, and religion. But it is worth noting that, precisely as Holy Writ, this story has been and is most often read in the midst of religious life, accompanied by just this sort of liturgy and invocation. That is, Genesis 2–4 is a religious story about the rise of religion, a self-referential etiology that amounts to a self-critique. Indeed, as if to underscore this self-criticism, J leads not only the story's protagonists, but also its readers and listeners, through a step-by-step descent that mirrors the fall portrayed in the account. That is, as we read and listen to the story, we move from (1) a narrative frame in which God seems to be present in all things (2:4b-25), through (2) an abrupt narrative break that itself portrays humanity's break — both *'adam's* and the reader's — from intimacy with God (3:1), into (3) a narrative frame in which God is pictured as a distant, local presence in the garden (Gen. 3), to (4) one in which God appears increasingly remote and capricious (Gen. 4), and finally "away" from humankind (4:16). The act of reading Genesis 2–4 may retrace for readers and listeners the very fall and invention of God that the story ostensibly recounts, pointing to the idea that these readers and listeners, far from merely looking or listening in on the story, are fully implicated in it. This is not "long ago and far away"; this is our story, too. Over the course of the narrative, J invites us to take up the protagonist's position (*'adam*'s anxious orthodoxy, Cain's confusion and protest) and thus to replay for ourselves the tragedy of religion, so that we may talk, read, and listen — *about* God. J invites us to reinvent God in our own image, and ourselves as if we live and work alone — in short, to fall. Moreover, J invites us to continually make the distance we continually fall "an observable fact of experience." Just as Michelangelo paints us into the picture as we stand on the Sistine Chapel floor, J effectively writes us into the story, reading our holy text, practicing our religion, finally raising our voices to "invoke the name of the Lord."

Therefore, I would suggest that a close reading of Genesis 2–4 may support, clarify, and extend Barth's critique of "worship" and "religion." When it is viewed in this way, the human predicament is fundamentally a liturgical predicament, a crisis constituted by the emergence and re-emergence of *leitourgia* in human life. However, Barth's case by no means entails an outright repudiation of worship. Indeed, if Barth casts human ruin as an indelibly liturgical problem, he also goes on to propose a likewise liturgical solution, to which I will now turn.

For Karl Barth, God is against religion. But this divine opposition takes the form not of an annihilating assault from above, but of a transformative undertaking from below and within. In Jesus Christ, God takes up worship and religion. God prays. God sacrifices. The sword, as we shall see, is remade into a plowshare, and thus through the thoroughly wretched human situation — our settlement that is also wandering, our flourishing that is also violent, and preeminently our worship that is also "fall" — God accomplishes the work of reconciliation and, at the last, redemption in Jesus Christ.

PART II

"We Pray by His Mouth"

The first edition of Karl Barth's *The Epistle to the Romans* appeared in 1919. By 1922, Barth had thoroughly revised the text for the second edition, so thoroughly, in fact, that in the new preface he wrote, "No stone remains in its old place."[1] Barth's studies in 1919 and 1920 both precipitated and informed these revisions: he read Franz Overbeck, Nietzsche, Plato, Kant, and Kierkegaard; the plays of Ibsen; the novels of Dostoevsky; and he studied the paintings of Matthias Grünewald. In particular, Barth was captivated by the crucifixion panels of Grünewald's *Isenheim Altarpiece,* where Christ, dead on the cross, is flanked on one side by his mother, his disciple John, and Mary Magdalene; and, on the other side, by John the Baptist, who is cradling a Bible and gesturing with his right hand toward Christ. Barth said that the latter was "pointing in an almost impossible way. It is this hand which is in evidence in the Bible."[2] So taken was Barth with this image that he had a copy of it on the wall over his office desk for the rest of his life.[3]

It is a gruesome picture. Christ's body hangs, large and imposing, on a crossbeam that bows with his weight. He is dead. His fingers are twisted with rigor mortis; his flesh is gray and green; his shoulders have almost

---

1. Karl Barth, *The Epistle to the Romans* (London: Oxford University Press, 1933), p. 2.

2. Eberhard Busch, *Karl Barth: His Life from Letters and Autobiographical Texts* (Philadelphia: Fortress, 1976), p. 116.

3. Busch, *Karl Barth,* pp. 114-16.

Isenheim Altarpiece: Crucifixion, **by Matthias Grünewald**

left their sockets. His head and body are bloodied, scarred, and studded with lesions and thorns. One of the earliest nocturnal depictions of the Crucifixion in Western art, Grünewald's masterwork seems a fittingly dark counterpart to the accounts of human ruin in both Barth's *The Epistle to the Romans* and J's narrative in Genesis 2–4. Here, we might say, the ultimate fruit of humanity's fall manifests itself in a single crime: the torture and killing of both genuine God and genuine human being. As we have seen in *Romans* and in Genesis, *leitourgia* emerges as the "work of people" unto death, a suicidal and homicidal turn away from God and toward a fierce and wretched alienation. Having first taken their own lives and then each other's, now human beings have brutally destroyed the Son of God.

But this devastating word of critique and condemnation, clear and uncompromising as it is, is not the last word on human work — for either Grünewald or Barth. There is another word. Fundamentally, for both the painter and the theologian this other word is the final word, God's word; indeed, it is "the Word of God" as flesh and blood and genuine human work in Jesus Christ. As the original and final Word, he is the one to whom all other words — preeminently the words of Scripture, including Paul's letter to the Romans — finally "point in an almost impossible way." For Barth, even the words indicting *leitourgia* in Romans and Genesis finally point to Jesus Christ; that is, even the dreadful news of humanity's fall finally points to the gospel.

Thus far we have seen how Barth argues that the "radical dividing of men from God" takes place as "worship" and "religion," and how a close reading of Genesis 2–4 may support, clarify, and extend this argument.[4] Now I wish to turn to Barth's account of God's reconciliation with humankind, in which *leitourgia* is taken up, fulfilled, and thus transformed in the work of Jesus Christ. For Barth, liturgy is not only the fundamental occasion of humanity's sin; it is also the fundamental occasion of humanity's return to God. Precisely as the epicenter of human trouble, *leitourgia* is where God's restorative, saving work takes place.

Consider Grünewald's *Crucifixion,* the painting before which Barth wrote not only the second edition of *Romans* but also the whole corpus of theological writing that followed it. It is, after all, a liturgical scene. Jesus' mother and Mary Magdalene — with postures strikingly similar to the

---

4. Barth, *Romans*, p. 241.

first woman's in Michelangelo's *The Creation of Eve* — take up the posture of prayer and supplication. Beside John the Baptist stands the Lamb of God, filling a eucharistic chalice with blood from a wound in his breast, and behind them both is a river, a likely reference to the river Jordan and thus to the sacrament of baptism. This suggests a positive valuation of worship as reconciliation — even in this picture of despair.

Moreover, the work itself is a panel of an altarpiece, designed by Grünewald for a chapel in the monastic hospital order of St. Anthony of Isenheim. That is, it was designed for use in worship by the sick. Christ's loincloth appears made of the old torn linen typically used for bandages in sixteenth-century France, and Mary Magdalene's anachronistic jar of ointment lies at her side. Originally, then, the afflicted came before this altarpiece to pray for healing, restoration, and for "salvation" in that sense (Latin *salvus,* "safe"). We may perhaps say that, by permanently placing the image over his desk, Barth himself effectively took up the posture of prayer and supplication in his theological work, the position of someone afflicted who is seeking salvation. Indeed, in the opening volume of his *Church Dogmatics,* Barth calls theology "an act of penitence and obedience," an endeavor that is only possible via the "attitude of prayer."[5] So Barth hung an altarpiece over his desk, an image originally designed for prayer in a hospital chapel.

Finally, it is worth noting that the *Isenheim Altarpiece* is a multilayered structure, with two sets of outer wings that close toward the center, like a cupboard within a cupboard. Grünewald painted his *Crucifixion* on the outside of the outer set of these doors, so that the work is only visible when the altarpiece is closed, as it would be, for example, during the Lenten season. Once the outer doors are opened up, however, a triumphant triptych is revealed: on the central panel, an angelic orchestra plays in celebration of the Madonna and child, and flanking this scene, the two outer wings — now open — display the Annunciation and the Resurrection. Thus, for Grünewald, the stark disgrace of crucifixion actually

5. Barth, *Church Dogmatics* (Edinburgh: T&T Clark, 1936-1975), I.1, pp. 22-23 (hereafter *CD,* page references cited in parentheses in the text). In later writings, too, Barth repeatedly returned to this theme: "It is imperative to recognize the essence of theology as lying in the liturgical action of adoration, thanksgiving, and petition. The old saying, *Lex orandi lex credendi,* far from being a pious statement, is one of the most profound descriptions of the theological method" (Barth, *The Humanity of God* [Richmond, VA: John Knox Press, 1960], p. 90).

"opens up" on the divine gifts of the Incarnation and Resurrection. Human defeat gives way to victory, Good Friday to Christmas and Easter.

Thus, inasmuch as Barth kept the Lenten image before him as he pursued his theological work, he also kept before him the hidden triptych, the saving work of Jesus Christ veiled within and behind the appalling work of humankind apart from God. Barth could not actually open up the reproduction over his desk, but the vertical seam between the panels, hope's thin line running through Christ's body, was always visible. In the same way, the tragic, violent work of worship — as intractable and apparently conclusive as it is — is penultimate for Barth, only an outer layer of double doors both concealing and revealing the ultimate, saving work of grace. In *The Epistle to the Romans,* Barth argues that human beings fall away from God through the "work of people" unto death. In *Church Dogmatics,* Barth also argues that human salvation takes place as this very work of people is taken up and transformed in the work of Jesus Christ, the "work of people-with-God" unto genuine human life.

Barth gave the fourth volume of his *Church Dogmatics* the title "The Doctrine of Reconciliation." In the first chapter of Part II, I highlight three aspects of his case: first, the claim that the divine will for human salvation "precedes" the divine will to creation (*CD,* IV.1, p. 9); second, the related idea that human salvation amounts to God's restoration of genuine human being as such; and third, Barth's account of the genuine human being as a being fundamentally covenanted with God, and thus as necessarily a "grateful" being. To develop this last idea, I turn both to Volume III of *Church Dogmatics,* "The Doctrine of Creation," and to the posthumously published drafts of an additional chapter for Volume IV, "The Doctrine of Reconciliation."[6] In these late drafts, Barth argues that true gratitude to God entails not only "thanksgiving" but also "praise and petition," that is, true gratitude entails the worship of God.

Along the way, I address two sets of questions to fill out the case: first, how should we understand "friendship" between God and human beings? Is friendship consistent with covenantal relationship, and in particular

---

6. For general treatment of this posthumously published material, see John Webster, *Barth's Ethics of Reconciliation* (Cambridge, UK: Cambridge University Press, 1995), and *Barth's Moral Theology* (Grand Rapids: Eerdmans, 1998), esp. pp. 151ff.; and E. Jüngel, "Invocation of God as the Ethical Ground of Christian Action. Introductory Remarks on the Posthumous Fragments of Karl Barth's Ethics of the Doctrine of Reconciliation," in *Theological Essays,* trans. J. B. Webster (Edinburgh: T&T Clark, 1989), pp. 154-72.

with the authoritative command "you shall not" that is so characteristic of biblical accounts of covenant, including Genesis 2? Second, since Barth is so critical of religion and worship, how should we understand his account of reconciled Christian life as thanksgiving, praise, and petition? Isn't this a contradiction? Has Barth changed his mind?

To help answer this latter set of questions, in the third section below I show how, for Barth, the choreography of genuinely human invocation — thanksgiving, praise, and petition — is carried out only by collaboration between human beings and the triune God. While the work of people alone amounts to a fall away from God, the work of people-with-God in Jesus Christ amounts to collaborative intimacy, a "meeting again" of creature and Creator, a reconciliation to God and thus to full humanity. To use Calvin's phrase, thanks to the ongoing work of Jesus Christ, Christians "pray by His mouth," and thus God reconciles even the tragic distance of prayer into a saving solidarity.

Finally, in the last two chapters of Part II, I sketch Barth's view, which is influenced decisively by Martin Luther, of Christian worship as simultaneously fall and reconciliation. To spell out this case, I turn first to Luther's so-called *simul* doctrine, and then to the idea that, for human beings, redemption ultimately means not only the transformation of *leitourgia,* but the end of it. In God's ultimate play of redemption, the disastrous work of people will no longer arise, and thus the reconciling work of people-with-God will no longer be necessary. The great Sabbath will begin at last, and prodigal humanity will return not to work but to rest with God, to intimacy with God, to love and joy and communion with God — in short, to "music and dancing" (Luke 15:25) and to celebration without end.

CHAPTER 3

Karl Barth on Worship as "Reconciliation"

1. The Work of Human Being

In Chapter XIII of Volume IV of his *Church Dogmatics,* a chapter entitled "The Subject Matter and Problems of the Doctrine of Reconciliation," Barth sketches his account of "the subject-matter, origin, and content of the message received and proclaimed by the Christian community" (*CD,* IV.1, p. 3). It is an announcement of human salvation, a report of God's movement and achievement of reconciliation with humanity. And this movement, Barth contends, is not merely a reaction to human failing, a remedial, reactive strategy subsequent to creation, in the face of an unfortunate creature spoiled by sin. Rather, it is contained within God's will and activity from the very first, from God's original creative act:

> The ordaining of salvation for man and of man for salvation is the original and basic will of God, the ground and purpose of His will as Creator. It is not that He first wills and works the being of the world and man, and then ordains it to salvation.... In the very fact that man is, and that he is man, he is as such chosen by God for salvation (*CD,* IV.1, pp. 9-10).

Thus, for Barth, the human being is nothing if not a being "ordained for salvation," that is, ordained to be God's covenantal "partner" and, as such, ordained for "the fulfillment of his being in participation in the being of God by the gift of God" (CD, IV.1, p. 10).[1] If human beings decline or oppose this ordination — as Barth says we do, decisively and irrevocably — if we "forfeit the predetermined salvation," then "in so doing man has lost his creaturely being" (CD, IV.1, pp. 10-11). In other words, Barth argues that what it means to be a human being is to be ordained to covenantal partnership with God and to "participate in the being of God by the gift of God." Any turn or departure from this relationship and participation constitutes "a supreme and final jeopardizing even of our creaturely existence" (CD, IV.1, p. 10).[2]

Human beings cannot rid themselves of this ordination to partnership with God. Therefore, Barth believes, we can never render ourselves inhuman or subhuman, whatever our rebellion may be. But we can and do, by declining or opposing this ordination, fail to live out the fullness of our humanity, the "fulfillment of [our] being" (CD, IV.1, p. 10). We take up a position against ourselves; we become our own adversaries. In sin, Barth suggests, the sinner "chooses his own impossibility" (CD, III.2, p. 136).[3] In this sense, a human being apart and away from God is no genuine human being at all; the loss incurred by humanity's fall amounts, in the end, to a

---

1. Barth does couple the terms covenantal "partner" and "participation in the being of God," but I take this coupling to suggest not a simple collapse or equivalence of the two terms but a close relationship between them. As I argue below, I take "invocation" to be the linchpin of this relationship, the link that holds together our work as God's partner on the one hand and our participation in God's triune life on the other. See also, e.g., Barth, CD, IV.1, pp. 8-10, 13-15.

2. See also CD, III.2, pp. 135ff., where Barth describes sin as "a mode of being contrary to our humanity," an "attack on the continuance of [human] creatureliness" (p. 136).

3. Barth calls sin an "ontological impossibility" for human beings: "[O]ur being does not include but excludes sin. To be in sin, in godlessness, is a mode of being contrary to our humanity. . . . If [a person] denies God, he denies himself. . . . He chooses his own impossibility." Thus, for Barth, the reality of sin in human life means that we enact our own impossibility, and thus render our own being radically convoluted, distorted, and alienated from its own genuine basis and character. In this way the sinner is, as Barth puts it, "impossible," "lost to himself," "incomprehensible to himself." But this contradiction, as a contradiction, includes not only the sinner's rebellion against the fullness of his humanity, but also his abiding humanity, his abiding ordination to exactly what he rejects and leaves aside. He is at once ordained and opposed to his ordination. If this were not so, sin would mean mere degeneration into a subhuman or nonhuman form; but for Barth, sin's tragedy is that we at once remain human and oppose our own humanity. In Barth's words, a human being "is indeed good and not evil. Even his sin cannot alter this fact. Sin means that he is lost to himself, but not to his Creator. . . . It does not mean that the being of man as such has been changed or replaced by a different being. . . . [R]eal man is not lost to God" (CD, III.2, p. 197).

loss of genuine humanity. Barth puts it this way: in sin the human being "has made himself quite impossible" in relationship to both "the redemptive grace of God" and "his created being as man." He has effectively "cut the ground from under his feet" (*CD*, IV.1, p. 10).

The anthropological dimension of this view, in which ordination to partnership with God and participation in divine being is constitutive of the ground of human being, is the first and crucial point I wish to highlight in Barth's case. In *The Epistle to the Romans*, Barth argues that genuine human being is constituted by intimate "friendship" and "dependence upon God"; in *Church Dogmatics*, he specifies this humanizing intimacy as "participation in the divine being," a "fulfillment" that renders the true human being "a being hidden in God" (*CD*, IV.1, p. 8).[4] Further, in *Church Dogmatics*, Barth argues that God ordains and creates humankind for salvation precisely because God, as "the One who loves in freedom," wills to give participation in the divine being, to bestow "redemptive grace"; for this very reason, God creates "a partner to receive it" (*CD*, IV.1, pp. 9-10).[5] That is, God creates and redeems because God wills to give Godself to another, that is, God wills to engage in loving intimacy. In this view, human beings are created to receive this grace and to enjoy this intimacy, in short, to hear God say, "Take what is mine — this final, supreme, unsurpassable gift; take it, it is meant for you" (*CD*, IV.1, p. 9).

The second point follows directly from the first, because the salvation to full humanity ordained in creation is, Barth contends, definitively delivered when the Word, present even at the creation, enters history as Jesus of Nazareth. That is, in Barth's account, God's saving action in Jesus Christ is not only the "restoration" to the original ordination human beings have forfeited, the "place of promise and expectation of the salvation ordained for us"; it is also that very salvation. What is achieved decisively in Jesus Christ — in God's life in history as a human being — is "nothing more nor less than the coming of salvation itself, the presence of the *eschaton* in all its fullness."[6] To put it differently, what is achieved

---

4. Cf. Col. 3:3: "For you have died, and your life is hidden with Christ in God."

5. This is true for Barth quite apart from humankind's subsequent fall; here "redemptive grace" means the perfection and fulfillment of created being, fallen or not. In other words, even prior to the mythic transgressions, 'adam, too, originally lacked this perfection and fulfillment, and thus could receive it as a gift. See *CD*, IV.1, pp. 8-10.

6. By referring to "the presence of the *eschaton*," Barth gestures, as he does so often in Vol. IV, toward an eschatological construal of the work accomplished in Jesus Christ: trad-

in Jesus Christ is the restoration of human being as such, in its most exalted and genuine form: "[W]e are awakened to our own truest being as
life and act." Therefore, though God acts decisively and unilaterally on
our behalf, for Barth this unilateral action "does not mean the extin-
guishing of our humanity, but its establishment." Thus Barth argues that
"our salvation, i.e., our participation in His being," amounts to nothing
less than the "establishment" of our humanity, the realization of our role
as God's covenantal "partner." It is only in this covenantal role, Barth
contends, that "the genuine being of man" is possible at all (CD, IV.1, pp.
14-15).

In what does this covenantal role consist? What work, in Barth's view,
does God's partner, the human being who participates in divine being,
properly discharge? This is the third point I wish to underscore in Barth's
account. The answer he provides, drawn in brief and general terms in
Chapter XIII and elaborated more systematically both in Chapter X and
in the posthumously published drafts for Chapter XVII, is this: God's
"covenant of grace"

> engages man as the partner of God only, but actually and necessarily, to
> gratitude. On the side of God it is only a matter of free grace and this in
> the form of benefit. For the other partner in the covenant to whom God
> turns in this grace, the only proper thing, but the thing which is uncon-
> ditionally and inescapably demanded, is that he should be thankful
> (CD, IV.1, p. 41).

According to Barth's understanding of the proper realization of the covenant between God and humankind, "Grace evokes gratitude like the voice
an echo. Gratitude follows grace like thunder lightning." Indeed, for
Barth, any deviation from this pattern can only signal disaster: "Only
gratitude can correspond to grace, and this correspondence cannot fail.

---

ing on the eschatological paradox of "already/not yet," Barth claims at once the definitive
arrival of salvation in the life, death, and resurrection of Jesus Christ and the nonetheless
provisional, as yet unconsummated character of that arrival, whose consummation will be
the Second Coming. Indeed, the very last sentence of the draft manuscript for a new chapter
in Vol. IV, published only after Barth's death, attests to the central position of eschatology
in Barth's thought: God's kingdom, he writes, "has come and will come," and even for the
one who is still an unbeliever, "Jesus Christ is his hope too" (see The Christian Life [Grand
Rapids: Eerdmans, 1981], p. 271).

Its failure, ingratitude, is sin, transgression. Radically and basically all sin is simply ingratitude" (CD, IV.1, p. 41).

Gratitude, then, as the "one but necessary thing which is proper to and is required of him with whom God has graciously entered into covenant," is nothing less than the primary and constitutive act of human being for Barth. For if the "genuine being of man" is realized only in covenantal partnership with God, and if the human work in that partnership is the work of thanksgiving, then gratitude is the crux and basis of genuine humanity, the "one but necessary thing" without which genuine human being does not and cannot arise (CD, IV.1, pp. 41-42). Barth puts it this way: "Just as there is no God but the God of the covenant, there is no man but the man of the covenant: the man who as such is destined and called to give thanks." Barth calls this person "the true man," as against the "man in himself," who regards thanksgiving to God as "a matter of his own freedom of choice." This alleged freedom Barth dismisses as illusory, arguing that in "real freedom" the human being "can only choose to be the man of God, i.e., to be thankful to God. With any other choice he would simply be groping in the void, betraying and destroying his true humanity" (CD, IV.1, p. 43). For Barth, "man can only be grateful man"; in this sense, too, he claims that, even though the dynamic pattern of salvation is primarily a pattern of divine initiative and power, nonetheless human beings "belong to the redemptive act" as "active subjects" insofar as we respond to God's gracious action. That is, we are "active subjects" insofar as "our human being, life and activity" take on "the form of the praise of God, of faith and love and hope" (CD, IV.1, pp. 44, 20).

Here Barth reprises a theme that he originally elaborated in Volume III of Church Dogmatics, "The Doctrine of Creation": in that earlier account he makes clear that humanity's genuine being as "grateful being" has its original, analogical basis in the triune divine life. That is, Barth suggests that God, as triune, is "one but not alone." "God exists," he says, "in relationship and fellowship. As the Father of the Son and the Son of the Father He is Himself I and Thou, confronting Himself and yet always one and the same in the Holy Ghost." God is both unity and community for Barth, an "I" and "Thou" in loving relationship and perfect intimacy.

This triunity helps explain, on Barth's account, the very act of creation itself. Because God is "not solitary" in se, God "therefore does not will to be [solitary] ad extra." Thus God originally and continually creates "a reality distinct from Himself," so as to enjoy fellowship not only within but also without the Three-in-One. To put it differently, divine love superabundantly exceeds the divine life. God wills to create and love another life, distinct from God, truly other — in Barth's famous phrase, "wholly other" — and also capable, on the basis of both this otherness and gracious divine gifts, of entering into genuine intimacy and friendship with God. In short, God wills to create and love a neighbor. And thus God creates the cosmos and its creatures, not because the divine life is incomplete, but because in love God freely wills to exceed completion. Divine love is not abundant; it is superabundant. It boils over. God's own "I" and "Thou," in their eternal encounter and in their eternal unity in the Spirit, do not comprise a closed circle but an open one.

And so the triune God, precisely because of this triunity, this superabundant life-in-relation, speaks the opening and continuous words of creation: "Let there be . . ." (Gen. 1:3). Like so many Christian exegetes before him, Barth finds suggestions of this triune creativity in the fact that God speaks in the plural in Genesis 1: "Let us make humankind in our image, according to our likeness" (Gen. 1:26) — and in the threefold report of that creative act in Genesis 1:27: "So God created humankind in his image, in the image of God he created them; male and female he created them" (see *CD*, III.2, p. 324; III.1, pp. 19ff.).[7]

But these verses report not only that God is one-and-plural, but also that men and women are originally created, as *Elohim* puts it, "in our image" and "likeness." Thus, in Barth's view, the divine fellowship creates a human partner, a neighbor made likewise to live in open fellowship and love: "God is in relationship, and so too is the man created by Him. This is his divine likeness" (*CD*, III.2, p. 324). From this angle it becomes clear that, for Barth, the original and intended divine-human intimacy — the "delicious freedom of intercourse" that so enthralled the younger Barth in Michelangelo's *Creation of Adam* — is an analogical repetition, an image of the intimate intercourse within and among the divine Trinity.

---

7. Barth is well aware, of course, that the original authors and editors of the priestly creation story may not have had in mind a triune picture of God; however, against the common interpretation that the plural "us" and "our" refer to "divine beings who compose God's heavenly court" (as the NRSV committee puts it), Barth points out that "Genesis 1:26 does not speak of a mere entourage, of a divine court or council which later disappears behind the king who alone acts. Those addressed here are not merely consulted by the one who speaks but are summoned to an act (like the 'going down' of Gen. 11:7), i.e., an act of creation." Thus in any case, for P, *Elohim* is in some sense genuinely plural — though the account is not explicit as to the number or extent of this plurality (see *CD*, III.1, p. 192).

However, since God and humanity are nonetheless distinct even in their intimate friendship, this is no "analogy of being, but of relationship." God's fundamental life-in-relation is analogically imaged in our fundamental life-in-relation; accordingly, God's relationship with us is imaged in our proper relationship with God and with one another. Made in the divine image, the human being is fundamentally and properly a being-in-encounter. Like the triune God, who is "one" but not "solitary," we also find our genuine humanity only in relationship: "It is not good that *'adam* should be alone" (Gen. 2:18) (*CD*, III.2, p. 324).

The whole of Barth's anthropology follows from this starting point. Precisely as *imago Dei*, humanity's "basic form," the form that makes human beings "capable of entering into covenant with God as the creatures of God," is the dynamic form of a meeting between an "I" and a "Thou" (*CD*, III.2, p. 224). Any genuinely human "I am," Barth argues, may be paraphrased, "I am in encounter" (*CD*, III.2, p. 247). In this view, the true human being is none other than the event of being in encounter, of being human by "being with" and "being for" another in mutual recognition and engagement. Among human neighbors, being human means meeting face to face in dialogue and care: seeing and being seen, openly welcoming and being welcomed, speaking and listening, calling and being called on, helping and being helped — all of this, Barth suggests, "gladly" and "freely" (*CD*, III.2, pp. 273-74).

This last feature, the free gladness of joy, Barth calls "the *secret* of humanity" (*CD*, III.2, p. 271). If this work — this openness and conversation and mutual assistance — is carried out as if in obedience to "an alien law imposed from without," if it is not carried out in sincere gladness and spontaneous freedom, then it is not humanity, but rather its empty shell (*CD*, III.2, p. 269). Humanity means this free encounter in mutual joy. Humanity means a reciprocal act of "being given and giving," a shared self-donation in which each "has quite simply been given the other" (*CD*, III.2, p. 272). Humanity means a "togetherness" in which "I" and "Thou" are "neither slave nor tyrant . . . but both are companions, associates, comrades, fellows and helpmates" (*CD*, III.2, pp. 269, 271). In short, they are friends: "I am not Thou, but I am with Thee. Humanity is the realization of this 'with'" (*CD*, III.2, p. 268).

Created in the image and likeness of the triune God, human beings are fundamentally beings in encounter, beings-with and beings-for their human neighbors. But they are also, and preeminently, beings with and for

God. For Barth, the human "I am in encounter" always means first and last that "I am in encounter with God." We are made, Barth observes, to encounter not only other creatures but also our Creator as "companions, associates, and comrades." God desires this friendship with us. God creates human beings as covenantal partners: for God this is a "covenant of grace," while for us it is a "covenant of gratitude."

It is clear that Genesis 1:26-27 is a kind of backdrop for this argument. Our gratitude images divine grace in a reciprocal, though asymmetrical, relationship. Just as among human neighbors, full humanity consists in both parties' "being given and giving" themselves to the other, between God and genuine human beings there is mutual self-donation. However, because of the radical distinction between creatures and Creator, this giving takes different forms. God bestows Godself in the form of benefit: chiefly, the divine presence with God's people, but also every "perfect gift" that makes for abundant life (James 1:17). Genuine humanity, on the other hand, bestows itself by imaging this gesture in the form of gratitude for these benefits: chiefly for the divine presence, but also for the divine gifts and divine life.

Thus Barth specifies his account of being human as "being in encounter": "[T]he being of man can and must be more precisely defined as a being in gratitude" (CD, III.2, p. 166). The particular encounter with God for which we are made, then, is the encounter of thanksgiving. In this way, says Barth, the mutual, asymmetrical self-donation between Creator and creature takes place. God gives Godself to the human neighbor, saying, "Take what is mine," ordaining her to "participate in the being of God by the gift of God" (CD, IV.1, pp. 9, 10). And genuine human beings, in and through their gratitude, acknowledge divine generosity and respond to it "gladly" and "freely."

But they may not respond in kind! For Barth, the form of human self-donation can in no way match or even approximate the divine form. Human beings cannot shower God with benefits from above, nor can they quite modestly present God with a single benefit from below. In short, they cannot themselves repeat the divine words "take what is mine" without making an utterly illegitimate claim on some particular "what" as their own in the first place. Only God, as creator and sustainer and provider of all things, can make this claim. But as we have seen, human liturgists, in a perfect reversal of gratitude, may explicitly or implicitly allege that their goods and services are "theirs" to give to God, not theirs inasmuch as they receive them from God, but rather fundamentally theirs for the giving. Barth's argument points to the idea that the act of "offering" benefits to God, for all its ostensible generosity, involves a tacit and presumptuous claim to possession: "Take what is mine." Take these goods, or, if I ostensibly recognize that these goods are already yours, then take this work, this very gesture of love and devotion with which I offer them. Or, if I recognize that even my devotion comes from you, then take this very recognition as evidence of my exceedingly devoted devotion, my exceedingly humble humility, and so on. "Take it," we insist, echoing Cain: "Take what is mine!"

The situation would be merely absurd, even comical — the recipient of a million-dollar gift returning a five-dollar bill to her donor as a sincere and solemn thank-you — were it not so tragic in its implications. Indeed, from this vantage point we may definitively charge Cain and Abel with trying to cash in, even so long after the fact, on the serpent's promise: "You will be like God" (Gen. 3:5). For each brother brings to God his own particular offering, his own particular show of human beneficence that apes, if only in iconic fashion, divine grace. Each one sets himself and his wares before God as if to say, "Take what is mine." If the conspicuously precious character of their gifts — the farmer Cain's "fruit of the ground" and the herdsman Abel's "fat portions" of the "firstlings of his flock" — does not conclusively mark their liturgy as an audacious impersonation of divine generosity, Cain's ensuing anger and violence surely do. "What is his" has been rejected, and he is furious. If he has thought otherwise, if he has realized in the first place that his offering is not his to give to God but rather already belongs to God, if he has admitted that not only his goods but also his very work of "generosity" are only his insofar as they are first of all God's gift to him (James 1:17), then he would either refrain from his offering at the outset or, when God shows no regard for what are after all divine gifts in the first place, he would refrain from his anger and his terrifying turn against his brother.

But he does not refrain. Instead, he makes his offering and thus makes his bid to take up the divine mantle and position alongside God, leaving the human mantle and position behind. He seeks to be colleagues with God, to confront God as an equal, as if to say, "One good gift deserves another." He seeks to make God a recipient of his own good graces, and himself God's benefactor; and, in this sense, he seeks to revolt, to turn heaven and earth upside down. Like his parents in the garden, he presides over the bounty of creation as if it were his own, giving what he can only rightly receive. Quite confidently he says to God, "Take what is mine." And thus he says, in effect, to his Creator and to himself and to his brother beside him, "I, too, am a God."[8]

God exposes and rebuffs this claim, but not with the outrage of a tyrant. After all, God is not put at risk by Cain's anxiety, confusion, and pride. Rather, it is the intended friendship between God and Cain that is at risk, and thus it is finally Cain's humanity that is at risk most of all. For these reasons, God acts, moving to interrupt Cain's pride and allay the fear his pride betrays. As we have seen, God assures Cain that his anger is unnecessary (Gen. 4:6-7); and even after Cain has murdered Abel, God provides him a last opportunity to repent and return to himself and to God. Indeed, for J and for Barth, God originally and finally desires neither sin's futility — the human attempt to secure something like divine power, to "be like God" — nor the distant relationship of czar and serf. Rather, God desires intimate friendship with humankind. The triune God creates men and women that they might live with God as God lives with them, together in a covenant of grace and gratitude. As the human-to-human relationship in its own way reflects, this covenant is to be an event of continual, mutual self-donation. But since divine and human "persons" are utterly distinct, the forms of donation can only analogically parallel each other. God gives all things; genuine human beings live as beings-in-gratitude. They do not offer God gifts in comic and tragic parodies of divine generosity. They are grateful. In short, they are human.

---

8. Though he does not mention Cain directly, Barth's account of human ruin in *The Epistle to the Romans,* the section entitled "The Night," opens with a polemic against religion and worship that may well be applied to Cain, and thus to human beings generally insofar as we, too, carry out Cain's liturgy: "We suppose that we know what we are saying when we say, 'God.' We assign to Him the highest place in our world: and in so doing we place Him fundamentally on one line with ourselves and with things. We assume that He *needs something*: and so we assume that we are able to arrange our relation to Him as we arrange our other relationships. We press ourselves into proximity with Him: and so, all unthinking, we make Him nigh unto ourselves. We allow ourselves an ordinary communication with Him, we permit ourselves to reckon with Him as though this were not extraordinary behavior on our part. . . . We confound time with eternity. . . . Our well-regulated, pleasurable life longs for some hours of devotion, some prolongation into infinity. And so, when we set God upon the throne of the world, we mean by God ourselves. In 'believing' in Him, we justify, enjoy, and adore ourselves" (*The Epistle to the Romans,* p. 44).

2. The Work of Gratitude

But what is the proper form of this gratitude? If thanksgiving is not the work of bestowing goods and services on God, what is it? What concrete shape does the event of glad and free self-donation to God take in genuine human lives? Barth puts it this way: the work of really being human is to receive divine gifts and "use what is received" — to be both "recipients and enjoyers."[9] To receive well and to enjoy well, that is the work of "being in gratitude."

As we have seen, J's account of the original human vocation may help specify this work. For receiving well and enjoying well entails not only collecting divine gifts but tending to them, cultivating them with care — tilling and keeping creation, in J's terms (Gen. 2:15). Moreover, for J, this task extends not only to the ready-made benefits already available, but also to the barren places that, for all their current desolation, contain the seeds of benefit planted by God (Gen. 2:8). Even Eden begins as a wasteland (Gen. 2:4ff.), and God's invitation to "freely eat" of the garden's fruit points to the spontaneous, delighted character of enjoying well: "Eden," after all, likely means "delight." In this view, God does not mean for us merely to consume creation's goods as merchandise, but fully to enjoy them as blessings. Just as in our giving and receiving of gifts in our human family, we receive divine gifts well if we embrace them into our care and revel in the pleasurable joy they are meant to provide. Accordingly, God does not coerce humanity into taking pleasure in Eden's fruit; rather, God invites them to do so, with all the hospitality of friendship: "You may freely eat of every tree in the garden" (Gen. 2:16).

But there is a command. Even blessings and delight have their limit. Indeed, it is arguable that limitation is one of the conditions for the possibility of enjoying a blessing at all, a line to mark the blessing off as blessing, to distinguish what is given from what is merely available, and thus to distinguish "freely eating" from mere eating. In any case, there is this limit in Eden: the fruit of one tree is withheld from the banquet.

And thus we may ask: While being in gratitude seems quite natural and fitting in response to permission and delightful gifts, what form does it take in response to prohibition? Obedience, surely. Compliance. Submission. But are intimacy and friendship possible under the sign of authority and command? Does a word of decree not establish or at least lay claim to a sce-

---

9. Barth, *The Christian Life,* p. 88.

nario wholly different from the gracious and grateful interplay of friends, namely, the dealings between sovereign and subject? Does not a clear and unmistakable distance open up between God and humankind after the announcement of the covenantal "you shall not" that was so prominent in the covenant at Sinai but also clear here at the creation? In short, is divine-human covenant compatible with divine-human friendship? Once the grateful receiving and enjoying of divine gifts is limited and thus determined by obedience to what indeed may appear as "an alien law imposed from without," how can being in gratitude remain both glad and free? Moreover, once God has delivered the command, how can human beings avoid interpreting it, questioning it, preaching it, honoring it, or dishonoring it? How can they avoid religion? Isn't the possibility of genuine friendship between God and 'adam jeopardized at just this point, that is, at the very outset?

Everything depends on the precise character of the command. In Barth's discussion of "the basic form of humanity," he argues that God, as Creator of humankind, indeed "imposes" this basic form as a kind of law that human beings must follow in order to be human at all. But as a determination, this command is, Barth says, "inward as well as outward":

> It is not therefore added to his essence, to the man himself, as though it were originally and properly alien to him and he to it, and at some level of his being he were not determined by it. He is not free in relation to it, but [only] as he is determined by it. He is himself in this determination (*CD*, III.2, p. 268).[10]

In other words, the "basic form of humanity" may be called a *constitutive command*. The procedure it names and requires is the event of human being; it makes the creature what and who she is. It constitutes her. Thus, with respect to following this procedure, she is not strictly free, as if she, already fully human, stood before the command as before a signpost at a fork in the road. Rather, she walks under the command as she moves along the road of humanity at all. She freely steps forward — that is, she is human — only to the extent that she is "determined" by this command. Being human, we might say, acting in accord with the basic form of humanity, is the condition of "human being."

10. Cf. Barth, *Ethics* (Edinburgh: T&T Clark, 1981), e.g., p. 209: "The demand of the Creator's command cannot be anything other than that of the most proper being of the creature."

Non-constitutive commands may also confront her, arising from all quarters; we may call these, by contrast, *legislative commands.* These are the signposts along the road. Great or trivial things may be at stake for her as she decides for or against following these signs, and she may obey or disobey them, variously reaping benefits and suffering consequences. But in these cases her full humanity, her genuine creaturely being itself, is not at stake. Her authentic humanity is jeopardized or preserved only in relationship to constitutive commands. Thus, for Barth, the command that human beings encounter each other in mutual openness and assistance is a constitutive command: at stake here is their full humanity. On the other hand, a command, say, to pay a particular tax or to stay out of a dangerous body of water or to arrive on time for a day of work — these may be legislative commands. Disobedience here may mean illegality, physical risk, or professional demerit; in any case, however, the delinquent's full humanity does not rise or fall with her decision.

Thus, for Barth, the "basic form of humanity" amounts to a constitutive command from God the Creator. If a human being disobeys this command — that is, if he violates his own basic form — he forfeits his full humanity, including his genuinely human freedom. He loses himself. He binds his own hands. In effect, he has "made himself quite impossible" (*CD,* IV.1, p. 10).[11] And thus this kind of command, Barth suggests, is fully consistent with friendship, since the command does not impose a law alien to humanity, as if from outside, but rather a law constitutive to humanity, as if from both without and within. Though originally issued from a locus distinct from humankind, it is not, strictly speaking, heteronomous. As a law of God given to the human being "as his own law, the law which he himself has set up, the law of his own freedom," it is both heteronomous and autonomous. "Only as such," Barth argues, is it understood and obeyed by human beings — "according to the intention of its Giver." Determined by this com-

---

11. Here again (see above, note 3), it is worth noting that, for Barth, the forfeiture of full humanity involved in sin in no way renders the sinner *sub*-human or *in*-human, but rather renders him, as Barth puts it, "impossible," "lost to himself," opposed to his own true being, identity, and character: "Our being does not include but excludes sin. To be in sin, in godlessness, is a mode of being contrary to our humanity.... If [a person] denies God, he denies himself.... He chooses his own impossibility." The sinner remains human, but the fullness of his humanity becomes for him a closed door, though his abiding humanity, that is, his ordination to full humanity, is never forgotten or withheld by God: "Sin means that [the sinner] is lost to himself, but not to his Creator" (see *CD,* III.2, pp. 136, 197).

mand, I follow not only a "law of God" but my own law as well, the law of my humanity, the law of being human that constitutes human being. Legislative commands confront us; constitutive commands, when followed, make us what we are as humans (*CD*, III.2, pp. 268-69).[12]

And so we may put the question this way: Is the original divine command in J's narrative — "of the tree of the knowledge of good and evil you shall not eat, for in the day that you eat of it you shall die" — a legislative or a constitutive command? If we read it as constitutive, then its delivery is not a prescription but a description of what is already established, a map of the world and a map of human being: "Here is your proper work amid this creation, the work of human being." On this reading, it is a command only in the sense of a "charge," a "commission," an "ordination" or "appointment" — all of which are legitimate translations of the Hebrew word J uses here: *sawah*. God does deliver a "you shall not," but God does so in order to describe both the substance and the limits of human vocation. "Here are the precincts of your work. Do this, and you will flourish — do that, and you will perish." Human life, precisely as vulnerable, creaturely life in a likewise vulnerable creation, is not without risks. Therefore, God gives *'adam* yet another gift: the gift of counsel, of guidance and warning, a word of wisdom. This only sharpens the irony, of course, when *'adam* eventually turns against God in an effort to "make one wise" (Gen. 3:6). Understood in this way, the command is not only consistent with hospitable friendship, but is a supreme expression of it. It is a word of welcome and advice. Like a host greeting a new guest, God provides, lovingly and crucially, the lay of the land, including the limits of safety and the limits of humanity itself. As such, the

12. Cf., e.g., Paul Tillich's conception of "theonomy," in which both "autonomy and heteronomy are rooted," and which means "autonomous reason united with its own depth." See Tillich, *Systematic Theology*, Vol. I (Chicago: University of Chicago Press, 1951), pp. 83ff.; see also Tillich, "Moralisms and Morality: Theonomous Ethics," in *Theology of Culture* (Oxford: Oxford University Press, 1959), pp. 135ff., 141ff. Cf. Franz Rosenzweig's distinction between command and law: a true command "knows only the moment" and is spoken by an "I" to a "thou," its paradigm being the lover's call, "Love me," while a law "reckons with times, with a future," and is spoken not by the lover but by a "third party," not by an "I" but by a "he." All orders, Rosenzweig argues, may be commands only if they follow from — and thus are "executions of" — the "one initial commandment to love [God]." For Rosenzweig, this first command (Deut. 6:5) grounds the possibility of all others, and "unlocks" the soul to God. See Rosenzweig, *The Star of Redemption* (Notre Dame: University of Notre Dame Press, 1970), pp. 176ff.

command is constitutive: it is issued from without but also from within. *Do this and be human.*

If we read it this way, God's remark is part of the inaugural divine call, the true human vocation; and it is the original event of divine friendship toward humanity that is imaged in every event of genuine human friendship toward a human neighbor. As God calls, we call on each other, marking and preserving our distinction from one another even as we open and reach toward intimacy. As Barth puts it, my human neighbor, too, for all his indelible externality, "is inward and intrinsic to me even in his otherness" (*CD*, III.2, p. 268). His commands, too, may name and require my vocation and thus in their own right may be constitutive for me, for my full humanity. When they are, when he constitutively commands me in care and hospitality, when he speaks from without but also from within me, from his position simultaneously external to me and "intrinsic to me even in his otherness," when he names the law of my humanity and encourages, even obligates me to live it out — then he acts as my "companion, associate, comrade, fellow and helpmate." Then he images God's stance of friendship with me. Then, in a word, he loves me.

Far from an alien law that disrupts the original covenant of friendship, the divine "you shall not" in Eden instead helps constitute that covenant. No less than the original gifts and permission, the command is also an act of friendship. God encounters 'adam in genuine love and intimacy, simultaneously external and intrinsic to human partners even in their "otherness." In this communion, God lovingly names and requires the proper vocation for humankind, the divine law that is also our own law, the law of our own freedom. On this reading, for J, human beings originally are by no means strictly naïve or innocent or ignorant before their meeting with the serpent. For they receive at the outset the very knowledge they require, a picture of their proper work (to till, keep, and freely eat) and a map of the creation with respect to that work's pleasures and risks (both the "you may" and the "you shall not"). Therefore, the divine command, as a constitutive command, completes the divine charge to 'adam to carry out the work of genuine human being. It seals the true human vocation, and it inaugurates divine-human friendship. As such, it is not an occasion for human submission but rather of human commission with God, of entry into the common life — the covenant of friendship between Creator and creature — for which humankind was created.

Moreover, this reading may also shed light on the serpent's disruptive work, since with his opening query he revisits and reinvents the divine in-struction, trading on the possible ambiguity between constitutive and legis-lative commands. For if the "you shall not" is reconstrued as a legislative command, and thus if human commission gives way to human submission, friendship will also give way to the strict heteronomy of sovereign and sub-ject. A clear breach opens up. As Aristotle puts it, once "one party is re-moved to a great distance" — as, he notes, "in the case of kings" — "the pos-sibility of friendship ceases."[13] But as we have seen, 'adam's conversation with the serpent — introduced and framed with the question, "Did God say. . . ?" — accomplishes just this removal, not only because it seems to pre-suppose that God is not present, but also because it effectively presents the prohibition not as a constitutive command but as a legislative one, issued not by a divine "Thou" that is both external and intrinsic to the human "I," but by a divine rule-maker, an exalted bureaucrat, a third party, merely ex-ternal and indeed "removed to a great distance." The serpent's question di-rects the discussion to the issue of what God did or did not say, and thus it invites 'adam to consider the command strictly as divine discourse, that is, as a divine fiat and thus as a legislative "alien law," a word spoken not by a friend but by a mere monarch — even, the serpent suggests, by a tyrant.

In other words, the serpent invites 'adam to hear God's command as one given not to constitute but rather to constrict human beings, to keep them from becoming like God. Indeed, both inside and outside today's reli-gious communities of interpretation, wherever the divine command in Genesis 2:15-17 is read as a legislative command; wherever it is heard as strictly heteronomous; wherever it is conceived as a decree issued strictly "from on high" and not also "from within"; wherever it is understood to set the stage for human beings to transgress a merely divine law and not also their own law of humanity — that is where the serpent's work continues apace. With every such reading, God is reinvented, if not as a tyrant then certainly as a mere king, "removed to a great distance"; therefore, the proper human vocation is likewise reinvented as submission and obeisance. The serpent may be condemned as the father of treason, but as long as that treason is conceived to be against a divine monarch and not a divine friend, the serpent quietly maintains his blank-eyed smile. In this way, J catches us in our own act of reading, as we ourselves retrace and replay the descent into distance, the fall away from friendship and intimacy with God.

13. Aristotle, *Nicomachean Ethics*, 1159a, 1-5.

In Barth's view, once this breach opens up, once the command registers as legislative, the act of genuine human being is ruled out for us. Obedience to a sovereign, no matter how dutiful, cannot be carried out gladly and freely, but only as mandatory, obligatory, and binding — and thus only more or less cooperatively and more or less reluctantly. To be sure, such obedience may very well be eager and enthusiastic; after all, Cain's near-namesake, *qana'* ("zealotry"), is only too happy to honor and obey. But the zealot's happiness, however fervent, is not gladness or joy; rather, it is joy's parody, in the oldest sense of that word: *para oide* ("subsidiary to song"). Joy is the song. To follow the divine command as a constitutive command means to follow it joyfully, as an almost musical "inner Yes" spoken in the spontaneous "freedom of the heart" (*CD*, III.2, pp. 267, 273). Apart from this joy, the "with" of intimate friendship dissolves into mere being-alongside. And since, for Barth, the "with" of fellowship makes for genuine humanity, apart from this joy and this freedom of the heart there is no genuine human being as such, but only empty motions, however "humane" they may appear (*CD*, III.2, p. 273).

Apart from this joy, we might say, there is only "acting human," not "being human." For Barth, once someone imagines himself to stand — already human — before a divine command as if before a signpost at a fork in the road, he thus presumes to "know the other possibility of either not obeying it at all or doing so reluctantly because he himself wills or can will something very different" (*CD*, III.2, p. 269). That is, he presumes that, first of all, he "neutrally" regards the command and only subsequently subjects himself to it, or ignores it, or half-heartedly negotiates with it, or what have you (*CD*, III.2, p. 266). But in this situation the command — as a *constitutive* command — is actually unknown; it is mistaken for a legislative order. "But if he does not really know it," Barth continues, "this means that he does not know himself. He is not himself but lost outside himself" (*CD*, III.2, p. 269). That is, Barth argues that, as soon as one friend is conceived to be "merely imposed or thrust" on the other,

> the encounter has almost the instinctive form of a "falling-out," i.e., of a secret or open reversal of encounter, or movement of retreat, in which a hasty greeting is exchanged and then the one seeks safety as quickly as possible from the other, withdrawing into himself for fear of violation and in the interest of self-assertion (*CD*, III.2, p. 269).

In this way, then, the first couple's interaction with the serpent confounds them into a fall that is also a "falling-out." They grasp and eat the fruit that will, they think, make them wise, and they stumble not into wisdom but into folly, forfeiting their original gift of self-knowledge. They withdraw into themselves in anxious self-interest and, like stars collapsing, they lose themselves as they withdraw. Their full humanity becomes a continually deferred possibility for them, a closed door. In Barth's interpretation of Michelangelo's *The Creation of Eve,* both the man's retreat into stupor and the woman's step forward into prayer are "reversals of encounter": crass secularism and crass religiosity, we might say, arise in the same scenario. Neither one takes the form of open encounter in gratitude and friendship; and thus neither one takes the form of full and genuine humanity.

For Barth, being in gratitude takes the form of receiving well, enjoying well, and obeying well, that is, obeying God's "you shall not" as a gift, a constitutive command delivered in love and friendship that resounds from without and from within, calling and recalling us to full humanity. And this gift, too, even this "you shall not," we can embrace into our care and can enjoy it for the pleasures it is meant to provide. We give thanks for it if we follow it, not as a legislative order, however prudent or sensible or fair we may take that order to be, but rather as a commission to full humanity, to being human in spontaneous gladness and the freedom of the heart.

Analogies for this form of gratitude are not hard to find. Watch a child receive a long-sought bicycle as a gift, for example, and watch the parents who give it to her. They want nothing more than for her to embrace the gift into her keeping as a blessing, to quit the house at once, without pausing to pay solemn tribute to her parents, much less to remove and gratefully present them with a pedal or a spoke as an offering! They want her to go outside and ride it, to revel in it and in her own strength, enjoying them both for all she is worth. To her parents, she is worth a great deal. And if they command her to ride only on quiet streets, to avoid the busy thoroughfares, they are not interrupting their love for her; rather, they are continuing it, heaping gift upon gift. Therefore, if she follows their command not as an interruption but as a continuation of her joy, she rides in thanksgiving. She receives even the command as a gift. She is grateful.

In the unfinished drafts for the posthumously published Chapter XVII of *Church Dogmatics,* "The Command of God the Reconciler,"

Barth develops his account of being-in-gratitude in covenant with God. For even the girl on her bike returns home from her ride, and she is not oblivious to her parents' generosity. She is aware of it and responds to it, her gratitude passing over into other forms of interaction. That is, in these manuscripts Barth argues that the founding work of genuine human life begins in *thanksgiving,* but also properly evolves into *praise* and *petition.* For Barth, these three gestures — understood together as *invocation* — comprise not merely a cluster but rather an integrated choreography of human response to God.

To spell out this case, Barth first revisits his concept of grateful humans, designating human beings as the "beings who owe [God] thanks and can and may and should thank him." In the covenant of grace, God calls on humankind to call on God, to return the echo of gratitude to the voice of grace, "to thank God and to thank him again and again — from this angle already invocation is a never-ending action — for all that he was and is and will be and all that he did and does and will do for them as his human children." This repeated and ongoing act of thanksgiving, Barth explains, "is to acknowledge as such a gift that someone else has freely given." Thus the "first motive" of human invocation of God, "which as a basic note decides and determines all that follows, is that they owe him the boundless acknowledgment of his free gift."[14]

This "first motive," however, if it is serious, cannot remain mere "acknowledgment," however appreciative that recognition may be. In Barth's view, genuine thanks always involves a second movement: "It must also entail the honoring, extolling, lauding, and praising of their Father as the Giver of this gift." True thanks entails praise. If thanksgiving is fundamentally an acknowledgment of God's free gift, Barth glosses praise as "specifically to confess and to make visible and audible the fact that God is worthy to be venerated and invoked as God." Once the gift is truly recognized as worthy, and the giving as free, then the Giver can only be recognized as worthy of laud and honor, of "visible and audible" signs of praise. Barth describes the invocational progression this way: "In the authentically required turn from God's benefits to his beneficence and finally to himself as the Benefactor, thanksgiving becomes praise." Not gratitude alone, then, but gratitude and praise together constitute human being in covenantal partnership with their Creator, and thus genuine human being

---

14. Barth, *The Christian Life,* p. 86 (hereafter *CL*).

itself. Moreover, Barth is clear that these two movements are to be understood less as distinct moments and more as distinguished aspects of a single gesture of invocation. Therefore, any distinction between the two can only be relative, as true thanks involves praise, and true praise, thanks. Taking as exemplary both the Psalter and Paul's epistolary greetings, in which the terms "thanksgiving" and "praise" are repeatedly coupled, Barth denies any "abstract separation of the two concepts." Thus it is not merely that praise follows thanksgiving as one discrete action follows another in sequence; but also, for Barth, thanksgiving and praise are to be understood as "merging" components, only analytically distinguishable, of the single invocational act in which they find their place (*CL,* pp. 87-88).

And yet there is a third and culminating aspect of this choreography. For Barth, as proper and required as this invocation is, it "will always take place within the painful limits of their humanity," and thus it

> can only be that of those who have total need of him and his further gifts. Even more, it can be genuine thanks and praise only in unreserved acceptance of this neediness of theirs, only as crying to God for his further free gifts, only as petition (*CL,* p. 88).

The "required turn" from thanksgiving to praise, then, is only possible in the context of an "unreserved acceptance of this neediness," our recognition not only of the worth of the gift and the worthiness of the Giver, but also of our own, the recipients', ongoing destitution and dependence on these gifts and this Giver. This recognition of need finds expression in a "crying to God" for further gifts. At stake here is the very propriety of the thanks and praise, and thus of the grateful assembly's humanity itself: as they give God thanks and praise while recognizing their own indigence, "they act in accordance with the situation between [God] and them," and this accord with reality allows them to "thank and praise him in truth" (*CL,* p. 89).

For Barth, therefore, the grateful praise of invocation that founds and constitutes the human being-with-God properly culminates in the act of *petition,* of "crying to God," indicating as it does the utter and ongoing dependence of the creature on the Creator. This is a culmination not only of invocation but of genuine humanity as such. It is for this reason, says Barth, that "the invocation of God the Father which Jesus taught his disciples in the Lord's Prayer takes the form of pure petition." This petition, far from diminishing or detracting from the thanks and praise, instead "gives definitive honor to their character as thanks and praise, when invocation is multiple petition presented to God with empty outstretched hands. Only thus is their invocation totally serious as the movement of men in their humanity turning to God in his deity" (*CL,* p. 89). Barth thus develops the human being's proper response to God's grace, the "one but necessary thing" that is her proper work as God's covenantal partner, as not merely gratitude but rather the whole pattern of human invocation: to acknowledge God's gifts as good and freely given, to visibly and audibly testify to God's generosity and excellence, and to cry out to God for further gifts with empty outstretched hands — that is, to give God thanks, praise, and petitionary prayer (*CL,* p. 88).

For Barth, this choreography of invocation is the event of humanity itself, the gesture that founds and constitutes genuine human being. Human reconciliation to God consists in being restored to this invocation, this genuine humanity, this covenant of gratitude — that is, this covenant of thanks, praise, and prayer — in response to God's covenant of grace. But we may ask, both in light of this account and also in view of Barth's critique of worship and religion: How is this invocation possible? Have we now reached an impasse? Given that human beings have made themselves "impossible" by turning away from God, and thus have "cut the ground from under their feet," where may they now stand and act and "invoke the name of the LORD" (Gen. 4:26)? And if they do find footing somehow, and set about the work of invocation, how can they avoid repeating the original rupture, the attempt to stand aright before God, and thus away from God? In short, how can they avoid religion?

Are not "thanksgiving, praise, and petition" religious, and are they not also *leitourgia* — indeed, the preeminent *leitourgia* of them all? Wouldn't Cain be able to protest that his offering of fruit was also a token of thanks and praise, and a request for further benefits? In any case, on what basis can any human being finally and thoroughly distinguish his own offering from Cain's? And if not from Cain's, then how can his be distinguished from 'adam's, the naked "taking" that Cain and Abel only mask as pious "offering"? In short, if human worship is "fall," doesn't human invocation just compound the trouble?

In the drafts for Chapter XVII of *Church Dogmatics,* Barth expounds in greater detail on his account of genuine human being and genuine human life with God. In so doing, he provides, I would argue, a way of coordinating his critique of worship, on one hand, and his claim that invocation constitutes genuine human being, on the other. To anticipate: Barth maintains that "true" human lives, "grateful" and fashioned in "the form of the praise of God," are indeed possible for human beings, but not strictly as their own achievements. Rather, just as he makes an anthropological case for understanding the human being as "the being engaged and covenanted to God" (*CD*, IV.1, p. 43), and in that sense fundamentally a "being-with," Barth likewise argues that the genuinely human work of invocation is only possible in concert with the work of the triune God, and in that sense it is fundamentally a "working-with." That is, the worship that amounts to reconciliation with God is not accomplished by human beings on their own: as we have seen, such unilateral liturgy presupposes and maintains an arrangement in which humanity is set over against God. Rather, worship as reconciliation is accomplished by human beings in concert with the triune God. The restoration to friendship with God and thus to true and full humanity is not a work of people as if alone, but rather a work of people-with-God, a radically collaborative event of renewed intimacy, fellowship, and communion precisely at the point of rupture, precisely in worship, precisely in human gratitude, praise, and prayer. Far from an impasse, then, the apparent tension between Barth's critique of worship as fall, on the one hand, and his account of worship as reconciliation, on the other, is for him the very framework and fulcrum of human salvation, the return to friendship and new life in God.

3. Conspiracy and Solidarity

Invocation, for Barth, is the founding human work. The "true man" is none other than the "grateful man." Calling on God in thanks, praise, and petition is the "one but necessary thing," the only proper and demanded labor for genuine human beings in covenant with God. In those unfinished drafts for Chapter XVII, Barth develops his view, suggested in Chapter XIII, that this foundationally human work — and thus genuine human being itself — cannot be carried out by the creature alone, but only in collaborative action with the triune God. To be sure, for Barth, this collaboration is one in which God is the founding and primary member; but it is also one in which the human partner, precisely as the active subject who follows and engages the divine dancer, finds her genuine balance, power, and freedom — that is, her humanity itself.

The breath of proper thanks, praise, and prayer to God, Barth suggests, is not merely human breath, but is a conspiring at once decisively divine and genuinely human. Likewise, the footing or ground of responsibility in proper invocation is not merely human ground, but rather a common ground of solidarity between God and creature. Barth thus sketches an anthropology in which human being, far from being strictly self-determined and independent vis-à-vis the triune God, instead finds its true life in concert with God, in working-with-God, a form of genuine human work that Barth calls "*ec*-centric."

Thus Barth's view of the genuine being and work of humanity amounts to this: the human being is one who calls on God, with God. That is, the human being is an invoking being who, in collaboration with God the Spirit's prior initiative and power, and in solidarity with God the Son's prior stance and standing, partakes of the triune divine life and work by thanking, praising, and petitioning God our Father and our Mother. In this view, the relational plurality of God's triune life is no less than the basis of human salvation: according to Barth's case, the personal plurality and substantial unity of God makes possible human invocation that is not over against but rather "in, with, and through." By taking up our calling into God's own calling — both God's "sighs too deep for words" (Rom. 8:26) and God's spoken prayer (e.g., Matt. 6:9-13) — God enfolds human work into divine work and thus reconciles humans to God by transforming the work of people into the work of people-with-God.

Let us return, then, to the questions Barth's case opens up. As we have seen, for Barth, genuine human being is constituted by invocation, the human response as active subjects to God's prior acts of grace. But who accomplishes this calling? In the first place, if gratitude is the foundational and constitutive human act, the event before and without which there is no genuine human being as such, then how does it arise in the first place? Moreover, how can human beings be "active subjects" and not at the same time submit to what Barth, earlier in *Church Dogmatics,* calls the desire to become a "being as subject," to possess "self-determination outside the divine predetermination" (*CD,* I.2, p. 314)? In other words, how can "active subjects" responding to God with thanksgiving, praise, and supplication avoid taking up a position over against God as "some second thing"? How can they avoid, in a word, religion?

Further questions arise from another angle. Barth himself maintains that all human calling on God "will always take place within the painful limits of their humanity." They cannot "deal on equal terms" with their Creator, nor can they "precede or anticipate him with something of their own that they bring and have to offer him." To be sure, God gives human beings the gift of freedom to turn to God, for "they can neither give it to themselves nor take it for themselves." But human reception and enjoyment of this freedom, both for Barth and for J, invariably take the form of forfeiture: "The use they make of it will always be misuse, by which the fellowship that he has created between him and them is totally and irreparably called into question." Following the first couple in the garden, human beings do attempt to take and give their freedom for themselves. Following the second generation east of Eden, human beings do bring and offer "something of their own," not only fruit and fat portions but works of all kinds, including the most sincere demonstrations of piety and reverence. Thus, disoriented as we are in Barth's view, ungrateful even in our alleged gratitude, caught up in the original and continual fall into the liturgies of Cain and 'adam, we may ask: How is the work of human thanksgiving — and thus the work of human being — accomplished at all? (CL, p. 88).

Indeed, Barth calls the event of human invocation "totally inconceivable," "the mystery of the covenant," "in its way no less a mystery than that of the incarnation and resurrection of the Lord" (CL, p. 89). For this "inconceivable" act to occur, says Barth, another "highly astonishing event" must precede and inform it, namely, "the fruitful meeting and the living fellowship of the Holy Spirit with them and with their spirits: their experience, perception, contemplation, and resolve" (CL, p. 90). Therefore, in a characteristic move, a fundamentally Augustinian one, Barth maintains that it is God's prevenient action toward God's creatures that allows them the freedom and wherewithal to properly call on God. According to this view, without God's "living fellowship" in the Holy Spirit, we cannot properly thank, praise, or pray to God. As creatures confounded in sin, we can only forfeit any opportunity to invoke God in this way; the "painful limits of our humanity" pervert even our best attempts. Even in our most delicate doxologies, our most assuredly humble offerings, our most profuse and impressive acts of penance, as long as we act as if alone, we are following Cain, that original human acquirer and maker of things — cities, social violence, and not least, full-blown religious worship.

But in the transformed situation brought on by "the fruitful meeting and the living fellowship of the Holy Spirit," the impossible becomes possible: "He, this Spirit of truth who is himself truth, God himself, the Kyrios, himself comes to help us in our weakness." Where for us thanksgiving, praise, and prayer only set us over against God, "the Spirit intercedes for us, with his own better sighing, which we can never express." And our human sighs are joined by God's own "sighs too deep for words" (Rom. 8:26). God meets us in "living fellowship," breathing with us in a conspiracy of reconciliation. Thus even the most confounded, divisive attempts at gratitude and praise are transformed and thereby rescued by the Spirit's intercession, a conspiring that guarantees God the Father's acknowledgment and hearing, for "how can he fail to recognize his own voice in the cry?" (*CL*, p. 86).

If taken alone, this last move in Barth's argument, the idea that God the Spirit's intercessions transform human prayers by allowing God the Father to recognize his own voice, seems to suggest an odd divine need to hear the divine voice in order to recognize it, or worse, a kind of divine narcissism. But if we consider this idea in light of Barth's critique of worship, another understanding comes into view. That is, if the root of human trouble is that through worship human beings set themselves over against God as some second thing, then this trouble is undone by God's gracious action not only toward human beings but precisely in and through them as they worship. In other words, if God the Spirit "comes to our help in our weakness" with God's own sighing, then how can we, not only praying-to-God but also praying-with-God, be set over against God? How can we be some second thing beside God if, in our very thanksgiving, God stands with us and as us? It is as though God, in the face of our bowing out and away from the divine embrace, lovingly collects us again, not by condemning or destroying our *leitourgia,* but by making it God's own — or rather, by taking it up into God's own triune life, God the Spirit calling on God the Father. We "fall" into prayer, but in the divine work of reconciliation God prays with us, with sighs too deep for words. We fall into invocation, calling out to God across the distance our very calling effects and maintains; but in the divine work of reconciliation, God calls with us, so that, "when we cry, 'Abba, Father!' it is that very Spirit bearing witness with our spirit that we are children of God, and if children, then heirs, heirs of God and joint heirs with Christ" (Rom. 8:15-16).

If we understand that, we may clarify and restate Barth's argument that God, by joining us in our cry, transforms merely human invocation by rendering it "recognizable": by joining us in our cry, God transforms merely human invocation — the worship that sets us over against and apart from God — into no less than an entrance into the triune divine life. The divine "with" overwhelms our "against," reworking our withdrawal into another way toward God. We turn from God, but God meets us in this very turning. In this view, then, *Immanuel* ("God-with-us") is an event that takes place first of all by transforming the original human gesture of separation itself — the invocational gesture of thanksgiving, praise, and prayer — into an event of intimate solidarity, companionship, and life together.

And so this transforming work is not only the work of God the Spirit for us, but also the work of Jesus Christ, the one whom "they shall name Immanuel" (Matt. 1:23). Indeed, in Barth's view, the Father hears in our human cry not only the Spirit's voice but also the Son's, and so the Father hears human thanksgiving not only because of the Spirit's sighing but "because, as he hears it, their weak and dissonant voices are sustained by the one strong voice of the one by whose Eucharist the inadequacy of theirs is covered and glorified in advance" (*CL*, p. 106). Apart from God, our *eucharistia* ("thanksgiving," the fundamental human act for Barth) can only be the interested, tragic eucharist of Cain, presented under a convincing guise of generosity and sincere thanks (convincing most of all, perhaps, to the presenter), but ultimately a bid for acquisition and security. With God, however, our eucharist is overcome and undertaken by God's own Eucharist, the thanks given by Jesus Christ on the night of his arrest (Luke 22:17, 19). Likewise, for Barth, God the Son joins us in not only our thanks but also our praise: "In their doubtful praise he hears *his* voice, his 'I thank thee, Father, Lord of heaven and earth' (Matt. 11:25)" (*CL*, p. 107). Likewise, in the case of their petitions, "in their voices with all their false notes the Father hears his pure voice" (*CL*, p. 108). Note that in each case the human speech, unsound as it may be, is not obliterated but sustained, strengthened, and accompanied by divine speech. Human beings do take their stand, but only by standing with God the Son, participating "in *his* calling upon *his* Father." Quoting Calvin, Barth puts it this way: "We pray as it were by His mouth" (*CL*, p. 105).

Amid the sweeping variety of Christian worship practices, there are perhaps few customs as widely and consistently found as the phrase that closes prayer, the declaration that is meant as a culmination: "We pray in

Jesus' name," "In the name of Jesus Christ we pray," or some equivalent variation that immediately precedes and introduces the final "Amen." Without rejecting what I take to be a commonly held understanding of this phrase for many Christians — that the phrase marks the prayer as Christian and not as, say, Muslim or Jewish — I want to suggest another view of this phrase's function in light of Barth's case, to wit: the phrase "in Jesus' name" refers to the "footing," or ground of responsibility, on which the speaker stands, the capacity in which she speaks, and the frame in which she acts.[15] For Barth, "true calling on the true God" can only be "participation in *his* calling." That is, it is an invocation established and maintained by the true calling of God the Son. God the Father's hearing us, Barth argues, is

> unshakably guaranteed by the fact that Jesus does not command them to pray in their own name but in his name, in the name of God's Son, their Brother, Jesus Christ, that in him they have their access to the Father, that they are adopted into fellowship with his praying (*CL*, p. 108).

Christ speaks and, through the power of the Holy Spirit, transforms our standing or stance vis-à-vis our Father and each other by adopting us into "fellowship with his praying." We pray, then, by taking up with Christ his standing, aligning ourselves with his stance, his position, his responsibility, and thus his "access to the Father."

And yet the Trinitarian emphasis in Barth's case, as well as his insistence on the priority and power of divine initiative in the covenantal relationship, requires that what appears to be our "taking up" Christ's footing must finally be described the other way around. To be sure, it is we who use the phrase "in Jesus' name we pray," but the phrase is an acknowledgment, not an achievement. It is Jesus Christ, precisely as God incarnate, who, through the power of the Holy Spirit, takes up our footing with us. We say "in Jesus' name," then, not because we ascend to his position, but because we recognize that he descends to ours, taking up our

---

15. For a treatment of this argument in light of sociologist Erving Goffman's work on "footing" and interaction, see Matthew Boulton, "We Pray By His·Mouth: Karl Barth, Erving Goffman, and a Theology of Invocation," *Modern Theology* 17:1 (2001): 67-83; see also Erving Goffman, "Footing," *Forms of Talk* (Philadelphia: University of Pennsylvania Press, 1981).

words into his Word, the divine Logos itself. Thus it is not so much that we stand or hope to stand in solidarity with Jesus Christ, but that he stands in faithful solidarity with us. In this sense, *Immanuel* means most fundamentally that we do not pray alone. We breathe and speak with God the Spirit, and we stand in responsibility with God the Son.

Therefore, the phrase "in Jesus' name" in Christian prayer involves an inversion of the commonplace linguistic pattern. On the one hand, the typical committee chairperson, declaring that she speaks "in the name" of her committee, thereby speaks on behalf of a larger group; on the other hand, Christians praying, asserting that they speak "in the name" of Jesus, do not thereby speak on behalf of Jesus. Instead, they are acknowledging, first, that Jesus stands with them: indeed, to the extent that the church is the body of Christ, Jesus stands in perfect solidarity *as* them, as they speak; second, that by virtue of the access this footing provides, the Holy Spirit speaks on behalf of them. Indeed, in Barth's view, in prayer we stand and speak only by way of a standing-with God the Son and speaking-with God the Spirit; this is solidarity and speech that is at once ours and not wholly ours. Remembering Barth's emphasis on divine priority in any collaboration, we might say that in the invocation of God we share both responsibility and authorship with the triune God — especially insofar as the Spirit "corrects" and "amends" our prayers. This is what Barth calls a "fulfillment, that is, a transformation, of the prayer itself." When it is understood in this light, the Christian practice of culminating prayer with some variant of the phrase "in Jesus' name" may be seen as a twofold discipline: first, it is a discipline of recognition that Christian prayer arises from the genuinely human form of life and work that Barth calls "living fellowship" with God; second, it is a discipline of formation toward that life and work, that is, it is Christian education.

Thus, in Barth's view, the act of proper invocation, the original and decisively human work, is carried out not by the human being working alone, but by a working-with-God in concerted action and "common life," though one where the divine partner stands in the prior and pivotal position (*CL*, p. 90). Barth's case, then, amounts to a picture of genuine human being and work as fundamentally being-with-God in covenant and working-with-God in living fellowship. Genuine human beings live, Barth contends, insofar as they stand with the Son ("in Jesus' name"), and call with the Spirit (both "Abba, Father!" and "sighs too deep for words" [Rom. 8:15, 26]). They give thanks and praise and petition, not in their own name but in the name of God's Son, standing aright before God the Father only insofar as they stand in Jesus' name, that is, only insofar as Jesus Christ stands for them and with them. Furthermore, taking the term *spiritual* to "denote only a new definition of the human spirit, of the whole of this spirit, by the Holy Spirit," Barth claims that genuine human beings "live spiritually" and, "to the extent that they live, *ec*-centrically." Through their genuine invocation they live a life centered (that is, subjectively entrusted, sworn, tethered, and rooted) neither in themselves nor in some other creature or finite locus, but "beyond themselves, clinging to God himself . . . and this only as they are freed to do so, and continually freed to do so, by the Holy Spirit" (*CL*, pp. 92, 94). For Barth, reconciled life with God means living *ec*-centrically in the power of the Spirit and the name of the Son, calling on the Father as child and heir, both fully human and fully centered in the divine Three-in-One. In the final analysis, Barth says, human beings neither are nor work alone.

Here, then, is Barth's account in Chapter XVII of the genuine human being, the active subject who responds to God in thanks, praise, and petition. She is fundamentally *ec*-centric, at once herself and centered beyond herself in God, neither divinized nor in any respect alone or apart from divine life. Breathing and calling with God in conspiracy, standing with God in solidarity, she is "a being hidden in God" (*CD*, IV.1, p. 8). But for all that, she is nonetheless — through this radical intimacy — again and at last fully human. She is distinct from God; she is a creature through and through. Indeed, if she were not, friendship would collapse into merger and identity, *Immanuel* collapsing into merely "God." But God does not desire to subsume or consume human beings; rather, God wishes to be in loving intimacy with them as creatures. For this to be possible, they must remain — or become again — creaturely, genuinely human active subjects. But their subjectivity, their spirit, must undergo "a new definition . . . by the Holy Spirit," decentered and recentered beyond themselves and in God's triune life. Like Michelangelo's first Adam, they must remain on earth, reclining in their created grace, distinct from their creator, but nonetheless looking and pointing and reaching out — centered in God.

We may understand Barth's critique of the fundamental human desire to become a "being as subject," to possess "self-determination outside the divine predetermination" (*CD*, I.2, p. 314) as a critique of the *en*-centric subject, the subject centered not beyond itself but in itself. Barth says that to become such a subject is the supremely and basically religious desire, the longing that makes religion, in all of its forms and variations and claims to the contrary, "still thoroughly self-centered" (*CD*, I.2, p. 315). In this view, in religion *'adam* longs to become and works to become a "being as subject," to make "the mystery of his responsibility his own mystery, instead of accepting it as the mystery of God" (*CD*, I.2, p. 314). That is, in religion human beings seek to make their responsibility, their ability to respond to God's grace as God's partner, their own possession, to "take full responsibility" for themselves, to be responsible in their own right and on their own feet, beside and apart from God. Here, says Barth, is religion's characteristic emblem and highest honor, for what virtue is more hallowed in human affairs than taking full responsibility for one's actions? But in Barth's account of properly human invocation and thus of properly human being, the ability to respond as God's covenantal partner is not human responsibility alone. To be sure, it is our responsibility; but even as such, it is neither our outright possession nor a gift we enact alone. Instead, it is a gift of God that we enjoy and play out by way of radical intimacy with God, "the fruitful meeting and the living fellowship of the Holy Spirit" (*CL*, p. 90). Therefore, our responsibility as human beings is, first and finally, "the mystery of God's responsibility," and only as such does it, through God's gracious gift, become the responsibility of human beings as well.

In this divine-human fellowship and common life, human beings respond to God and thus are responsible to God; but they only do this work with God, who meets them and joins them with better sighing and better standing. Conspiring with God the Spirit, standing with God the Son, we call on God as "Abba, Father!" That is, standing with the Child of God as children of God, we call on God as Creator and parent, no less "Mother!" than "Father!"[16] We are unable to respond in this way apart from the triune God; we are, in a word, irresponsible. In communion with the triune

16. Indeed, according to the biblical witness, the way is clear to name and portray all three divine persons with woman-centered language: "Spirit" as *ruah* or *shekinah,* the common (and grammatically feminine) terms translated "spirit" throughout Hebrew Scripture (e.g., Gen. 1:2; Ps. 17:8); "Son" as "Sophia" (Prov. 8) or as mother, i.e., as human mother to humanity (Luke 23:37); and "Father" as "Mother," i.e., as divine mother of creation (John 3:4-5; Isa. 66:13; Hos. 13:8). See Elizabeth Johnson, *She Who Is: The Mystery of God in Feminist Theological Discourse* (New York: Crossroad, 1992), esp. pp. 76-103; see also Sallie McFague, *Models of God: Theology for an Ecological, Nuclear Age* (Philadelphia: Fortress, 1987), esp. pp. 97-123.

God, we respond with authentic invocation — true thanks, praise, and petition to God — and thus we live as the *ec*-centric beings God means for us to be. Barth says that the "mystery of human responsibility," the "mystery of the covenant," takes place in human life and work. God calls us, and responds with us; God gives us our vocation and lives it out with us, indeed, precisely as "God-with-us." By way of this gracious divine action, we live it out as well — as genuinely human, genuinely responsible, active subjects, thoroughly *ec*-centric, centered in God.

Therefore, this invocation — and thus this eccentricity — is by no means limited to a particular precinct of human activity for Barth, but instead characterizes all properly human activity as such. That is, as the foundational gesture of human being, invocation is no mere starting point or touchstone for genuine human work; instead, it should encompass and inform that work, for God "wills" for human beings "that their whole life become invocation of this kind" (*CL,* p. 85). Far from being an action discharged, for example, merely during Sunday morning worship, or merely during hymn singing, and so forth, invocation is, for Barth, a gesture within which every human gesture can and must find its place in the Christian life. Just as religion, that is, worship as fall, is in Barth's view a broad category that includes all "moral and legal ordering," so salvation, that is, worship transformed into reconciliation by God's gracious gifts of conspiracy and solidarity, is lived out over the full sweep of human life — and through thanksgiving, praise, and prayer without ceasing (1 Thess. 5:17). God's covenant of grace, and its claim upon us, is thoroughgoing. Indeed, Barth argues that, for both Christian communities and their individual members, genuine obedience to God's call consists in human lives lived in the movement of invocation:

> [Christians are obedient] when explicitly or implicitly, directly or indirectly, their thought and speech and action finds itself in this movement; or, to speak in greater detail, when it presents itself as a form of the praise of his gift, his giving, and himself as the free Giver, and as a form of the prayer which, in every respect, it is always necessary that they address to him (*CL,* p. 108).

For Barth, what God "expects and wills" for Christians is this invocation without ceasing, this "action of obedience accomplished as their Christian life" (*CL,* p. 42).

The preposition here is worth emphasizing: Barth's case is not that invocation is an act of obedience *in* Christian life, but that it takes place *as* that life itself. Explicit invocation — practices of table grace or Sunday morning worship services, for example — may and should occasion that life and routine, but the whole form of Christian life, not only explicitly but also implicitly, Monday morning as well as Sunday morning, "finds itself in this movement." For both the individual and his community, says Barth, thanks, praise, and petition "must precede, accompany, and follow the whole of his life's work," as the "epitome and common denominator" of all that God requires of human beings. "This life of calling upon God," Barth says, "will be a person's Christian life" (*CL,* pp. 42-44). In "great and little things alike, both inwardly and outwardly," and carried out as "concretely as [our] rising up and lying down, coming and going, eating and drinking, working and resting," genuine invocation — that is, the Christian life — is lived and worked out (*CL,* p. 108).

To put it differently, Christian life is a life of worship as reconciliation that is made possible by divine initiative and accompaniment, but that is nonetheless carried out by human beings in collaborative, intimate partnership with the triune God. This intimate work is indeed an entrance into "participation in the being of God by the gift of God," the covenantal intimacy to which human beings were and are ordained even in creation. Thus this intimate work is no less than an entrance into God's salvation for humankind. Indeed, as the work of invoking God the Father in solidarity with God the Son and conspiracy with God the Spirit, it is a participation in the triune divine life, an event in which we are "hidden in God" (Col. 3:3) by standing with Christ, sighing with the Spirit, and calling on God our Father and our Mother. That is, genuine human being is restored to us, our salvation takes place, not by virtue of our own better sighing, no matter how eloquent, simple, or heartfelt our words may be, but by the Spirit's.

Likewise, genuine human being is restored to us — that is, our salvation takes place — not by virtue of our own standing aright, but by the Son's standing, in which we participate at his disposal and by way of his gift and command to "pray like this," not in our name but in his. Barth says that in Christian life, that is, in genuine human life, we sigh with the Spirit and we stand with the Son. Thus the "mystery of invocation," and hence the "mystery of our responsibility," is a reality in human life. This is the basis on which we actually and properly call out to our Creator; and this is the basis on which we actually and properly return to ourselves, that is, we return both to the peace and friendship with God for which we are made, and to the peace and friendship with each other that images God's friendship with us, mutually calling on one another in openness and care.

For Barth, therefore, worship as reconciliation, the proper form of Christian life, is correctly carried out neither as a response to salvation (a duty of the saved) nor as a means to salvation (a duty of the damned seeking reprieve). Instead, it is the life of salvation itself, the very event of reconciliation between God and human beings, made possible and carried out graciously and decisively by God, but in such a way as to establish human beings as genuine partners and friends, collaborators in the event by conspiracy and solidarity. The God who wills salvation for human beings, Barth argues, wills "that their whole life become invocation of this kind," that is, that their whole life, as "concretely as [their] rising up and lying down, coming and going, eating and drinking, working and resting," become a life of thanksgiving, praise, and petition, that is, a life of worship as reconciliation, a life of calling on God by God's power and in God's name. Just as Barth paints the human predicament as a fundamentally liturgical predicament in his picture of religion, his view of reconciliation between humanity and God is likewise liturgical. Worshiping as if alone, we fall unto death; worshiping through Jesus Christ and the Holy Spirit, we are restored to the life for which we were made by God our Father and our Mother.

Far from being some particular precinct of human activity, or even a "dimension" of that activity, worship — as both fall and reconciliation — is for Barth the very form of human work. Embroiled in sin, that form is twisted tragically inward, *ec*-centric, a parody of life, a masquerade finally issuing in Cain's murderous "rising up" (Gen. 4:8). Through God's saving work in Jesus Christ and the Holy Spirit, human life is restored to its original integrity: re-turned outward, *ec*-centric in freedom, courage, and joy, and reopened into peace, friendship, and partnership with God and neighbor. It is toward these ec-centric lives, Barth suggests, lives lived "as a form" of praise and prayer, that God both calls us and frees us; for it is in our answering God with and through God, our collaborative invocation, that we find ourselves genuinely and fully human, reconciled to God and neighbor, and incorporated into the triune divine life.

For Barth, this saving incorporation into God's life is no ad hoc strategy on God's part, no mere reaction to sin as if the great physician dreams up the cure according to the disease. Rather, the disease — religion, or worship as fall — is in fact a distorted, disastrous form of the originally intended friendship, a ruinous departure from the blessed living fellowship with God. Therefore, the cure — our salvation — is a return to that fellowship, to that health and abundance of life (John 10:10). In other words, in Barth's view, 'adam is first of all created for this intimacy with the triune God, this conspiracy (Gen. 2:7), and this solidarity and common work (Gen. 2:15). That is, 'adam is created in the image and likeness of the triune God, a creature fit for being-with-God by calling on God our Father and our Mother through God the Spirit and God the Son. Salvation for human beings means being restored to this originally intended common life, this intimate fellowship and partnership. It means undoing worship-as-fall, in which humans worship God — that is, act and live — as if they are alone, as if they are over against God, as if they are speaking and working on their own in en-centric isolation and self-sufficiency. It means a new dawn, the transformed event of worship-as-reconciliation, in which human beings worship God — that is, act and live — with God and through God, in conspiracy and solidarity. It means, in a word, repentance, a return toward friendship, toward reunion and intimacy between God and humanity, and thus a turning away from the dark night of religion, that grim parody of friendship that ends in violence.

But dawn is not the day. Human salvation may have begun, and decisively begun, in the divine and human history of Jesus Christ. Genuine human life, reconciled with God, lived ec-centrically by the Spirit and in the name of the Son, may now actually take place. The "mystery of invocation" may be a reality in human speech and work. Religion may be undone by God's gracious action, leitourgia taken up into God's triune life, and thus humanity actually and irrevocably returned from a stance over against God to a stance of intimate friendship with God, hidden in God, conspiring in the Spirit and standing with the Son. All this Barth attests without reservation. But religion, he insists, carries on, and not just outside the Christian church; it carries on in the Christian church, and preeminently there. No less within Christian communities and Christian lives as outside them, the liturgies of 'adam and of Cain, of fear and maneuver and violence and betrayal, carry on. Christian life, says Barth, involves not only religion's continual undoing, but full-blown religion as well. Christians — and for Barth, Christians most of all — still set themselves beside and over against God. They are still religious. They still withdraw. They still move afresh to shore up their allegedly independent positions. If their worship is reconciliation, Barth says, it is also fall. If they are reconciled, they are also sinners, through and through. Christ may have come to them already, but they still await Christ's coming, and stand in need of it no less than do any of their neighbors.

In Chapters 4 and 5, I turn to this paradoxical heart of Barth's case. First, I sketch how Luther's so-called *simul* doctrine, according to which the genuine Christian is both fully a sinner and fully righteous, frames and informs Barth's construal of Christian life. In particular, I argue that, for Barth, Luther's decisive theological move is his expressly liturgical account of the *simul* as the act of repentance. And, finally, I spell out the idea, suggested by Barth's liturgical account of Christian life, that worship — both as fall and as reconciliation — is provisional and temporary, and thus will one day come to its finale. Barth never finished Volume IV of *Church Dogmatics,* "The Doctrine of Reconciliation," and never began his planned fifth volume, "The Doctrine of Redemption." But these titles alone suggest that, for him, reconciliation is by no means the final movement of the divine symphony. Therefore, to close this book, I explore the idea that, while reconciliation for human beings means a life of calling on God, of invocation, of *leitourgia* transformed into participation in the divine life, of thanks, praise, and petition without ceasing — while reconciliation means all of these things — redemption will mean the end of them, the ceasing of prayer, and with that cessation, humanity's last and promised entrance into new life with God. This new life was originally intended in Eden, that garden without a temple, and one day will be finally realized in what John of Patmos called "the New Jerusalem," that city without a temple, "for its temple is the Lord God the Almighty and the Lamb" (Rev. 21:22). According to this view, the final victory over religion — eschatologically anticipated in Christian life but finally consummated only when even Christian life passes away — will take place not as our reconciliation but as our redemption, not as invocation but as Sabbath, celebration, and communion. The end of God's creative and redemptive work is not only reunion but also jubilation and delight, "music and dancing" (Luke 15:25).

CHAPTER 4

Martin Luther and Christian Life

Almost to the year, four centuries before Karl Barth began his commentary on Romans, Martin Luther began his. After his lectures on the Psalter, Luther's earliest academic lectures were on Paul's letter to Rome. And even in these early texts, which Luther wrote before the Ninety-Five Theses, his celebrated and notorious disputations, and his excommunication in 1521, there are outlines of a doctrine crucial to Luther's later theological work, and also formative for Barth's.[1] Now commonly known by Luther's phrase *simul iustus et peccator* (or more simply by the *simul*), the doctrine amounts to this: a genuine Christian is at the same time fully a "sinner" and fully "righteous," simultaneously "holy and profane, an enemy of God and a child of God."[2]

In this chapter I sketch this doctrine as Luther spelled it out, particularly highlighting the distinctly liturgical character of his thinking and the sense in which it points to a fundamentally penitential — and finally baptismal — portrait of Christian life. For Luther, if the genuine Christian is at once "always righteous" and "always a sinner," she is also "always a penitent," and as such she lives out a way of life in which she is "continually baptized anew." Understood in this way, I argue, Luther's doctrine of the

1. On Luther's influence on Barth generally, including the decisive importance of the *simul* in Barth's thought, see George Hunsinger, *Disruptive Grace: Studies in the Theology of Karl Barth* (Grand Rapids: Eerdmans, 2000), pp. 279-304.

2. *Luther's Works,* ed. Jaroslav Pelikan and Helmut Lehmann (St. Louis: Concordia Publishing House, 1963), 26: 232 (hereafter *LW,* page references cited in parentheses in the text).

simul is an interpretive key for understanding how Barth's apparently conflicting construals of worship — as fall and as reconciliation — may be fruitfully held together.

I. Martin Luther's *Simul*[3]

Generally, Luther's *simul* belongs to his well-known doctrine of justification by "faith alone." For Luther, the believer's faith and trust in God's promises of salvation — and his faith alone, apart from any works of mercy, piety, or righteousness — unites him to Christ and thus involves him in a peculiar relationship. Early in his theological work *The Freedom of a Christian* (1520), Luther calls this relationship "communion" with Christ, and describes it in nuptial terms: faith, he says, "unites the soul with Christ as a bride is united with her bridegroom," thus rendering them "one flesh."[4] "And if they are one flesh," Luther continues,

> and there is between them a true marriage — indeed the most perfect of all marriages, since human marriages are but poor examples of this one true marriage — it follows that everything they have they hold in common, the good as well as the evil. Accordingly, the believing soul can boast of and glory in whatever Christ has as though it were its own.

In other words, since in marriage "the wife owns whatever belongs to the husband," the believer can "boast of and glory in" not her own righteousness but Christ's righteousness as if it were her own, or rather, indeed as her own, but only by way of this "most perfect of all marriages," this "joyous ex-

---

3. This doctrine appears throughout Luther's work, e.g., *LW* 25: 258ff.; *LW* 27: 231; and *LW* 26: 232: "Thus a Christian man is righteous and a sinner at the same time [*simul iustus et peccator*]." For discussion of this, see, e.g., Heiko A. Oberman, *Luther: Man Between God and the Devil* (New Haven: Yale University Press, 1989), pp. 184, 320; Paul Althaus, *The Theology of Martin Luther* (Philadelphia: Fortress, 1966), pp. 242ff.; Alister E. McGrath, *Luther's Theology of the Cross: Martin Luther's Theological Breakthrough* (Oxford: Basil Blackwell, 1985), pp. 133ff.

4. Here Luther refers to Eph. 5:31-32, where Paul cites and comments on Gen. 2:24: "'For this reason a man will leave his father and mother and be joined to his wife, and the two will become one flesh.' This is a great mystery, and I am applying it to Christ and the church."

change." In itself, Luther insists, "the soul is full of sins, death, and damnation." But as wedded to Christ through faith, the soul may nonetheless properly conceive of itself as "endowed with the eternal righteousness, life, and salvation of Christ its bridegroom." The believer is still "full of sins" — and these sins, even as Christ now bears them, are still "her sins" — but since she now wears "the wedding ring of faith," these very sins "cannot now destroy her": "[S]he has that righteousness in Christ . . . which she can confidently display alongside her sins in the face of death and hell." In this way, as a bride of Christ, the believer may rightly understand herself to be fully righteous without losing sight of the fact that she remains, considered apart from Christ, fully a sinner. Her sins and her righteousness — that is, her standing as sinful and her standing as justified — are thus pictured alongside one another, simultaneous and thoroughgoing, joined together by the believer's "wedding ring of faith," itself, like all wedding rings, a gift from her beloved.[5]

Elsewhere in his theological work, however, Luther portrays the *simul* not in the quasi-mystical terms of "one flesh" and nuptial "communion," but rather in terms emphasizing difference and divine mediation. In his first *Lectures on Galatians* (1519), for example, he portrays Christ not as a bridegroom but as an advocate: a believer's sin "is not imputed to him. This is because Christ, who is entirely without sin, has now become one with His Christian and intercedes for him with the Father" (*LW* 27: 227). As he does in *The Freedom of a Christian*, Luther writes here of a unity between Christ and believer — they have "now become one" — but here the saving choreography of the union is intercessory, not conjugal. As an advocate, Christ mediates between the faithful and the Father. Similarly, Luther frequently trades on biblical images of "covering" — from Boaz covering Ruth with his cloak (Ruth 3:9) to a mother hen covering her chicks with her wing (Matt. 23:37) — to illustrate how Christ's saving righteousness is both intimately protective and extrinsic to the believer (*LW* 25: 265; *LW* 26: 231). In his later *Lectures on Galatians* (1535), he puts it this way: Christ's righteousness "is not in us in a formal sense, as Aristotle maintains, but is outside us, solely in the grace of God and in His imputation" (*LW* 26: 234).[6] That is, like a cloak or a mother bird's wing, or in-

5. Luther, *The Freedom of a Christian,* in *Three Treatises* (Philadelphia: Fortress, 1970), pp. 286-89.

6. Cf. his formulation a year later, in 1536: "The righteousness of Christ, since it is outside of us and foreign to us, cannot be laid hold of by our works" (*LW* 34: 153).

deed, in another figure, "like an umbrella against the heat of God's wrath," or a cover that serves as "shield and defense," Christ's righteousness intervenes and mediates on behalf of believers, sheltering and caring for them in their distress and trouble (*LW* 34: 153 [1536]; *LW* 32: 28 [1521]). "Christ protects me," Luther writes, "and spreads over me the wide heaven of the forgiveness of sins, under which I live in safety" (*LW* 26: 231-32). Under Christ's wing, so to speak, believers are nonetheless desperate, vulnerable sinners; but under Christ's wing, they are also graciously — and externally — forgiven and accepted.

Luther clarifies and qualifies his account of matrimonial union in "one flesh,"[7] a picture that might otherwise suggest an inherent or intrinsic transformation to righteousness on the part of the believer.[8] As Heiko Oberman has argued, Luther's emphasis on the "outside" or "alien" character of Christ's righteousness distinguishes his doctrine of justification from those put forward by his teacher Johann von Staupitz, and indeed by the namesake of Luther's own monastic order, St. Augustine.[9] For these teachers, a believer's justification means that in some respects he is himself actually transformed and made righteous; but for Luther, the justified believer remains thoroughly a sinner. He is "reckoned" or "accounted" righteous not because he himself is righteous in any respect, but only and strictly because of the divine imputation of Christ's righteousness, which

7. It is worth noting, however, that the matrimonial picture in *The Freedom of the Christian* is not devoid of difference or distinction between Christ and the believer. Luther does write, following Ephesians and Genesis, of "one flesh"; but the "joyous exchange" is, after all, an *exchange,* and thus it presupposes not a merger or identity but instead shared intimacy between two distinct partners.

8. For a recent and intriguing study arguing that justification as "communion" and inherent transformation to righteousness for the believer is in fact the best way to read Luther, and thus that a new rapprochement may be possible between Lutheran and Eastern Orthodox Christians, see Carl E. Braaten and Robert W. Jenson, eds., *Union with Christ: The New Finnish Interpretation of Luther* (Grand Rapids: Eerdmans, 1998). The burdensome question for such an argument, of course, is just what to do with passages in Luther that emphasize the "alien" character of Christ's saving righteousness and, indeed, perhaps most pointedly, with passages that emphasize the *simul* itself. Can an Orthodox conception of *theosis* really be squared with Luther's account of the Christian as at once "holy and profane, an enemy of God and a child of God" (*LW* 26: 232)?

9. For a discussion of this point, see Oberman, *Werden und Wertung der Reformation* (Tübingen, 1977), pp. 110-12; also Oberman, *The Dawn of the Reformation* (Grand Rapids: Eerdmans, 1992), esp. pp. 104-25. See also Alister E. McGrath, *Luther's Theology of the Cross,* pp. 134ff.

itself is both outside and foreign to him (*LW* 34: 153). "On [Christ's] account," Luther says, and on no other, "God overlooks all sins and wants them to be covered as though they were not sins." Thus believers live, as sinners, "under the curtain of the flesh of Christ (Heb. 10:20) . . . to keep God from seeing our sin" (*LW* 26: 232 [1535]).

And yet Luther's overall picture of human justification before God is more complicated, finally, than a divine imputation of Christ's righteousness to believers. In the passage just cited, for example, in which the external and strictly imputed character of Christ's saving righteousness is so vividly drawn, Luther also maintains that "on [Christ's] account God reckons imperfect righteousness as perfect righteousness" (*LW* 26: 232 [1535]). The phrase "imperfect righteousness" is striking. In view of Luther's argument that a believer, though justified, is nonetheless fully a sinner, we may ask, What is "imperfect righteousness"? Why doesn't Luther simply say, as he seems to in his *simul* doctrine, "On Christ's account God reckons sinfulness as perfect righteousness"? Likewise, on the very page where he says that "the righteousness of Christ . . . is outside of us and foreign to us," he also argues that this "righteousness, since it is without defect . . . does not allow our beginning righteousness to be condemned" (*LW* 34: 153 [1536]). Again we may ask, What is "beginning righteousness"? Why doesn't Luther say, "Christ's righteousness does not allow our sinfulness to be condemned"? If believers are thoroughgoing sinners, if Christ's righteousness is in no way "infused into the soul" (*LW* 26: 233), but rather an external curtain or cover for the soul's past and present sins, then why does Luther mention "imperfect" or "beginning" righteousness at all?

Here we enter a centuries-old debate among Luther's interpreters, between those who read his theology of justification as most fundamentally an account of God's "imputation" of saving righteousness to believers, and those who read it, instead, as an account of God's "impartation" of that righteousness to believers.[10] The best reading, I would argue, does justice to both aspects of Luther's thought. As we have seen, his repeated emphasis on the foreign and external character of Christ's righteousness

---

10. Oberman, *The Dawn of the Reformation,* p. 122. Oberman suggests a way to combine the two "seemingly irreconcilable alternatives of imputation and impartation" by way of a distinction in Roman law between *possessio* and *proprietas,* i.e., by arguing that, for Luther, saving righteousness is the believer's possession, but not her property (see Oberman, *Dawn,* pp. 121-25).

seems to exclude any merely "impartational" account of justification; but his case, replete as it is with figures and terms, such as "imperfect righteousness" and "our beginning righteousness," which point to some noteworthy change on the part of believers, resists merely "imputational" accounts as well.[11] That is, it resists any account of justification that fails to include — alongside the decisive and saving imputation of Christ's righteousness *extra nos* — the crucial impartation of a beginning righteousness *in nobis,* and thus the form of life through which this beginning is lived out as Christian life. For Luther, the Christian does not merely huddle, sinning away, beneath Christ's wing. The Christian believes. And this faith gives her life a particular — and as we shall see, an expressly liturgical — form and choreography.

Let us return to those striking terms "imperfect righteousness" and "beginning righteousness." By these Luther means, first of all, "faith in Christ." In his *Lectures on Galatians* (1535), he says, "In us there is nothing of the form or of the righteousness *except* that weak faith or the first fruits of faith by which we have begun to take hold of Christ" (*LW* 26: 234; italics added). In other words, a believer's "weak faith" or "first fruits of faith" is the single exception to her otherwise thoroughgoing lack of righteousness. Thus her faith is not only her beginning in trusting God and "taking hold of Christ"; it is also her "beginning in righteousness" (*LW* 34: 153),[12] the inaugural glimmer of her own new creation. It is only a glimmer; in itself, Luther insists, this beginning is utterly insufficient for salvation, worthy only of being condemned (*LW* 34: 153). Nonetheless, it is a real and consequential beginning. As we have seen, Luther denies the idea that Christ's righteousness is "in us in a formal sense"; but he also explicitly

11. For another such figure, see Luther's repeated use of the so-called Good Samaritan text in Luke 10, in which "the sinner" is identified with the dying man on the side of the road, and Christ is identified with the Samaritan. The sinner is in the process, Luther explains, of being made righteous (i.e., being nursed back to health) and thus is not yet fully righteous (i.e., fully healthy): "he is both sick and well at the same time" now that Christ "has begun to cure him." But precisely as a narrative scenario in which the sinner returns to health by degrees, this account suggests gradual, intrinsic transformation to righteousness for the believer (see, e.g., *LW* 25: 260).

12. Compare, for example, Luther in *The Disputation Concerning Justification* (1536) — "His righteousness, since it is without defect . . . does not allow our beginning righteousness to be condemned" (*LW* 34: 153) — with his *Lectures on Galatians* (1535): "God reckons this imperfect faith as perfect righteousness for the sake of Christ. . . . For because faith is weak, as I have said, therefore God's imputation has to be added" (*LW* 26: 231-32).

identifies faith itself as none other than "our 'formal righteousness'" imparted by God: "a cloud in our hearts, that is, trust in a thing we do not see, in Christ" (*LW* 26: 130 [1535]).

This "cloud in our hearts" is, for Luther, a necessary but insufficient condition of justification. There are two things, he says, that "make Christian righteousness perfect: the first is faith in the heart," and "the second is that God reckons this imperfect faith as perfect righteousness for the sake of Christ," for "because faith is weak, as I have said, therefore God's imputation has to be added" (*LW* 26: 231-32). That is, while too weak to warrant saving forgiveness, faith is nonetheless "our beginning righteousness," the gesture joining believers to Christ, on whose account "God reckons imperfect righteousness as perfect righteousness" (*LW* 26: 232).[13] To be sure, this gesture — believers' imperfect faith and thus their imperfect righteousness — is by no means strictly their own achievement, but rather a "work of God" and a "gift of God," "poured into [them] by hearing about Christ by the Holy Spirit" (*LW* 34: 153, 160). But precisely as a divine gift, precisely as God's impartation of "faith in Christ" to human beings, rendering them "faithful," this gesture takes shape in Christian life, quite simply and modestly, but also definitively and consequentially, a "beginning in righteousness" that is not extrinsic but rather intrinsic to them. For believers, Luther contends, however weak and imperfect their faith, the tide has turned. Clinging to Christ in trust, believing sinners receive and take up a new beginning.

What new beginning is this? As Christian life, what is the shape and character of this beginning? In *The Disputation Concerning Justification* (1536), Luther portrays the believer's beginning in terms of a pilgrimage: "For we perceive that a man who is justified is not yet a righteous man, but is in the very movement or journey toward righteousness." That is, as for so many Christian thinkers in late medieval Europe, for Luther a Christian is a *viator,* a pilgrim, fundamentally en route. As such, he is "not yet righteous." Thus, in the following sentence, Luther concludes, "Therefore, whoever is justified is still a sinner." But as a believer, he is not only reckoned righteous by God — via an imputation of Christ's righteousness — and thus justified; he is also himself on the way, "in the very move-

13. See also p. 234: "To take hold of the Son and to believe in Him with the heart as the gift of God causes God to reckon that faith, however imperfect it may be, as perfect righteousness."

ment or journey toward righteousness." He has set out by the grace and gift of God, and his new beginning means a new path for him. Christ is for him a curtain that ensures his salvation. But behind the curtain, so to speak, his "beginning in righteousness," however weak and imperfect, takes shape. In faith, his pilgrimage begins.[14]

Luther argues here that the divine gift of faith in Christ means the impartation of a "beginning righteousness," itself imperfect and utterly insufficient for justification, but nonetheless involving crucial consequences for the believer. She changes, not as a cause but as a consequence of God imparting faith to her. Indeed, as part and parcel of that impartation, she embarks on a new "movement or journey," and so her life takes on a new form. On the one hand, Luther characterizes her pilgrimage as a pilgrimage toward righteousness; on the other hand, though, he is clear that this approach, albeit a beginning in righteousness, in no way changes her status as a sinner. Not only is this beginning weak and imperfect; it also deserves in itself — that is, apart from Christ's mediation — only to be "condemned" (LW 34: 152-53).

And so, for Luther, this new movement and form of life must be a sinner's form of life. The pilgrim must not make any claims to righteousness whatsoever, to progress, to self-improvement or escape beyond the precincts of sin. And yet, paradoxically, this form of life must also be a beginning in righteousness. As a faithful pilgrimage, it must involve trust in God and God's promises. Indeed, bearing in mind Luther's well-known formula, justification by faith, this form of life, as faithful, must in some sense be "righteous." In short, this form of life must be *simul iustus et peccator*. In other words, from this point of view, the *simul* doctrine must be not only confessed but also undertaken as a path, as indeed a movement or journey. But if a Christian were to live out the *simul* as a way of being human, what form would that life take? What — or who — would that person become?

14. See *LW* 34: 152-53: "23. For we perceive that a man *who is justified* [*by faith*] is not yet a righteous man, but is in the very movement or journey toward righteousness. 24. Therefore, whoever is justified is still a sinner; and yet he is considered fully and perfectly righteous by God who pardons and is merciful. 25. Moreover, God forgives and is merciful to us because Christ, our advocate and priest, intercedes and sanctifies *our beginning in righteousness.* 26. His righteousness, since it is without defect and serves us like an umbrella against the heat of God's wrath, does not allow our *beginning righteousness* to be condemned" (italics added).

2. Penitential Life

Luther answers: that person becomes a penitent. That is, she becomes in no respect less of a sinner, but rather continually acknowledges and confesses precisely that she is none other than a sinner. And at the same time, as a penitent, she trusts that she is in no respect condemned or abandoned by God, but rather lives and walks under the "wide heaven of the forgiveness of sins" that Christ "spreads over" her (*LW* 26: 232). She trusts that she is reckoned and accepted as "righteous." And in that sense she lives *simul iustus et peccator*. Early in his theological work, in his *Lectures on Romans* (1515-16), Luther puts it this way:

> [R]epentance is the medium between unrighteousness and righteousness. And thus a man is in sin as the *terminus a quo* and righteousness as the *terminus ad quem*. Therefore if we are always repentant, we are always sinners, and yet thereby we are righteous and we are justified . . . that is, we are nothing but penitents (*LW* 25: 434).

As he does twenty years later in *The Disputation Concerning Justification*, here Luther portrays the Christian life as a pilgrimage from sin toward righteousness, but in such a way that the pilgrim never leaves the territory of sin. He is always a sinner: he travels from sin, but also "in sin." Therefore, his "journey toward righteousness" can only be undertaken and carried out by way of a continual recognition, first, that he is a sinner, and thus, second, that his journey is no pilgrim's progress. That is, on this journey he is not justified by degrees, or made progressively righteous according to his approach. On the contrary, it is as though he continually stops at church confessionals along the way, like any good medieval pilgrim, no less a sinner at one than he was at the last. To be finally forgiven and deemed righteous by God, he requires the gracious imputation of Christ's righteousness, the imputation to which faith testifies, and without which his own beginning — his own weak faith itself — could only be "condemned" (*LW* 34: 153). His continual confession, then, is always also a cry for deliverance and salvation, always *Kyrie eleison* ("Lord, have mercy").

On the other hand, if the sinner travels "in sin as the *terminus a quo*," she also travels in "righteousness as the *terminus ad quem*." That is, her faithful "journey toward righteousness" is also her "beginning in righteousness," weak and imperfect, to be sure, but nonetheless a beginning. She clings to Christ. She takes up her journey as a sinner but also as a bride. And her "wedding ring of faith," though it does not justify her in itself, indicates and constitutes the turn in her life, the divine gift of a new beginning in righteousness, on the basis of which Christ mercifully spreads out above her the "wide heaven of the forgiveness of sins." As a "cloud in her heart," her faith lives in her as her "formal righteousness" (*LW* 26: 130 [1535]), only begun and as yet insufficient, indeed condemnable, but assuredly begun and assuredly consequential for her. Now her life takes form as repentance, as *Kyrie eleison.* Now her life takes form as confessional prayer.

For it is her weak and imperfect faith, after all, that gives rise to her *Kyrie eleison* in the first place. Without faith, in Luther's view, her awareness of her own sin would take shape not as penitence but as impenitence, as hatred of God and flight from God — as it did for Adam, says Luther, "when he fled the voice of God calling him and sought a shady hiding place" (Gen. 3:8-10) (*LW* 34: 172).[15] In short, without faith a sinner's sin appears to her as cause for shame, self-protection, hatred, and fearful retreat. For Luther, only through the gift of faith can contrition take place as trusting approach, as penitence, as *Kyrie eleison.* Further, Luther argues that faith not only provides the basis on which our recognition that we are sinners becomes penitential; it also provides for that very recognition. That is, as a gift of the Holy Spirit, faith discloses to a believer her own standing as a sinner in the first place, and so initiates her repentant contrition: "A contrite heart is a precious thing, but it is found only where there is an ardent faith in the promises and threats of God."[16] Trusting "the truth of God's threat," Luther argues, is the "cause of contrition"; trusting

15. According to Luther's account, it is precisely at this point of hateful flight, itself induced by "the work of God's law," that a human being is mercifully seized by God, and given the gift of faith in God's promises: "Thus, when man is in flight, God lays hold of him and has mercy on him and says, 'You shall not die' [2 Sam. 12:13] . . . [and] gives him faith and the Holy Spirit" (see *LW* 34: 172, 174). It is worth noting, however, that this promise ("You shall not die") evinces the ambiguity of religion in compact form, since it is spoken both by Nathan in 2 Samuel and, crucially, by the serpent in Genesis (Gen. 3:4). In any given case, then, it is an open question as to whether the promise is actually delivered by a prophet or a snake.

16. Luther, *The Babylonian Captivity of the Church,* in *Three Treatises,* p. 210 (hereafter *BC,* page references cited in parentheses in the text).

"the truth of [God's] promise" is the "cause of consolation." Thus, in both respects, a believer's trust in God makes her penitence possible. In other words, faith provides both the insight that leads to the sorrow of contrition and the loving solace that allows sorrow to manifest itself, not as hatred and fear but as genuine repentance.

Indeed, for Luther, penitence is no mere possibility allowed by faith, but rather follows faith without fail: "Once faith is obtained, contrition and consolation will follow inevitably of themselves" (*BC,* p. 210). To put it differently, "once faith is obtained," the believer will live and work as a penitent, that is, she will live and work *simul iustus* (thus her continual consolation) *et peccator* (thus her continual contrition). Her transformation into the posture and life of penitence, her shift into *confessio,* is itself part and parcel of her shift into faithfulness, her "beginning in righteousness," her living reception of the gracious gift of faith imparted to her by God.

In Luther's view, then, the genuine Christian is "always a sinner, always a penitent, always righteous [*semper peccator, semper penitens, semper iustus*]" (*LW* 25: 434). The believer's continual gesture of penitence, of *Kyrie eleison,* is thus the form of work mediating the *simul* in the Christian life, a kind of medium, as Luther puts it, between *peccator* and *iustus* (*LW* 25: 434). Following inevitably upon faith, he suggests, penitence is no less than faith's living form, the human choreography of a sinner's trust in God. Therefore, for Luther, what may appear on the theological page as a conceptual paradox — *simul iustus et peccator* — emerges in liturgical life as not only a coherent practice but a way of life and work, the genuinely Christian way of being human: "We are nothing but penitents" (*LW* 25: 434). That is, for Luther the *simul* is no merely dogmatic discipline whereby we dialectically attribute contraries to the faithful.[17] Rather, for

---

17. Luther repeatedly calls the *simul* an offense to "reason," but he does not do so because of the doctrine's apparently paradoxical character, as if a violation of Aristotelian logic were at issue. Rather, "reason" rejects the *simul,* Luther argues, because "reason . . . declares that righteousness is a right judgment and a right will. Therefore this inestimable gift excels all reason, that without any works God reckons and acknowledges as righteous the man who takes hold by faith of His Son" (*LW* 26: 234). In other words, the *simul* is an offense to the "reasonable" idea that God saves not God's own enemies, i.e., sinners, but rather God's friends, those who themselves have "right judgment and a right will." As so often in his writing, Luther does not mean, by "reason," formal logic or human rationality per se, but something closer to what we might call "the reasonable," or conventional common

Luther, the *simul* is fundamentally an act and a bearing, a pilgrim's way and carriage, a practice of living out human life in both the shadow of sin and the light of God's promises. In short, the *simul* is the life of penitence, the genuine Christian life. Trusting that God forgives us *(iustus),* we confess that we are sinners *(peccator);* and confessing that we are sinners *(peccator),* we trust that God forgives us *(iustus).* As nothing but penitents, genuine Christians are nothing but *on the way,* "not yet righteous." Their continual repentance, after all, is a continual recognition of this fact. Nonetheless, they are "in the very movement or journey toward righteousness." Like the prodigal son arising from the swine fields, they are simultaneously sinners afar off and sinners headed home (Luke 15:18-20a).

As Luther develops this position, however, he makes clear that this repentance, central as it is to his account of justification, is by no means justification's "efficient cause." The direct cause of justification, Luther insists, is always "the Holy Spirit, who breathes where he wills [John 3:8]" (*LW* 34: 171),[18] but human repentance nonetheless plays a crucial role as justification unfolds in Christian life. Precisely as the form of life inevitably following from faith (*BC,* p. 210), repentance is "necessarily required" in justification, though not as a direct cause (*BC,* p. 172). That is, according to Luther's mature theological work, penitence is a necessary condition of the saving forgiveness of sins, but it is not therefore the direct cause of that forgiveness, for "many things are necessary which are not causes." In other words, while faith inevitably takes shape for Christians as penitential life, penitence itself is never a guarantee, never a technique for producing or coercing God's forgiveness: "When contrition has been established" — that is, established by God "through the revelation of sin" — "justification does not always follow, as in the case of Judas [Matt. 27:3-10]." Indeed, Luther argues, far from an independent actor able to compel divine forgiveness by my own acts of piety, instead "I am the raw material and subject to divine action. Those whom [God] wants to justify, he justifies freely."

---

sense. For a general discussion of Luther on reason, see Brian Gerrish, *Grace and Reason* (London: Oxford University Press, 1962).

18. Notably, here Luther calls "the condition of penitence" "not the efficient cause of justification," but "a certain *beginning*" (italics added). Likewise, in his account of baptism (itself, for Luther, a kind of inaugural "penance"), he writes: "As soon as we begin to believe, we also *begin* to die to this world and live to God in the life to come" (italics added); see Luther, *The Babylonian Captivity of the Church,* p. 191.

Thus Luther argues that penitence is a necessary component of justification by faith, not as a means to effect justification but as a necessary condition or feature of the scenario in which justification graciously takes place. Show me justification, says Luther, and I will show you penitence. As to whether any given penitent is justified, however, only God determines that: "God justifies whom he wishes." Luther thus clarifies the basis of God's saving action, and he specifies the character of the penitent's cry: never a human claim, maneuver, command, or deserving feat, it is always properly an acknowledgment of guilt and a plea for divine mercy and deliverance (*LW* 34: 171-73).

In summary, for Luther, a believer's faith in Christ, and thus his repentant "beginning in righteousness," is graciously *imparted* to him by God; Christ's righteousness, however, which "intercedes and sanctifies our beginning in righteousness" and thus makes for human salvation, is graciously *imputed* to him by God (*LW* 34: 153). Decisively, human salvation takes place as the imputation to the believer of Christ's righteousness, itself outside and foreign to him, like a mother bird's wing protecting her young. But from the believer's point of view, this same event unfolds as the Holy Spirit pours into him faith in Christ, and thus imparts to him a beginning in righteousness, a *metanoia,* an inevitable and necessary, yet also weak and imperfect, transformation to a faithful life of repentance. Once this shift into penitential life is an event for the believer, he can in no way save himself; rather, he waits and calls for salvation both (1) as a child of God who believes in God's promises, who believes that "the kingdom of God is at hand," and (2) as an "enemy of God," a thoroughgoing sinner, who lives a life of *confessio* and repentance. That is, he waits and calls as a penitent, *simul iustus et peccator.* The believer's discipleship thus takes shape as a continual hearing of the New Testament's opening sermon: "Repent, for the kingdom of God is at hand" (Matt. 3:2, 4:17). Repentant, he is always a sinner; believing God's promises, he is always righteous. And the medium between these two simultaneous standings, the form of life that makes for his pilgrimage, is his continual liturgy of repentance.

As we have seen, Luther spells out this liturgical account of the *simul* in some detail in his *Lectures on Romans* (1515-16) and in *The Disputation Concerning Justification* (1536); but we may also trace it throughout his theological work. In his early writing, for example, the figure of Christ "covering" believers' sins is gleaned not only from Ruth and Matthew but also, and particularly, from Psalm 32: "Happy are those whose transgression is forgiven, whose sin is covered./Happy are those to whom the LORD imputes no iniquity" (v. 1).[19] In Luther's reading, by "those whose transgression is forgiven," the psalmist is referring to those who faithfully live *simul iustus et peccator,* full-blown sinners whose sin is covered, to whom sin is not imputed (see, e.g., *LW* 25: 258). But this psalm, as Luther points out both in his commentaries on the Psalter and elsewhere, ties this divine forgiveness to human confession: "I said, 'I will confess my transgressions to the LORD,' and you forgave the guilt of my sin./Therefore let all who are faithful offer prayer to you" (Ps. 32:5-6). Commenting on these verses, Luther suggests that the practical form of the *simul* is penitential:

> For inasmuch as the saints are always aware of their sin and seek righteousness from God in accord with His mercy, for this very reason they are always also regarded as righteous by God. . . . [E]very saint is a sinner and prays for his sins. Thus the righteous man is in the first place his own accuser (*LW* 25: 258).

The young Luther expounds the *simul* with a picture of a kneeling saint, "always a penitent" — that is, always faithful and thus both contrite and consoled. Continually, the saint is "in the first place his own accuser," and "for this very reason" he is "always also regarded as righteous by God."

But this passage is also exemplary of the younger Luther's tendency to ostensibly identify confessional humility with the direct cause of justification, using relatively unguarded terms he would later qualify: "God forgives through His nonimputation [of sin] out of His mercy toward all who acknowledge and confess and hate their sin and plead to be cleansed from it." Here the believer's continual *confessio* — her acknowledgment, confession, and "pleading to be cleansed" — seems to be the basis of her continually being forgiven: "Before God they are righteous because He reckons them so *because of their confession of sins*" (*LW* 25: 258, 259; italics added). As we have seen, however, Luther later clarifies this language, identifying more precisely the basis of God's gracious reckoning not with penitence per se, but with faith, the trust in God that finds form in penitence — indeed, that makes penitence possible. And yet, even as he clari-

19. For the place of Psalm 32 in Luther's thought, see, e.g., *LW* 25: 246, 259, 264-72; *LW* 26: 109.

fies his case, he does not discard concrete practices of penitence at all, or detach them from his account of God's justification of human beings. On the contrary, these practices remain "necessary for the remission of sins," even if this necessity is now clearly characterized as in no way a "cause and meritorious basis of salvation" (*LW* 34: 172, 173).

As early as 1520, Luther puts it this way:

> Beware, then, of putting your trust in your own contrition and of ascribing the forgiveness of sins to your own remorse. God does not look on you with favor because of that, but because of the faith by which you have believed his threats and promises, and which has effected such sorrow within you. Thus we owe whatever good there may be in our penance, not to our scrupulous enumeration of sins, but to the truth of God and to our faith (*BC*, p. 211).

Divine "favor," Luther argues, is granted "because of the faith by which you have believed." But this very faith effects penitential sorrow, and so is unimaginable, for Luther, without it.

In other words, Luther refines his early accounts by specifying the key basis of justification — the basis, that is, for God's gracious reckoning of sinners as righteous — not as faithful penitence, but as faith itself, that is, the trust that makes for penitence in Christian life. Therefore, practices of confession are still bound up inseparably with faith and thus with human salvation, still necessary for justification, but not as justification's "efficient cause." His early claim, for example, that sin "is not imputed as sin to those who call upon Him and cry out for His deliverance" (*LW* 25: 259-60), still holds in the later writings, but now with the proviso that God's mercy is not given on the basis of those calls and cries, but rather on the basis of the believer's "faith alone," the very faith that is nonetheless necessarily and inevitably pronounced as penitential invocation. To put it succinctly, penitence is not the cause of justification for Luther, but it is necessary for it; therefore, those whom God wishes to justify, God makes penitents.

As we have seen, what is at stake for Luther in this discussion, even at its most technical, is his theological anthropology and ethics, that is, his account of Christian life. For Luther, the genuine Christian, always a sinner and always righteous, is thus fundamentally always a penitent. This is decidedly not to say, Luther insists, that the genuine Christian "frequently practices the ecclesial rite of penance." What Luther provides in this account is not a picture of human life generously peppered with penitential practices; rather, it is human life *as* penitential practice. Ecclesial rites of penance — in which, incidentally, Luther found great value (see *BC*, pp. 206ff.) — were of secondary importance. Primarily, Luther sought to spell out a penitential form of life through which all Christian activity could be carried out and understood. Indeed, in the first two of his well-known Ninety-Five Theses (1517), Luther points to just this argument:

1. When our Lord and Master Jesus Christ said, "Repent" [Matt. 4:17], he willed the entire life of believers to be one of repentance.
2. This word cannot be understood as referring to the sacrament of penance, that is, confession and satisfaction, as administered by the clergy (*LW* 31: 25).

In his later "explanations" of the Ninety-Five Theses, Luther says that, properly understood, Christ's call to *metanoia* (repentance) — precisely as a call to "assume another mind and feeling, recover one's senses, make a transition from one state of mind to another, have a change of spirit" or a "change of heart" — can only "involve one's whole life." Notably, Luther appeals to the Lord's Prayer at that point: "We pray throughout our whole life, and we must pray, 'forgive us our debts' [Matt. 6:12]; therefore, we repent throughout our whole life . . . unless anyone may be so foolish as to think that he must pretend to pray for the forgiveness of debts." In an argument he would return to throughout his theological career, Luther contends that the church's own *lex orandi* ("law of prayer") should be matched by a corresponding *lex credendi* ("law of belief"), namely, the belief that Christian life is always and fundamentally penitential life, a life of continual confession and appeal, a life of praying "forgive us our debts" (*LW* 31: 84-85).

3. Baptismal Life

And yet this "whole life" of Christian penitence is also and ultimately, for Luther, a whole life of Christian baptism.[20] In *The Babylonian Captivity of*

20. For Luther's theology of baptism, see Ruben Josefson, *Luther on Baptism* (Hong Kong, 1952); see also Vilmos Vajta, *Luther on Worship* (Philadelphia: Fortress, 1958).

the Church (1520), Luther situates penance under "the sacrament of baptism," and once more he emphasizes the continual and thoroughgoing penitential character of Christian life. First, he describes baptism as a kind of inaugural "penance" (*BC*, p. 179), the opening and fundamental human confession and divine promise of saving forgiveness in a Christian's life, to which all of a person's subsequent acts of repentance can only return and "remember": "When we rise from our sins or repent, we are merely returning to the power and the faith of baptism from which we fell, and finding our way back to the promise made to us [at our baptism], which we deserted when we sinned" (*BC*, p. 180). And this returning, in Luther's view, is by no means intermittent and occasional, but rather ongoing and basic: "You have been once baptized in the sacrament, but you need continually to be baptized by faith, continually to die and continually to live" (*BC*, p. 192). For Luther, following Paul in Romans, believers "baptized into Christ Jesus" were "baptized into his death," so that, rising with Christ, "[they] too might walk in newness of life" (Rom. 6:3-4). Submersion in baptismal water "signifies that we die in every way" and, in turn, re-emergence from that water signifies that "[we] rise again to eternal life." But this dying and rising, for Luther, is no one-time event: "Our whole life should be baptism" (*BC*, pp. 191, 193).

Luther portrays the Christian life as not only penitential life, but also, and finally, as baptismal life. The genuine Christian is indeed "always a penitent," but her ongoing repentance can only be an ongoing return to faith in God's baptismal promises, an ongoing dying and rising with Christ, and in that sense an ongoing baptism: "For we are indeed little children continually baptized anew in Christ" (*BC*, p. 197). For Luther, just as baptism is "the first sacrament and the foundation of all the others" (*BC*, p. 181), so baptismal life is the most fundamental reality of Christian life: "One thing only," he writes, "has been enjoined upon us to do all the days of our lives — to be baptized, that is, to be put to death and to live again through faith in Christ." Accordingly, Luther says, Christians are "given over to baptism alone" (*BC*, p. 193).

But this picture of baptism, as an ongoing and thoroughgoing "actual death and resurrection," is also a picture of the *simul*. That is, the baptismal life Luther outlines, in which the believer is at once continually "put to death" on account of his sin, and continually brought "to live again through faith in Christ" on account of God's grace, is a life lived *simul iustus et peccator*. Indeed, the typical ecclesial rite of baptism is itself a vivid portrait of this situation: a sinner publicly repents, and then, precisely as a sinner, receives the gifts of baptismal water and communal welcome. As Luther has it, the rite is a kind of synoptic preview of Christian life as a whole: "Once baptized in the sacrament . . . we need continually to be baptized more and more, until we fulfill the sign perfectly at the last day" (BC, p. 192). Thus Luther's account of baptism is fundamentally an eschatological account, begun today but fulfilled "at the last." Thus he again portrays Christian life as itinerant life. For the baptized believer, the baptismal ceremony may be behind him, but his baptismal life unfolds before him like a pilgrim's path. And this life, as we have seen, is the life of a penitent, a life of continually returning to faith in God's baptismal promises, and thus of being "baptized more and more." For the believer remains, even after the rite, an acknowledged sinner. "Continually baptized anew" in the "spiritual baptism" of faith (BC, p. 191), the believer lives *simul iustus et peccator,* and journeying on his way, he trusts and prays, as a penitent under "the wide heaven of the forgiveness of sins."

Up to this point, we have examined Luther's liturgical account of the *simul* — as penitential, and finally baptismal, life — as if it applies primarily to individual believers. But Luther also crucially appeals to the doctrine in his ecclesiology. In his later *Lectures on Galatians* (1535), he affirms that "the church has no spot or wrinkle [Eph. 5:27] but is holy," though this purity, he insists, is utterly "invisible, dwelling in the Spirit," concealed and covered "with weaknesses, sins, errors, and various offenses." Like the individual believer, then, the church is "holy, though only through faith in Jesus Christ," and even then in such a way as to be nonetheless embroiled in sin: "It is not yet holy in the sense of being delivered and rescued from all evil desires or of having purged out all wicked opinions and errors" (LW 27: 84-85). In short, for Luther, the church is *simul iustus et peccator.* And to ground this argument, Luther turns again — as he had nearly two decades earlier, in explaining his Ninety-Five Theses — to the Lord's Prayer: "The church always confesses its sin and prays that its trespasses may be forgiven [Matt. 6:12]; it also [in the Apostles' Creed] 'believes in the forgiveness of sins.'" Thus, in Luther's view, for the church no less than an individual believer, the *lex orandi* (law of prayer) discloses the Christian situation: "Not that sin is not in us, as the sophists have taught when they said that we must go on doing good until we are no longer conscious of any sin; but sin is always present, and the godly feel it." In this sense, the church — *iustus* "only through faith in Jesus Christ," and

peccator in its abiding weaknesses, sins, and errors — is at once a communion of saints and a communion of sinners. Therefore, Luther argues,
"even though the church is holy, it still has to pray: 'Forgive us our debts'"
(*LW* 26: 66). And so for the church, no less than an individual believer, the
simul is lived out in an expressly liturgical form, namely, in penitential life,
continual *confessio*, the ongoing "baptism in the Holy Spirit" (Luke 3:16)
that is inaugurated for the church at Pentecost and that abides until "the
last day."

In the scheme of Luther's thought, the theological centrality and importance of his liturgical account of the *simul* should by now be clear:
from his early *Lectures on Romans* (1515-16) to the late *Lectures on
Galatians* (1535), and from the early Ninety-Five Theses (1517) to the late
Disputation Concerning Justification (1536). For Luther, Christian life is
lived out as a continual baptism, a penitential pilgrimage affording no advance in saving righteousness, nevertheless amounting to both a "beginning righteousness" and a "journey toward righteousness." And the chief
advantage of this journey, says Luther, is that it may involve the believer in
repeated and deepening awareness of her actual situation, that is, awareness of her own desolation apart from God's gracious generosity and
care.

In other words, throughout his theological work, Luther promotes a
penitential posture and carriage, a baptismal way of life, finally with an
eye to fostering a particular version of Christian humility. In his late *Lectures on Galatians* he says: "It is extremely beneficial to the faithful to be
aware" of their own sin, "for it will keep them from being puffed up by a
vain and wicked notion about the righteousness of works, as though they
were acceptable to God on its account" (*LW* 27: 85). That is, precisely because genuine Christians — both individually and as an ecclesial body —
continually confess by saying, "forgive us our debts," they are thereby
continually "not in a position to trust in [their] own righteousness, for
[they] are aware of the uncleanness of the flesh." The choreography of
confession, so to speak, properly contravenes the choreography of arro-
gance and supremacy, not only interrupting it but also working to inhibit
its emergence in the first place. Indeed, Luther goes so far as to say that
sin's "uncleanness" itself "remains in [the believer] *to keep him humble,* so
that in his humility the grace and blessing of Christ taste sweet to him"
(*LW* 27: 86; italics added). Thus, for Luther, the baptismal, penitential life
lived out by genuine Christians is in the end a discipline for cultivating a

particular form of humility, a practical choreography and so a way of life in which they may find themselves less often "in a position to trust in [their] own righteousness" and more often in a position to trust in God. "For the more aware they are of their weakness and sin," Luther says, "the more they take refuge in Christ, the mercy seat" (*LW* 27: 86). And the more they take refuge in Christ, in turn, the more they take up a particular posture and bearing, not just penitential life and work but a particular style of penitential life and work.

What style? Luther puts it this way:

> Thus a Christian remains in pure humility. He really and truly feels that there is sin in him and that on this account he is worthy of wrath, the judgment of God, and eternal death. Thus he is humbled in this life. Yet at the same time he remains in a pure and holy pride, by which he turns to Christ. Through him he strengthens himself . . . and he believes that he is loved by the Father, not for his own sake but for the sake of Christ, the Beloved (*LW* 26: 235).

The penitent's "pure humility," in this view, follows from his recognition of his own sin; and this recognition is possible only by way of the divine gift of faith. Without faith, his incipient recognition emerges as misrecognition, in the form of defense, denial, prevarication, and hateful retreat — just as Adam, says Luther, "fled the voice of God calling him and sought a shady hiding place" (Gen. 3:8-10) (*LW* 34: 172). Having received the gift of faith, however, the sinner's recognition may emerge as full-blown and sincere, in the form of admission, sorrow, and a contrite approach toward God — in effect reversing Adam's program of evasion (*BC*, p. 211). At the same time, Luther argues, the penitent is not only "contrite" but also "consoled" because of his faith in Christ, that is, because of his trust in the divine promise of forgiveness in Christ. No less than his contrition, his consolation follows inevitably from this trust (*BC*, p. 210).[21] And on this basis he "remains in a pure and holy pride."

Indeed, it is just this holy pride and pure humility that constitute his posture as always a penitent in the first place. The penitent is the one who, as *semper peccator*, confesses his sin in pure humility, and at the same

---

21. "Once faith is obtained, contrition and consolation will follow inevitably of themselves."

time, as *semper iustus,* turns to Christ in holy pride. And these gestures, notably, are neither sequential nor ultimately separable; rather, they are mutually constitutive, inevitably arising together from trust in God. Consolation makes way for vulnerable contrition, and vice versa. Thus, for Luther, the doctrinal *simul* corresponds to a liturgical one: simultaneous "pure humility" and "holy pride," the penitent's way of baptismal life.

Thus Martin Luther, the theologian who was so well known for his attack on "works righteousness," spells out a theology that is ultimately designed to engender and encourage a distinctive form of work. That is, precisely by denying that human beings are in any respect justified by works, Luther promotes a particular program for Christian life: the "humble pride" of the penitent, as opposed to its contrary gesture, the arrogant insecurity of self-righteousness, what Paul calls "boasting" (Rom. 3:27). Luther launches his attack on works righteousness as part of a campaign to portray Christian life as a baptismal, penitential pilgrimage, full of great sorrow but also full of great consolation and joy; full of daily dying but also full of daily rising to new life. In short, Luther portrays genuine Christian life as a "journey toward righteousness," the crucial condition of which is that those journeying in no way claim righteousness for themselves. Rather, they travel in pure humility and holy pride.

And if this pilgrim's work of penitence, this way of continual baptism, is the liturgical form of life entailed by Luther's doctrine of *simul iustus et peccator,* then this work's contrary, the form of life Luther seeks to oppose and undo, is likewise liturgical: the self-righteous work of boasting and self-congratulation. It is this contrary liturgy that Luther sets out to dismantle in his attack on works righteousness. From this point of view, then, Luther's well-known battles over *lex credendi,* battles he spent his life fighting, were finally and fundamentally battles over *lex orandi.* For, in his view, at stake in the contest between justification by faith ("penitence") and justification by works ("boasting") is nothing less than Christian prayer and thus Christian life, the appropriate posture and carriage that pilgrims ought to take up and live out. In a word, what is at stake for Luther in this liturgical contest is the question of Christian *praise.*

In his first *Lectures on Galatians* (1519), written as his mature theology was beginning to come into focus, Luther, speaking to God, puts it this way: "Man will praise, glorify, and love Thee when he realizes the goodness of Thy mercy and does not, in his self-righteousness, praise himself.

For those who [claim to be] righteous . . . do not praise Thee, but praise themselves" (*LW* 27: 185). Here, then, is the key battleground on which Luther's critique of works righteousness theology is carried out: the doxological battleground, the question of orthodoxy understood less as "right opinion" and more as "right praise" *(ortho doxa)*. For Luther, to say that we are justified by works is to say that we are justified by ourselves, indeed that "we have done it!" In effect, it is to celebrate ourselves apart from God: here doxology resounds as a jubilant (if implicit) shout of self-congratulation. And this scenario is the very picture of sin for Luther, of human being "deeply curved in upon itself," using all things strictly "for its own purposes" (*LW* 25: 291, 345), so that even our "hallelujah!" — indeed, especially and fundamentally our "hallelujah!" — is rendered an idolatrous boomerang, no longer "Praise God!" but rather "Praise us!" or "Praise me!"[22] At stake for Luther, then, in his struggle against justification by works is the proper orientation of human doxology, and therefore of human being, that is, the proper orientation of worship and the permanent risk of idolatry.

In a key passage in the later *Lectures on Galatians* (1535), Luther counsels a desperate "afflicted sinner," first affirming that his acknowledgment of his sin "is one step toward health," for which he should thank God, and then exhorting him to believe in Christ, his liberator and physician. "If you believe," Luther continues, "you are righteous, because you attribute to God the glory of being almighty, merciful, truthful, etc. You justify and praise God. In short, you attribute divinity and everything to Him" (*LW* 26: 233). That is, Luther encourages this afflicted sinner to trust God, to believe that Christ "saves sinners," and so to transform his anxiety into faithful penitence, that is, into genuine contrition and consolation, pure humility and holy pride. And crucially, Luther assures him that if he so believes, if he takes up this penitential posture as the form and act in which his life takes place, then he "praises God." Then he worships properly, justifying not himself but God. Then his "hallelujah!" resounds in its true form.

A sinner's fundamental *metanoia,* in this view, is finally doxological: from "boasting" to "penitence," from self-righteous praise of himself to self-emptying praise of God. The latter gesture is self-emptying because it refers all righteousness, all divinity — indeed, as Luther puts it, "every-

22. "Hallelujah," from the Hebrew *hallelu* ("praise") + *Yah* ("God").

thing" — to God. And yet this praise does not foreclose, abandon, or erase his humanity, but rather establishes it. For just as the one who praises God points away from himself, attributing all righteousness to God, so God attributes Christ's righteousness to him. As Luther puts it to the desperate man, "His righteousness is yours." For Luther, believers "attribute divinity and everything" to God, and God attributes divine righteousness — indeed, in its own way, "divinity and everything" — to them. On the human side, this "joyous exchange" is lived out as jubilant praise, a continual chorus of "hallelujah!" and "Amen!" On the divine side, the same exchange plays out as loving generosity, as bounty, as gifts of life and merciful care. And thus faith's doxology is self-emptying, but not self-destructive; on the contrary, in this doxology human beings live out genuinely human lives by divine grace.

Luther's account of penitence and the baptismal character of Christian life is thus also an account of praise: "He who humbly repudiates his own righteousness and confesses that he is a sinner before God truly glorifies God, proclaiming that He alone is righteous" (*LW* 25: 200).[23] Moreover, Luther says, it is by way of this penitential doxology that human being — "deeply curved in upon itself" in sin — begins to unfurl at last. The vicious circle of self-righteousness, of self-praising-self, is undone. Now the creature, precisely as a penitent returning again and again to her baptism, lives as a self-praising-God. In Karl Barth's terms, *en*-centric closure begins to open out into *ec*-centric life, that is, into genuine human life in genuine praise. The fist of sin gives way to an open human hand.

---

23. See also Vajta, *Luther on Worship,* pp. 156ff.

CHAPTER 5

God Against Religion

1. A Theology of Invocation

The modern category of "religion," as Barth uses it, was, of course, unavailable to Luther; yet it is possible to trace parallels between Barth's critique of religion and Luther's critique of works righteousness. As we have seen, Luther launched his doctrine of justification by faith as a broad attack on the Christianity of his day, which he eventually judged to be not simply mistaken but no less than the chief demonic power on earth. Luther vowed to "constantly cry out" against the idea that "we have forgiveness of sins and eternal life . . . through the observance of [Christian] traditions" rather than strictly "through [Jesus Christ's] death and resurrection." Such Christianity, he cried, is anti-Christianity, the domain of "the Antichrist," and "I shall announce that all your ceremonies and religion are not only a denial of God but supreme blasphemy and idolatry."[1] Luther identified the present power of sin and death in the world not with non-Christian activity but with Christian activity — or rather, with activity masquerading as Christian, works righteousness cloaked in the consummately religious forms of "brotherhoods, indulgences, orders, relics, forms of worship, invocation of saints, purgatory, Masses, vigils, vows, and the endless other abominations of that sort"

---

1. *Luther's Works,* ed. Jaroslav Pelikan and Helmut Lehmann (St. Louis: Concordia, 1960-1974), 26: 224 (hereafter *LW,* page references cited in parentheses in the text).

(*LW* 26: 222). Satan, wrote Paul, comes disguised as an angel of light (2 Cor. 11:14).

But this camouflage, Luther goes on to insist, though certainly at its most cunning and effective within Christianity, is by no means limited to Christian quarters. For him, works righteousness — the "supreme blasphemy and idolatry" — is evident not just in wrongheaded Christianity but in other religions as well. He puts it this way: "If all the religions and forms of worship under heaven that have been thought up by men to obtain righteousness in the sight of God are not condemned, the righteousness of faith cannot stand" (*LW* 26: 231). Put conversely, Luther's argument for the righteousness of faith amounts to a condemnation of "all the religions and forms of worship under heaven" that are designed to "obtain righteousness in the sight of God." In other words, Luther's argument for the doctrine of justification by faith alone amounts to a condemnation of sin's patently religious form in human life.

In a characteristic expression, in his *Lectures on Romans,* Luther describes the extremity of human sin as not an escape from religion, but rather an escape into it:

> [O]ur nature has been so deeply curved in upon itself because of the viciousness of original sin that it not only turns the finest gifts of God in upon itself and enjoys them . . . indeed, it even uses God Himself to achieve these aims, but it also seems to be ignorant of this very fact, that in acting so iniquitously, so perversely, and in such a depraved way, it is even seeking God for its own sake (*LW* 25: 291).

For Luther, the ultimate "viciousness of original sin" manifests itself precisely in a self-serving form of seeking God. Therefore, in his view, it is not as if sinners merely hoard divine gifts and then flee or reject God and religion, leading profane lives of wickedness or debauchery. On the contrary, for Luther the depths of sin are evident precisely in so-called sacred precincts. There sinners, far from fleeing or rejecting religion, set about the task of achieving their aims *through* religion. There sinners, far from fleeing or rejecting God, set about "seeking God for its own sake." Sin may take other forms, of course, but for Luther the tragedy of sin is finally and preeminently a religious tragedy. It is idolatry, not atheism or brute profanity. It is primarily "brotherhoods, indulgences, orders, relics, forms of worship, invocation of saints, purgatory, Masses, vigils, vows, and the endless other abominations of that sort" (*LW* 26: 222). It is perverted praise, misdirected glory, self-bestowed, and disastrously and "deeply curved in upon itself."

For Luther, of course, this critique of "all the religions and forms of worship under heaven" applies to every religious community but one, namely, Christians who confess Luther's doctrine of justification and live, act, and worship in light of it. Luther attacked the Christianity of his day, but he did so from what he considered to be a Christian theological position that was safe from his own critique. All forms of worship must be condemned, he says, *except* for those forms in which salvation is genuinely and absolutely attributed to God in Jesus Christ. Thus his attack on religions and forms of worship was not wholesale. He condemned Masses, for example, not to dispose of them altogether, but to reform, reframe, and reorient them according to his doctrine of justification. As we have already seen in the case of penance, Luther by no means rejected key Christian practices and forms of worship; instead, he subordinated them to faith with respect to salvation, and he maintained their indispensability with respect to Christian life.

But in so doing Luther laid out an alternative orthodoxy, an alternative version of Christian life, and this alternative, of course, is itself potentially open to his own charge. That is, it is potentially open to being understood and practiced as a new technique for "obtaining righteousness in the sight of God."[2] "Having faith in Christ," one might say, may become a new product peddled in Barth's "emporium of religion," a new answer to the question, What then must I do?

In this light, Barth's critique of religion may be read as a thoroughgoing extension, even a radicalization, of Luther's attack on works righteousness. If Luther (and the Reformers generally) launched an attack on works righteousness aimed at "all the religions and forms of worship under heaven" *except* what they considered to be proper Lutheran (or Re-

---

2. Luther would vehemently deny this charge; whether he can successfully do so is a complex question, and one I leave for another day. For my purposes here, it is enough to say (1) that Luther's doctrine of "the righteousness of faith" is plausibly open to being understood and practiced — with greater and lesser degrees of awareness — as yet another (well-disguised) form of works righteousness, whereby one exalted work ("having faith in Christ") is the recipe for "obtaining righteousness in the sight of God," and (2) that in many Christian communities today (inside but certainly also outside Lutheran churches) it is understood and practiced as such.

formed) Christianity, Barth launches a similar attack, but he subjects all religion, with no exception, to his critique.

We may understand Barth as following through on the Reformation's founding and driving insight, the claim that human sin takes the form not of areligiosity or even antireligiosity, but rather precisely of religiosity, of well-orchestrated attempts to "obtain righteousness in the sight of God." Barth's distinctive version of this insight, in effect, is to say that this kind of religiosity is the only kind available. He insists that there is no higher or purer or simpler or otherwise better religiosity. Works righteousness is not a deviant or distorted form of religion; it simply is religion. Further, Barth argues that religion, as the "last and most inevitable human possibility," is finally unavoidable for human beings exiled "east of Eden." That is, there is no higher or purer or simpler or otherwise better non-religiosity, or so-called secularity, or what have you. Thus works righteousness is, for Barth, not a deviant or distorted form of exilic or fallen human life; it simply is exilic human life. In a word, it simply is exile. As *leitourgia,* works righteousness is the event of exile from God, its basis and its ongoing, ruinous, and ubiquitous maintenance.

In Barth's view, then, the Reformers were quite correct to expose and attack works righteousness; but they were all too correct, since Reformed religion is unmasked by the same exposé. Reformed religion, even the religion of "faith alone," is still the religion of Cain (the original Reformer!): it is a doomed attempt to present God with a precious gift ("faith alone") in order to win divine favor, to obtain righteousness in the sight of God. Therefore, as Barth puts it in *The Epistle to the Romans,* "a like resentment must be applied to the totality of that new thing which they erect upon the ruins of the old."[3] God is not against every religion but one; God is against religion. Thus for Barth, whenever we pronounce judgment against a neighbor's works righteousness, that is, against her religion, the verdict and sentence we declare is also our own. Or, to shift the metaphor: Protestants have correctly diagnosed the disease, but the epidemic has engulfed the whole hospital. Everyone is afflicted.

Similarly, just as we may read Barth's critique of religion as a development and extension of Luther's critique of works righteousness, we may read Barth's view of reconciliation as a development and extension of Luther's ultimately doxological portrait of Christian life. As Luther has it, a

3. Barth, *Epistle to the Romans,* pp. 241-42.

reconciled human being is "always a penitent" and thereby "truly glorifies God" by attributing all righteousness to God alone. This view follows from Luther's understanding of the crisis of sin as principally a crisis of religious boasting, arrogant works that are designed to earn and retain divine favor. In Barth's work, too, a reconciled human being lives her life "as a form of praise," though for him the doxology of reconciliation is first of all thanksgiving, and only then praise and petition, since in his view, "only gratitude can correspond to grace," and so "basically all sin is simply ingratitude."[4] Thus, from different starting points, both Luther and Barth sketch human reconciliation with God as fundamentally doxological, and a reconciled human being as a being centered in God, fundamentally and continually upheld by gracious divine gifts, and thus engaged in a radically intimate "exchange" (Luther) and "friendship" (Barth) between creature and Creator. In both accounts, the shape of human salvation is a graceful movement from self-enclosure to *ec*-centricity (Barth), from a twisted posture "deeply curved in upon itself" (Luther) to an open posture of doxology and invocation.

On one hand, then, there are parallels and points of contact between Barth's critique of religion and Luther's critique of works righteousness; on the other hand, both theologians also put forward doxological accounts of human salvation. But these similarities point again to an apparently paradoxical pair of claims: first, the idea that worship constitutes humankind's fall away from God, and, second, the idea that worship constitutes humankind's reconciliation and return to God — in lives of thanksgiving, praise, and prayer. In short, these accounts describe worship as both fall and reconciliation. In Chapter 4 we saw how the contrast between these two descriptions may be understood, not as a contradiction but as a clear opposition marking out the brink and hinge of God's saving work, and thus the brink and hinge of human salvation. Precisely as humanity's fall, *leitourgia* is, after all, the expected locus of God's graceful rescue, the scenario in which the divine work of reconciliation must and does take place. It is only fitting that God's healing activity should occur in the fatal wound itself, that human salvation should mean the transformation of the "fulcrum of sin"[5] into the fulcrum of reconciliation, withdrawal into approach, separation into intimacy.

4. Barth, *Church Dogmatics,* IV.1, p. 41 (hereafter *CD,* page references cited in parentheses in the text).

5. Barth, *Romans,* p. 248.

Accordingly, Barth argues that by the Spirit's conspiracy and the Son's solidarity, our work over against God becomes work through God the Spirit and with God the Son. Thus the dynamics of alienation are lovingly and mercifully recast into dynamics of participation in divine life and genuine humanity. Exactly along the rift of separation, the fault line where human liturgists attempt to carve out a fantastic and devastating "us-without-God," God fashions the final and saving "God-with-us," the consummate *Immanuel.* Through the saving work of Jesus Christ, the *leitourgia* (work of people) is remade as the work of people-with-God.

Thus God stands with human beings in radical intimacy, in friendship, even in their very attempt to stand over against God. To put it another way, in love and mercy God enters into solidarity with sinners — and finally with sin. God becomes "a curse for us" (Gal. 3:13). In Jesus Christ, God enters into religion, into *leitourgia,* the work of people against and apart from their Creator, precisely in order to return and reconcile them with God. God is against religion, but for humanity. Indeed, building up from Barth's case, we may say that the Incarnation, God's life in history as a human being, does not take place in order for God to assume and redeem history or humanity as such, for these have already been created and deemed "very good" (Gen. 1:31). Rather, the Incarnation takes place in order for God to assume and redeem a particular, ubiquitous, disastrous form of human life, what Barth calls "the last and most inevitable human possibility," what we might call "the form of a slave" (Phil. 2:7), the form of *leitourgia,* the work of people unto death. The Incarnation takes place in order for God to assume and redeem worship and religion.

We can see this in the Gospel accounts of Jesus, the rabbi who both takes up and in the strongest terms repeatedly critiques the religious life of his day. Thus the Gospel accounts of Jesus, the religious man who adopts and transforms the whole length and breadth of that religious life, from baptism to prayer to the Passover meal. Finally, on the cross, Jesus adopts the quintessentially religious maneuver, the act of *sacrifice,* literally, the act of allegedly "making sacred."[6] In this view, God assumes, in Christ, this particular form of life (worship and religion) in order to oppose it from the inside out, to revolutionize it, to return us to friendship,

---

6. "Sacrifice," from the Latin *sacer* ("sacred") + *facere* ("to make"). Perhaps here is the height (or rather, the depth) of Cain's liturgy, he being the consummate human "maker of things."

and so ultimately to "redeem us from the curse" (Gal. 3:13), that is, to redeem us from worship and religion once and for all.

In Barth's view, humanity's fall is finally a fall to our knees, a fall into prayer. With this gesture, human beings set themselves over against God as "some second thing," staking out in their kneeling a specious sovereignty and a tragic, destructive attempt at separation and security. Therefore, the divine work of reconciling humankind to God means fundamentally transforming human prayer, renovating its foundations, reworking its basic choreography so that it no longer takes place as *leitourgia* in the name of human beings apart from God, but rather takes place as the work of Jesus Christ. It is in the name of God, to be sure — and thus excluding any separation from God — but preeminently it is in the name of *Immanuel* (God-with-humanity). As the work of Jesus Christ, prayer is truly divine work; and as the work of Jesus Christ, it is truly human work as well. It is the work of humanity-with-God, the perfect reversal and reconciliation of *leitourgia*. In Jesus Christ, at once Son of God and Son of humanity, all attempts at separation between creature and Creator are overcome, that is, overcome exactly insofar as Christ undertakes these very attempts and refashions them.

Thus even in the case of prayer, the prototypical picture of human alienation masquerading as intimacy, God does not annihilate the offending gesture. God reconciles it: God takes up and takes on the form of human estrangement from God, the form of worship, and thus transforms it into participation in God. God prays. Jesus Christ undertakes and overcomes prayer, worship, and religion. And thus we, by divine grace and never strictly by our own achievement, "pray by His mouth." Just for this reason, and just in this act, human alienation and exile, loneliness and sin, are undone. It is precisely in prayer that we are reconciled to God, that is, God and humanity reconcile (from the Latin *re*, "again," and *concilium*, "meeting"). Precisely in prayer, the very picture of departure, we meet again.

And yet this reconciling prayer, for both Barth and Luther, is no isolated or special act in human life, one episode alongside others. Instead, as Barth puts it, the invocation of God is a comprehensive "movement" within which all human "thought and speech and action" must find its place.[7] At the outset of his lectures on the Lord's Prayer, Barth refers to

---

7. Barth, *The Christian Life*, p. 108.

Paul's directive "pray without ceasing" (1 Thess. 5:17), and he concludes, with Calvin, that "language is not always necessary" in prayer. Therefore, Barth suggests, any sharp distinction between spoken or explicit forms of prayer and more implicit forms of prayer is dubious, and we should instead conceive of prayer as "at once word, thought, and life."[8] That is, at every moment, in every thought and word and act, human life is always invocational and doxological. In *Church Dogmatics,* Barth elaborates this view only briefly; but we may take it as a starting point to sketch an invocational account of human life.

Across the whole range of our activity, implicitly or explicitly, we give thanks and praise and confess and pray. And when we do, the open questions are: In whose name? To whom? and Toward what end? When we eat a piece of bread, for example, we do so always from a particular (usually unarticulated) point of view, on a particular footing, and thus in a particular style and form: we acquire it as a prize by our own economic ingenuity; or we steal it as plunder by our own cunning; or we seize it as part of a struggle for survival; or we receive it begrudgingly as our due; or we accept it gratefully, as a gift from a friend; or we consume it carelessly, as an entitlement; or we devour it opportunistically, as a kind of fuel. In every case, the eating itself is involved in larger invocational patterns: sometimes thanksgiving to a neighbor, or thanksgiving to ourselves; sometimes praise of a benefactor; sometimes praise of our own good work. Whether we recognize it or not, we do live unavoidably and comprehensively in these patterns of gratitude, congratulation, confession, petition, and so on. We appreciate, we acclaim, we admit, we appeal. And as Barth (with Calvin) points out, "language is not always necessary" for these patterns to take place, since they are "at once word, and thought, and life." We say, with and without words, "Thank you," "I am responsible," "Bravo!" and "Please. . . ." No matter how mundane, every one of our gestures finds its place in these and other invocational patterns, as will the whole range of our gesturing, the complex choreography we eventually live out. But again, everything hangs on the basis, direction, and purpose of this invocation: "In whose name?" "To whom?" and "Toward what end?"

In the exile and separation of sin, human beings deliver thanks, congratulations, and petitions in our own name, to our own doorsteps, and

8. Barth, *Prayer* (Louisville: Westminster John Knox, 2002), p. 7.

for our own sake. In this way we live "deeply curved in upon ourselves." We send and receive the same post. We speak with earnest and loving concern — into a mirror. Wittingly or unwittingly, we pray to ourselves and by ourselves, and in so doing, we turn away from both God and neighbor. Our whole life takes the form of this deep curvature, this *en*-centricity, this isolation and exile. Though we can make a show of our alleged relationships with our neighbors and with God, repeatedly thanking and applauding and petitioning them, we do so strictly on our own terms. We openly or secretly or unconsciously thank ourselves for our own skill, applaud our own feats and capacities, and ask others for goods in variously veiled attempts to commandeer and control those goods, so that we may flourish apart from our benefactors.

Here, then, is an invocational account of sin: we thank, praise, and pray to ourselves, and so we "live to ourselves," and finally "die to ourselves" (Rom. 14:7). In this scenario, our brothers and sisters can only appear to us as Abel appears to Cain, as competitors and adversaries. Our prayers, and thus our lives, take place not as acknowledgments of need and common life, but as private bids for partisan security and power, a thousand little acts — and a thousand larger patterns — of violence.

To transform such *en*-centric prayer, then, to rework these "deeply curved" patterns of invocation into open and intimate patterns of invocation, that is, into patterns of friendship, is to transform whole human lives and communities. Therefore, to actually pray in the name of Jesus Christ (something we can only actually do by God's graceful gift) is no less than to live in that name. This is true both individually, so that "it is no longer I who live, but it is Christ who lives in me" (Gal. 2:20), and together, so that our bodies are members of one another, and, finally and decisively, of Christ's body, the church. In this way, Jesus Christ reworks our "living and dying to ourselves" into "living and dying to God" (Rom. 14:7-9). Thus the renovation of prayer accomplished in the Incarnation amounts to a wholesale renovation of human life, of all "thought and speech and action" so that human being may take place centered not in itself but in God, no longer *en*-centric but genuinely *ec*-centric. And thus prayer in Christ's name, as an event of reconciliation with God, is no Sunday morning antidote to the poisons of the workweek. It is instead a way of life, both weeklong and lifelong, a life in Christ's name, a thoroughgoing and comprehensive transformation of which baptism provides an ongoing foretaste and portrait: dying to death and rising to new life.

From this vantage point, then, the familiar Christian soteriological picture of Christ covering sinners like a mother hen covering her chicks may be reconceived. Christ transforms the catastrophe of worship by entering it, assuming it, and providing it with a new basis, a new direction, and a new purpose. (1) *A new basis:* prayer to God, the fatal procedure carried out in the name of a creature as if apart from the Creator, is reworked into a procedure carried out in the name of Jesus Christ, the person — both true human being and true God — in whom such separation between humanity and God is decisively ruled out. (2) *A new direction:* as carried out in the name of Jesus Christ, the unilateral movement away from and over against God is reworked into a triune pattern with God the Son, through God the Spirit, and to God our Father and our Mother. (3) *A new purpose:* as a gesture carried out in the name of Jesus Christ and thus caught up in God's triune life, prayer's choreography of alienation is reworked into a choreography of participation, that is, fall is reworked into reconciliation.

Accordingly, Christ covers human sin not so much as a mother bird's wing protects from above, but rather as a complete set of clothing may cover and transform a human being's whole body, activity, and life. Thus reconciled human beings, as Paul puts it, "put on Christ" (Rom. 13:14). Or, from another angle entirely — and bearing in mind the pervasive character of such a shift in basis, direction, and purpose — we may say that Christ covers human sin as musicians cover a familiar piece of music, preserving its ostensible structure but also transforming it thoroughly, from its basic foundations to the farthest reaches of its style and signature. Our liturgies, the liturgies of 'adam and Cain, are now marked by a different name. Now Christ, the new 'adam and also the new Cain, carries out our work with us and for us, not destroying the human work of prayer but rather assuming it, undertaking it in God's name, and thus making it God's own.

In *Church Dogmatics,* Barth's word for this kind of assumption is *Aufhebung,* which is typically translated "abolition."[9] Following Hegel, Barth uses this term to mean not merely cancellation, as the English word suggests, but also both preservation and transcendence. The related German verb is *aufheben,* translatable as (1) "to raise or lift"; (2) "to keep"; or

---

9. See, e.g., Barth, *Church Dogmatics,* I.2, p. 280: "The Revelation of God as the Abolition [*Aufhebung*] of Religion."

(3) "to abolish." And in typically Hegelian fashion, he simultaneously keeps all three meanings in view.[10] "Abolition," then, provides only a partial — and therefore misleading — translation. "Sublation" is a common alternative in English,[11] and as we have seen, other possibilities are available, including parallels from music ("covering"), semiotics ("transfiguration"), hermeneutics ("translation" or "citation"), sociology ("reframing" or "incorporation"), cultural studies ("co-option" or "assimilation"), philosophy of science ("paradigm shift"), and parallels from the Bible itself, where in Matthew's Gospel, for example, the term "fulfillment" signals both continuity and a decisive change in course (Matt. 5:17).

As Barth uses it, *Aufhebung* indicates a "taking up," an assumption that (1) lifts or raises worship to a new, superior level insofar as it reframes and refounds it, providing it with a new basis, direction, and purpose; (2) preserves worship insofar as it is assumed and not merely vanquished or eliminated; and (3) ends or abolishes worship insofar as it radically refigures and transforms it. Consider how one scientific picture of the world is "taken up" into another (e.g., Newtonian physics taken up into Einsteinian physics), at once preserving, contradicting, and transforming the prior picture. Alternately, symbols of oppression are often taken up by an oppressed community as a symbol of liberation, preserving their significance precisely in order to overturn it: one example is the Nazi "pink triangle," which was originally used to identify homosexuals in concentration camps, and which is now often taken up as a symbol of pride and solidarity in gay and lesbian communities. A New Testament example was the Roman empire's cross, a devastating instrument of violence and terror that was taken up by the early church as a consummate instrument of peace and reconciliation. In ways variously analogous to each of these "takings up," worship and religion are taken up and transformed in the life of Jesus Christ.[12] They are in-

10. The English word "lift" may give some indication of this semantic range, since "to lift" can mean both "to raise up" and "to cancel, cease, or annul," as in "lifting" a ban or blockade. Similarly, the English phrase "hold up" can mean both "to manually raise" and "to stop," as in "holding up traffic." The range of the German term *aufheben* also includes a third meaning: to preserve.

11. Following Hegel scholars, Garrett Green suggests "sublation"; see Green, "Challenging the Religious Studies Canon: Karl Barth's Theory of Religion," *The Journal of Religion* (Oct. 1995): 477.

12. As George Hunsinger has noted, the whole structure of Jesus' life, death, and resurrection may be understood in these terms: "*Aufhebung* is the Hegelian pattern of affirming,

corporated into his body, and thus into divine life. Even in their inhumanity, human beings are gracefully preserved, raised up, and thus transformed into their genuine humanity, that is, into their participation in God. If we keep in mind two meanings of the English word "lift" (both to *raise,* as in "lift a glass," and to *annul,* as in "lift a ban"), we may say that God's saving act for humankind is to "lift religion" once and for all.

2. The End of Christianity

It is possible, of course, to understand this argument as a simple vindication of Christianity, a claim that acts of worship undertaken by Christians, in contrast to those acts undertaken by non-Christians, are covered or lifted by God in Jesus Christ. And, in one sense, Barth intends just this kind of vindication: God's reconciliation of humankind in Jesus Christ is, after all, the Good News proclaimed in Christian preaching. But alongside the vindication, Barth registers a simultaneous critique as he repeatedly returns to the idea that, no less than their non-Christian contemporaries, Christians also stand empty-handed and in need of God and God's grace. In fact, Barth's critique of religion as the "fulcrum of sin," a critique that applies, he says, without qualification to the Christian religion, means that, if we draw up a list of those most in need of divine rescue, we should list Christians first of all.

Indeed, Barth's critique of Christianity is at the heart of his notorious revolt against the so-called liberal theological traditions in which he was trained. In brief, Barth charges liberal theology and culture with conceiving of God, in effect, as a high-ranking member of human society — a supreme member, to be sure, but a member nonetheless, and thus domesticated. As he expresses it in *Romans,* Christians "suppose that we know what we are saying when we say, 'God.' We assign to Him the highest place in our world: and in so doing we place Him fundamentally on one line with ourselves and with things."[13] The God of liberal theology, Barth argues, is a domesticated God, a house God, a God finally conceived as an

---

canceling, and then reconstituting something on a higher plane (a pattern whose underlying metaphor would seem to be 'incarnation, crucifixion, and resurrection')." See Hunsinger, *How to Read Karl Barth: The Shape of His Theology* (New York: Oxford University Press, 1991), pp. 85-86.

13. Barth, *Romans,* p. 44.

aspect or highly exalted personality in human experience, and thus as a God who can be placated and satisfied and enjoyed and to some degree controlled by human beings in their ingenuity, in their nobility, in their piety — that is, in their religion. Barth argues that in religion "we press ourselves into proximity with [God]: and so, all unthinking, we make Him nigh unto ourselves."[14]

Barth's interpreters often gloss this critique as primarily an effort to champion divine sovereignty and freedom, to recover a sense of God as by no means "on one line with ourselves and with things," but rather as, in his famous phrase, "wholly Other." And so it is. But Barth means to clarify this doctrine of God only with a view to clarifying the scope and severity of humanity's dilemma, our situation apart from God. In other words, for Barth, the chief problem with any domestication of God is not that God is misunderstood, but that God is missed altogether, and that human beings, precisely in their alleged dealings with God, are actually deeply curved in upon themselves. The cathedral walls Christians build up on all sides, Barth insists, are in fact prison walls. Exactly where we claim to "press ourselves into proximity" with God, Christians repeat the fatal separation.

Thus Barth's critique of religion is not first and foremost a critique of religion in general from a Christian standpoint: first and foremost, it is a critique of Christianity. In a lecture on nineteenth-century Christian theology in Europe, Barth put it this way: "Grace, which the theologians of the time described so beautifully as free, did not remain free for them. They claimed it as a right, a certainty, a possession of the Christian, the so-called believing Christian."[15] This kind of Christian claim to possession, in Barth's view, amounts to its own reversal (i.e., to forfeiture) since whatever I possess as a right, as a feature of my own being or technical skill (by virtue of my own "believing," for example), is just to that extent no longer free regarding me. I claim it. It is mine. Therefore, when I issue this kind of claim, I do not possess God's free grace; on the contrary, I move decisively to reject it and leave it aside in my very act of claiming it as a right.

Again, at stake here for Barth is not ultimately divine freedom, which for Barth is secure in any case, but human freedom — and, most promi-

14. Barth, *Romans,* p. 44.

15. See "The Word of God in Theology from Schleiermacher to Ritschl," in *Theology and Church* (London: SCM, 1962), p. 216.

nently, Christian freedom. Since the free grace I allegedly possess can be thereby neither "free" nor "grace," my claim to possession is a serious mistake, an act of idolatry, and thus an act of my own Christian incarceration. Precisely as a Christian, I bind my own hands and hem myself in. Precisely as a Christian, though I may beautifully describe grace as free, when I claim to possess it as a right or a certainty or an inevitable result of my own impeccably Christian technique, I deeply curve myself around my supposed prize, like a fist clutching a precious gem, though I am clutching nothing at all. In fact, I am empty-handed, an empty fist clutching only my own impeccably Christian pride.

"It is not against faith that we are warned," Barth writes near the end of *The Epistle to the Romans,*

> but against OUR faith; not against the place that has become visible where men can stand and live, but against OUR taking up a position there and proceeding to live out our lives there; not against freedom and detachment, but against their ambiguous appearance in OUR lives, against the certainty with which WE advance in freedom and in detachment. The warning is uttered against any position or manner of life or endeavour that WE think to be satisfactory and justifiable, as though WE were able in some way or other to escape the KRISIS of God.[16]

For Karl Barth, this "we" and this "our" may apply, in the second place, to all people; but for him, concretely and in the first place, these terms apply to Christians. From this point of view, we may add the following: it is not against religion that we are warned, but against "our" religion, against Christianity. And this for two reasons.

First, as Barth puts it in *Church Dogmatics,* Christianity is always "one religion with others," and so it sits squarely under the critique of religion in general (*CD,* I.2, p. 298). When Christians imagine or protest or hopefully suggest otherwise, we merely demonstrate our own religiosity, our own desperate scrambling to avoid the shadow that falls across all religious life, "as though WE were able in some way or other to escape the KRISIS of God."

Second, Barth argues that the critique of religion — as "unbelief, idolatry, self-righteousness" (*CD,* I.2, p. 324) — applies across the religious

16. Barth, *Romans,* p. 504.

board, but most damningly to Christianity. "It does not affect only other men with their religion," he writes. *"Above all* it affects ourselves also as adherents of the Christian religion" (*CD*, I.2, p. 300; italics added). In Christianity, we find "the same self-exaltation of man which means his most profound abasement" that is found in other religions; but in Christianity this abasement takes its most radical form, because "this time it is in place of and in opposition to the self-manifestation and self-offering of God." That is, Barth argues that every religion erects its own "great and small Babylonian towers," but in Christianity we build them up not against an empty sky but actually against heaven itself, actually against God's forgiveness and reconciliation in Jesus Christ (*CD*, I.2, p. 327).

According to this view, the very truth of God in Jesus Christ means that Christian idolatry — in which we reject this truth in a way no other religion can or does — is the epitome of idolatry: the Christian religion is the epitome of religion, and thus Christian sin is the epitome of sin. To be sure, sin may be found throughout the emporium of religion, but in Barth's view, "in the history of Christianity, just because it is the religion of revelation, the sin is, as it were, committed with a high hand. . . . For contradiction against grace is unbelief, and unbelief is sin, indeed it is *the* sin" (*CD*, I.2, p. 337; italics in original). Barth says that humanity's "contradiction against grace," our commitment and recommitment of *"the* sin," is never so clear and catastrophic as it is in Christianity.

Thus, in a striking appropriation and reversal of the familiar Christian claim that Christianity is the "highest" religion,[17] Barth argues that this very height — the fact that Christianity actually has to do with God — means that Christianity above all falls under the divine "KRISIS" and judgment. For Christians, then, our dubious distinction is that precisely as adherents of "the true religion," we ourselves are the true sinners, the true idolaters, the truly religious men and women on earth, and thus the ones most truly in need of God's grace and salvation. Christianity, in this view, is the highest religion on earth in the same way the Tower of Babel was the highest tower. To miss this crucial point, to merely carry forward the mantle of Christianity with triumphant confidence and good cheer, is to miss the fact that, in any case, Christians continually withdraw into the depths and injuries of religion. We continually take up afresh the fatal po-

---

17. See, e.g., Friedrich Schleiermacher, *The Christian Faith* (Edinburgh: T&T Clark, 1989), pp. 31ff.

sition. Barth frames the point in *Romans:* "The man therefore who, armed with the knowledge of the Epistle to the Romans, himself advances to the attack, has thereby failed to perceive the attack which the Epistle to the Romans makes upon him."[18] To put it another way, this kind of advance ignores or attempts to erase what Barth calls "the impenetrable ambiguity of human life — even of the life of the Christian and of the Christian Community."[19]

With the idea of the impenetrable ambiguity of Christian life, we arrive at the very heart of Barth's theological work. And from this vantage point we can see clearly how fundamental Luther's doctrine of *simul iustus et peccator* is for Barth as he spells out this ambiguity. Christianity is "the true religion," as Barth puts it plainly in *Church Dogmatics,* "only in the sense in which we speak of a 'justified sinner'" (*CD,* I.2, p. 325). On its own feet and by its own lights, Christianity stands alongside other religions, ignorant and disastrous: "No religion is true. It can only become true . . . in the way in which man is justified from without; i.e., not of its own nature and being, but only in virtue of a reckoning and adopting" (*CD,* I.2, p. 325). Like religious man and woman, religion itself can stand aright only by way of divine forgiveness and gracious reconciliation, only by way of God covering human beings in their ongoing sin and self-abasement. Christianity, Barth contends, is a religion of unsurpassed "unbelief, idolatry, self-righteousness," of "great and small Babylonian towers" built up against heaven, of the "work of people" par excellence. Thus Christianity is the featured product, done up in lights, at the very heart of the emporium of religion. In these respects, Christianity differs from other religions and philosophies of life only insofar as it outdoes them in religiosity, only insofar as it commits the same sin "with a high hand," and with the most acute "contradiction against grace." Only as such, and continually as such, is Christianity adopted by God, reconciled by God, lifted (i.e., elevated, preserved, and ended) by God in Jesus Christ. Only as such can it be called "the true religion."

Consequently, in Barth's view, Christianity is simultaneously adopted and condemned, saved and abolished, *iustus et peccator.* On the basis of the Lord's Prayer's petition "forgive us our debts," Luther argues that both the individual Christian and the Christian church as a whole are

18. Barth, *Romans,* p. 505.
19. Barth, *Romans,* p. 505.

justified only as abiding sinners, and thus they properly live as abiding penitents. Every time Christians pray this prayer (at least weekly, for most Christians), we recall, affirm, and reenter the penitential posture. Likewise, Barth describes the Christian life in terms of sin and ongoing confession: "There can be no more question of any immanent rightness or holiness of this particular religion. . . . The Christian cannot avoid abandoning any such claim. He cannot avoid confessing that he is a sinner even in his best actions as a Christian" (*CD,* I.2, p. 338).[20] For the Christian religion no less than for individual Christians, the proper way of life can only be the penitent's way, the path on which human beings "live by grace" (*CD,* I.2, p. 338). Indeed, Barth goes so far as to say that even the word "Christian," indicating as it does a supposed relationship to Jesus Christ, can never be properly uttered as a confident "grasping at some possession of our own." It can only be uttered properly as "a reaching out," "an inquiry," and hence finally as "a prayer" (*CD,* I.2, p. 349). At bottom, if I say that I am a Christian man, or that my religion is the Christian religion, I do so only as an invocation, only as an entreaty. I am asking, not telling. I am praying, and, as with every one of my prayers, the truth of what I say remains an open question. So "impenetrably ambiguous" is the Christian life, says Barth, that even its identifying name, even this word "Christian," can at most be assigned the precarious — and indeed, the deeply ambivalent — status of a prayer.

The ambivalence indicated in the name "Christian life" pervades that life, and it may be found and traced out at every level. The individual Christian, particular Christian communities, and Christianity as a whole are always, Barth suggests, *simul iustus et peccator,* and they should be described from both directions. Again, Christians, their communities, and their religion are not sinners because they fail to rise to their own standards of conduct and piety; they are sinners precisely because they rise to these standards all too well, precisely because they are Christians, Christian communities, and the Christian religion. It is not deviant or decrepit forms of Christianity that are actually opposed to God and God's grace. It is Christianity itself, considered well and done well, that is so opposed. It is Christianity at its allegedly most honorable, most decorous, and most revered that is so opposed. Bearing in mind Barth's expansive,

---

20. For Luther's references to the Lord's Prayer, see, e.g., *LW* 26: 66; *LW* 31: 84-85.

invocational account of liturgical life, it is Christian worship that is so opposed.

Thus we cannot say, "If only we were better Christians!" On the contrary, we must say again and again that the better Christians we are, the more we stand in need of divine rescue, because the genuine Christian, Barth insists, "cannot avoid confessing that he is a sinner even in his best actions as a Christian"; moreover, with exactly these best actions, he commits sin with a high hand (*CD,* I.2, pp. 338, 337). To borrow Luther's terms, the genuine Christian cannot avoid the stance of the penitent, for she is "always a sinner, always a penitent, always righteous" *(semper peccator, semper penitens, semper iustus).*[21] At every turn, she must constantly confess that, if she is justified, she is simultaneously a thoroughgoing sinner; if her community is a community of saints, it is simultaneously a community of sinners; if her religion is the true religion, it is simultaneously the religion of unbelief, idolatry, and self-righteousness without peer. This emphatically rules out Christian triumphalism, or as Paul puts it, Christian "boasting."

At the same time, however, and just as emphatically, Christian shame and despair are likewise ruled out. For, at every turn, the genuine Christian must constantly confess and rejoice that, if she is a thoroughgoing sinner, she is simultaneously justified by God's grace; if her community is a community of sinners, it is simultaneously a community of saints by God's grace; and if her religion is the religion of unbelief, idolatry, and self-righteousness without peer, it is simultaneously "reckoned and adopted" by God's grace, that is, reckoned and adopted by God's prodigal love and mercy in Jesus Christ, who enters, adopts and lifts religion once and for all.[22]

---

21. *LW* 25: 434.

22. For now, I leave aside the complicated question of whether Christians properly confess that salvation in Jesus Christ includes all human beings, Christian or not. Suffice it to say, however, that the view outlined here — that Christianity is the worst offender against God among religions, and is graciously forgiven and "adopted" as such — would seem to point toward an account of universal human salvation, on the principle that "if the worst, then also the better." That is, since Christians are by no means the cream but rather the very depths and dregs of human religiosity, the fact that God rescues and welcomes the dregs would suggest that God also rescues and welcomes the whole barrel. Thus Christianity, as a "light to the nations," is less like a shining temple on a mountaintop, beckoning the townsfolk to climb to its remarkable height, and more like a light deep in the valley below, witnessing that even the ones supposedly farthest from heaven are reconciled by God to God (the

Finally, from this vantage point we can also see how Luther's doctrine of the *simul* may serve as an interpretive key for reading Barth's account of worship as fall — together with his account of worship as reconciliation. Bearing in mind how important the *simul* is in Barth's thought, we may say that worship is simultaneously fall and reconciliation for him. Indeed, it is as if Barth picks up and extends Luther's liturgical account of the *simul*, which Luther expressed exclusively in terms of penitence, and applies it to worship generally, and thus to human life generally — not only confession but thanksgiving, praise, and petition as well. Penitence remains fundamental for Barth, a kind of keynote for the whole range of gestures in worship and thus in human life. But now the whole range is explicitly taken into account. Furthermore, now the whole architecture of Christian life, both in its continual fall and in its continual reconciliation in Jesus Christ, may be framed and conceived in liturgical, invocational terms. Now the *simul* may be understood as mediated in and through Christian liturgical life.

On the one hand, in worship we fatally fall away and apart from God; on the other, in worship God reconciles us to participation in divine life and hence to genuine humanity. Therefore, we properly call Christian worship "reconciliation" only in the sense that we speak of justified sinners: just as God justifies sinners in such a way that they remain sinners through and through, God reconciles liturgists in such a way that they remain liturgists through and through, carrying out *leitourgia* and thus requiring reconciliation precisely because they are and continue to be confounded and hazardous, set over against God as some second thing. Worship is reconciliation, then, only insofar as God takes up and transforms worship in order to reconcile it, to reconcile fallen and falling humanity, religious humanity, liturgical humanity, humanity dead set on "standing aright" before and away and apart from God.

According to this theology of invocation, therefore, wherever Luther and Barth refer to "justified sinners," we may refer to "reconciled liturgists," or perhaps better, to "reconciled enemies." And again, even as the phrase "justified sinner" indicates someone who is justified and nonetheless a sinner, the phrase "reconciled enemy" indicates someone recon-

---

Christmas stories in Matthew and Luke may be read as prototypical here). In brief, in this view, Christian witness amounts to this: if God can love and save Christians, surely God loves and saves everyone! But full development of this argument must wait for another day.

ciled to God who is nonetheless an enemy of God, who nonetheless opposes God, who worships, sins, and so who falls even as he is reconciled. To borrow again from Luther, any Christian liturgist is simultaneously "holy and profane, an enemy of God and a child of God."[23] Barth's description of both worship as fall in *The Epistle to the Romans* and worship as reconciliation in *Church Dogmatics* may be fruitfully read together. Framed and understood as a version of *simul iustus et peccator,* these accounts provide promising groundwork for a systematic theology of invocation.

The broad outlines of this groundwork are as follows. In their theologies of justification, both Luther and Barth exclude two possible Christian claims: first, the claim that, since Christians are justified, they are no longer sinners (here Luther and Barth answer: *semper peccator*); and second, the claim that, since Christians are always sinners, they are not justified (here Luther and Barth answer: *semper iustus*). Therefore, in the invocational theology sketched here, we likewise exclude two claims: first, the claim that, since Christian liturgists are reconciled to God through worship, they no longer fall into *leitourgia;* and second, the claim that, since Christian liturgists invariably and profoundly fall into *leitourgia,* they are not actually reconciled to God through Christian worship. In our thanksgiving, praise, and petition, we retrace and replay the original and continual human attempt at separation from God: we contradict ourselves and our Creator; we withdraw from divine friendship and try to take up a position on our own, beside and against God, and hence also (as J so masterfully unveils in Genesis 3 and 4) beside and against one another. And simultaneously, in this view, through our thanksgiving, praise, and petition, God graciously reconciles our *leitourgia* by reworking it into participation in the triune divine life. God transforms the work of people into the work of people-with-God, the work of *Immanuel,* the work of Jesus Christ, that is, the work of genuine humanity, human beings living and moving in conspiracy, solidarity, and friendship with their Creator.

As we have seen, Luther portrays his *simul* doctrine variously: in matrimonial terms (the "joyful exchange" between husband and wife), in intercessory terms (Christ advocating on behalf of the faithful), in protective terms (Christ covering believers from divine wrath), and in liturgical terms (penitence mediating between *iustus* and *peccator*). In *Church Dog-*

23. *LW* 26: 232.

matics, Barth portrays the *simul* primarily in terms of juridical acquittal;[24] but in his view of Christian worship, another figure emerges: the *simul* is pictured as mediated by Christian liturgical life. Christians' worship — that is, their whole life, all their moral and legal ordering and all their invocational choreography, all their thanking and acclaiming and asking and admitting — is now given a new footing, direction, and purpose. Now they pray and live not in their own name, but in the name of Jesus Christ. They are thus covered by this name, since the nominal basis on which they stand and act is fundamentally reworked. Now they give thanks and praise not over against God, but with God the Son in solidarity, through God the Spirit in conspiracy, and to God our Father and our Mother. Thus they are covered by this new direction and choreography, since they live now as beings "hidden in God" (*CD*, IV.1, p. 8), "taken up" and enveloped within the triune divine life.[25] As such, now they worship for reconciliation's sake, indeed "for Jesus' sake." Thus they are covered by this new sake, this new purpose, and this new hope.

In this view, then, the *simul* takes shape through human beings living Christian liturgical lives. On one hand, in all of their thought and speech and action, human beings, including and especially Christians, fall into worship and religion. They fall into prayer. They carry out *leitourgia,* working and living supposedly on their own feet, in their own name, and for their own sake. On the other hand, owing strictly to God's gracious work in Jesus Christ and the Holy Spirit, in all of their thought, speech, and action, Christians are simultaneously reconciled to God. They are taken up into God's triune life; they carry out the work of people-with-God, working and living not in their own name but in Jesus' name, and not for their own sake but for Jesus' sake. On this basis, and on no other, they are enjoined to "rejoice always," to "give thanks in all circumstances," and above all to "pray without ceasing" (1 Thess. 5:16-18). On this basis, and on no other, they are enjoined to take up the posture pictured at the very heart of the Sistine Chapel ceiling, to take their place in the first woman's congregation, to pronounce her unceasing prayer that God may remake, reconcile, and finally redeem.

24. See, e.g., Barth, *CD*, IV.1, p. 574: "Justification begins as man's acquittal from sin, from his being as a sinner. . . . [I]t is God's righteous sentence on him, because he is still not righteous but unrighteous, because he is still the old man and not yet the new. It is *iustificatio impii*."

25. Cf. Col. 3:3: "For you have died, and your life is hidden with Christ in God."

So let us return, at last, to Michelangelo and the image with which we began. Though Barth does not mention it, another interpretation of *The Creation of Eve* is possible, compelling, and consistent with an account of Christian worship as simultaneously fall and reconciliation. As we have seen, Michelangelo placed the picture centrally, and thus prominently, in his sequence of scenes from Genesis. Though its counterpart, *The Creation of Adam,* is today far better known, it is *The Creation of Eve* that is actually the focal point of the ceiling, and thus focal for the sanctuary. As such, it occupies a kind of pivot point in the chapel, and through Barth's eyes, we saw how this crucial position may indicate that the scene depicts the decisive turn, or fall, of humankind into worship and religion. Adam lies collapsed in an awkward stupor. Eve leans forward in a desperate prayer. God stands earthbound beside and apart from them both, dour and distant.

But now we may see with other eyes; rather, we may see twice with Barth's eyes, taking up a point of view made possible by his account in *Church Dogmatics* of worship as reconciliation, and finally by his appropriation of Luther's *simul* doctrine. For the Sistine Chapel, it turns out, is dedicated to the Virgin Mary.[26] And this fact, along with the longstanding theological tradition of conceiving not only Jesus Christ as "the second Adam" but also Mary as "the second Eve," allows for another interpretation of the fresco, one that simultaneously includes both Barth's view of the scene as fall and a view of the scene — likely intended by Michelangelo himself — as reconciliation.

That is, if we view the scene typologically, with Adam and Eve serving as types or foreshadowings of Christ and Mary, then the picture has a double resonance. As a portrait of humanity's fall, it depicts the first Adam, who has indeed fallen into an awkward stupor, and the first Eve, who is lunging into prayer, attempting to stand on her own feet apart from God even as she "presses herself into proximity with Him," as Barth puts it, "in a manner at once terrible and presumptuous."[27] And yet as a portrait of humanity's reconciliation, the picture simultaneously depicts the second Adam, Jesus Christ, lying dead at the foot of his cross. Indeed,

---

26. In 1483, under Sixtus IV (for whom the chapel is named), the chapel was dedicated to Mary; Perugino's fresco, *The Assumption of the Virgin,* was originally the altarpiece. See Hibbard, *Michelangelo* (New York: Harper and Row, 1974), p. 100; Charles Seymour, Jr., ed., *Michelangelo: The Sistine Chapel Ceiling* (New York: Norton, 1972), p. 70.

27. Barth, *Romans,* pp. 44, 247.

one of the chief indications that Michelangelo intended the picture to be seen in this way is the stark, apparently dead, cruciform tree against which the man's body leans, a tree that is surely out of place in the lush Garden of Eden, but is reminiscent of Paul's reference to Christ's crucifixion in Galatians 3:13: "Cursed is everyone who hangs on a tree."

Thus, in the figure of the first Adam, the second Adam — or better, the last Adam — is also visible here at the culminating point of his reconciling work, the death into which all Christians are baptized (Rom. 6:3). And likewise, in the figure of the first Eve, the last Eve is also visible. According to this way of typologically viewing the fresco, Mary, who is often understood as a type of the church, emerges from Christ's wounded side. The first Eve may intone the fatal first prayer, but the last Eve — Mary, or the church — intones the saving last prayer, the prayer born of Christ's own body, and therefore, we may add, taken up and transformed by the Holy Spirit in divine conspiracy. Eve's first prayer is undertaken and overcome by Mary's (the church's) last prayer, the climactic scene in salvation history for a chapel dedicated to Mary. And yet, as the picture itself manifests, these "firsts" and "lasts" are not sequential: they are simultaneous, visible typologically at the same time. Therefore, just as the fresco simultaneously includes both portraits, so Christian life simultaneously includes them: the first and the last, Adam and Christ, Eve and Mary, our fall and our reconciliation.

The Christian life is thus set forth in a single image. In Adam we fall; in Christ we are reconciled. In Eve's prayer, we set ourselves against God as enemies; in Mary's prayer, the church's prayer prayed and lived out in the name of Jesus Christ, proceeding from his body, and in conspiracy with the Holy Spirit, God reconciles us as children. The tragedy of prayer and the miracle of prayer, the work of people and the work of people-with-God, the wretchedness of sin and the joyful hope of reconciliation — this single image, with its double aspect, is thus a picture of *simul iustus et peccator.* If we interpret it this way, its placement at the center of the chapel ceiling is no surprise. In a sanctuary devoted to Mary, as well as to the sketching of the whole sweep and drama of Christian history, it is only fitting that the central image be *The Creation of Eve,* a scene typologically pointing to the "creation of Mary," that is, to the creation of the church, and hence finally to Christ's creative work of reconciliation with humankind.

We have called Mary's (or the church's) prayer "the last prayer." Undertaking and overcoming the first prayer (a prayer that also belongs above all to the church, the fatal prayer of separation), this last prayer in the name of Jesus Christ means our reconciliation with God, as God the Son takes our place with us in solidarity, and God the Spirit breathes with us in conspiracy. It means that our worship and religion are "lifted": raised up, preserved, and abolished. And this third dimension of Barth's *Aufhebung,* the dimension of abolition, only promised and foretasted in God's work of reconciling humanity, is full-blown and decisive in God's redemption of humankind. Our *leitourgia,* lifted in the divine work of reconciliation, is finally and thoroughly swept away in the divine play of redemption. We may truly speak, then, of a last prayer, a prayer after which there will be no more prayer.

3. The Play of Redemption

Karl Barth did not live to write his planned fifth volume of *Church Dogmatics,* "The Doctrine of Redemption," but the spirit, direction, and substance of his case points to the idea that Christians can and should conceive of the Christian life, that is, Christian liturgical life, as provisional and temporary. In other words, Barth's work points to the idea that Christians properly confess that Christianity will end. Liturgy will end. Prayer and praise and thanksgiving will end. Inasmuch as God promises not only to reconcile but also to redeem humankind, the work of reconciliation will, in the end, pass away — and so will worship. Human beings will not live as *simul iustus et peccator* forever. At the end of days, they will live strictly *iustus;* or better, they will live wholly beyond the *simul's* schema of *iustus* and *peccator,* since these descriptions will no longer apply (or even arise as possibilities). What will arise instead is intimate friendship. What will arise instead is "the delicious freedom of intercourse," the ecstasy of loving communion. What will arise instead is jubilation, with its riot of beauty, joy, and delight.

Therefore, the work of people will not only be undertaken and transformed, not only overcome and covered; it will end. And accordingly, the divine work of undertaking and transforming the work of people, of overcoming it and covering it with the work of people-with-God, will end as well. Indeed, in this view, at the end of days, all work will end, giving way to rest, to play, to Sabbath, and thus to genuine celebration. This is the dearest Christian hope and the greatest Christian joy: that Christianity itself will pass away.

Biblically, this idea is consistent with J's portrait of the Garden of Eden as a place replete with blessings, but without an altar. It is consistent, too, with J's report of God's call on humanity as a call to "till and keep" the garden and "freely eat" its fruit, but by no means to worship God. In short, as the exquisite lyrical and metrical symmetries of Genesis 1 suggest, creation itself is a kind of temple, a place where God means to dwell in friendship with humanity. But originally — and properly — there is no temple in creation. Likewise, the idea that God's redemption of humankind involves liturgy's end is consistent with the graphic vision of the New Jerusalem recorded by John of Patmos in the book of Revelation: "I saw no temple in the city, for its temple is the Lord God the Almighty and the Lamb" (Rev. 21:22). In a kind of amplification and radicalization of the Incarnation, here God arrives on earth and sweeps away "the first things" and inaugurates ultimate friendship between God and humanity: "See, the home of God is among mortals. God will dwell with them; they will be his people, and God will be with them, wiping every tear from their eyes. Death will be no more; mourning and crying and pain will be no more, for the first things have passed away" (Rev. 21:3-4). The first things, the first Adam, Eve, and Cain, the first worship and religion, the first work of people unto death — these will give way to the last things, to the eschaton of *shalom,* to the rest and play of people unto life. Thus, both in the original creation in Eden and in the new creation in the New Jerusalem, God will be "all in all" (1 Cor. 15:28), and no temple will be found. God and human beings will dwell together, face to face and within one another, in friendship and communion.

This idea is also consistent with the biblical polemic against worship found in the Hebrew prophets. Amos and Micah, for example, vehemently dismiss "festivals," "solemn assemblies," and liturgy's "ten thousands of rivers of oil"; instead, they call for "justice," "righteousness," "kindness," and "walking humbly with your God" (Amos 5:21-24; Mic. 6:7-8).[28] The idea that God's redemption of humankind involves the end

---

28. This blistering critique of worship is typically softened by Christian exegetes who rather hastily explain that YHWH is not opposed to worship per se, only to worship undertaken by unjust persons or in some connection with unjust social arrangements (as if any other kind of worship were possible in the world as we know it), or by those who insist that

of liturgy allows us to read this polemic in eschatological perspective, pro-phetically naming and anticipating the last things, when God and human-kind will indeed "walk humbly" together in friendship, and when temples and festivals, sacrifices and anointings will be no more.

Finally, the idea that liturgy will end is consistent with the complex biblical portrait of divine covenant. For while the biblical history of God's covenantal life with human beings often includes divine commands to worship God (as, for example, in the Mosaic covenant at Sinai), in the overall scriptural scheme these covenantal forms are marked as provisional, slated to be ultimately fulfilled and relativized by a new covenant. For Christians, of course, this new covenant is decisively announced, sealed, and eschatologically promised in Jesus Christ (Luke 22:20); but the proclamation of a new covenant does not belong to the New Testament alone. It is also prophesied by Jeremiah: "The days are surely coming, says YHWH, when I will make a new covenant with the house of Israel and the house of Judah. . . . I will put my law within them, and I will write it on their hearts; and I will be their God, and they will be my people. No longer shall they teach one another, or say to each other, 'Know YHWH,' for they shall all know me" (Jer. 31, 33-34).

Barth calls the Jeremiah covenant "the final word in matters of the di-vine covenant with Israel. In the light of the last days, it describes it as the covenant of the free but effective grace of God" (*CD*, IV.1, p. 34). The "ba-sic form" of humanity, for Barth, is the event of "being in encounter," a face-to-face meeting in dialogue and care: seeing and being seen, openly welcoming and being welcomed, speaking and listening, calling and being called on, helping and being helped — and all this "gladly" and "freely" (*CD*, III.2, pp. 273-74). This holds true, Barth says, in the case of human friendships, but these friendships also analogously "image" the friend-ship between creatures and Creator for which human beings were and are created. That is, God makes each human being to be a partner in loving intimacy with human neighbors but also and especially with God, to en-

---

the apparent critique of worship is only apparent, only a colorful hyperbole meant to under-score God's demand for social justice. But the texts themselves read differently: YHWH does not say, "Give me festivals only if you let justice roll"; rather, YHWH says, "I hate your festivals! Let justice roll!" Indeed, these texts suggest that, for many of the prophets, festi-vals and sacrifices are not just inferior alternatives to justice, kindness, and humility, but work to subvert and oppose them. Barth's critique of worship, in short, opens up a more plausible and fruitful reading of this polemic. See also, e.g., Hos. 6:6; Isa. 1:11-17; Jer. 6:20.

ter into a togetherness in which "I" and "Thou" are "neither slave nor tyrant . . . but both are companions, associates, comrades, fellows and helpmates." In short, they are friends in spontaneous freedom and mutual joy (*CD,* III.2, pp. 269, 271). And this free joy, which Barth calls "the *secret* of humanity" (*CD,* III.2, p. 271), means that the event of genuine human being is never carried out as if obedient to "an alien law imposed from without" (*CD,* III.2, p. 269). On the contrary, for me as a true human being, the neighbor with whom I am in encounter "is inward and intrinsic to me even in his otherness" (*CD,* III.2, p. 268). He sees me and is seen by me, calls me and is called by me, helps me and is helped by me — both from without and from within, so to speak. Thus, if he issues me a command, it is what we have called a "constitutive command," resounding from a point at once external to me and "inward and intrinsic to me." If we speak of "lawgiving" in this relationship, then we must speak of a law given extrinsically, but also inwardly and intrinsically, as a "law of my own freedom" (*CD,* III.2, p. 268). Quoting YHWH, Jeremiah puts it this way: "I will put my law within them, and I will write it on their hearts" (Jer. 31:33).

Precisely as such, the new covenant promised in Jeremiah is, for Barth, "the final word in matters of divine covenant with Israel"; for here the covenantal law is at once explicitly divine law ("my law") and radically inward and intrinsic to God's people ("within them"). Indeed, as Jeremiah puts it, this law will be made so much "their own" that teaching — *torah,* instruction, and thus, in Barth's terms, religion — will be obsolete. "Talk about God," that perilous gossip invented in Eden, will be plainly unnecessary, "for they shall all know me, from the least of them to the greatest" (Jer. 31:34). As partners in this covenant, human beings will live with God in genuine intimacy, spontaneous freedom, and mutual joy, as God's companions. Thus, in Barth's view, this "new and eternal form of the covenant means the ending of the fatal controversy between God and man," but hence it also means "the ending of the corresponding necessity" for the "human opposition between wise and foolish, prophets and people, teachers and scholars, the *ecclesia docens* and the *ecclesia audiens*" (*CD,* IV.1, p. 33). In a word, it means the ending of religion. The sprawling emporium will at last close its doors. The glittering question over its gates — What then must I do? — will no longer trouble human beings, for God's law will be within them, as ordinary and native to them as the beating of their hearts.

As a supremely constitutive command, the covenantal command will take the form of friendship, the form of love. And while "love never ends," the trappings of religion, which Paul paraphrases as "prophecy, tongues, and knowledge," will thus reach their finale (1 Cor. 13:8) (*CD*, IV.1, p. 33). That is, owing to "the completely changed conditions of the last time, [the prior covenantal] form will certainly be altered, and so radically that it will no longer be recognizable in that form" (*CD*, IV.1, p. 32). A new form will emerge in its place, a "new covenant." Thus, according to Jeremiah, the covenantal command will become "inward and intrinsic"; the prophet strikingly describes the immediate outcome of this new arrangement not as immaculate and dutiful human behavior, but as the cessation of religious instruction, the end of prophecy, the end of religion, and thus, we may add, most fundamentally the end of liturgy. At the last day, human beings will rest once and for all from their work of people. The exilic condition of "toil" (Gen. 3:17) will be lifted at last. The ultimate Sabbath, full of joy and celebration and delight — indeed, as Luke puts it, full of "music and dancing" (Luke 15:25) — will begin in glory. In effect, Jeremiah is prophesying the end of his own vocation, and by pointing to this prophecy as the "final word" on divine covenant, Barth does the same. Even theology — especially theology — will end!

Barth calls this covenant of friendship the "perfect covenant," the divine covenant's "new and proper form," and the "final word." "But at the same time," he argues, "it is also the first word in these matters." That is, though the Jeremiah covenant points to an eschatological "complete change in the form of the covenant," it also lays bare "what the divine covenant with Israel had been in substance from the very first." This substance, Barth continues, "was not simply absent in the 'old' covenant — or in the one covenant in its old form. . . . It was only hidden" (*CD*, IV.1, pp. 33-34). In other words, Barth argues that the Jeremiah covenant at last discloses the substance of the divine covenant itself, a substance only indirectly or imperfectly discernible in prior forms. Here again, Barth plays with the idea of *Aufheben,* maintaining that in the Jeremiah covenant, the divine covenant "is upheld, that is, lifted up to its true level . . . given its proper form . . . [and] far from being destroyed it is maintained and confirmed. There is no question of a dissolution but rather of a revelation of the real purpose and nature of that first covenant" (*CD*, IV.1, pp. 32).

Thus, according to Barth, prior covenantal forms are properly understood in light of the Jeremiah covenant. At every stage in the history of God's dealings with Israel, the "real purpose and nature" of the divine covenant was and is this covenant of friendship, of intimate partnership in mutual freedom and joy. Therefore, this theological vantage point allows, first, for an affirmation of each covenantal stage, inasmuch as the new covenant prophesied by Jeremiah entails not a displacement or opposition to prior forms, but a clarification of them — or an *Aufhebung,* a raising up, a preservation, and a transformation of them. Prior covenantal forms, then, however contrary to the Jeremiah covenant they may appear, are actually formal variations under which the true covenantal substance is variously hidden. And second, this theological vantage point also allows for a crucial hermeneutical key for understanding covenantal history. By taking up a position alongside Jeremiah, we may properly conceive of the various forms of divine covenant with Israel in "eschatological perspective" and thus recognize more readily the covenantal substance hidden within them. We may see, for example, that God issued the inaugural command in the biblical narrative — the renowned prohibition in the Garden of Eden — precisely in this spirit of friendship and intimacy. Ironically, perhaps, precisely by pointing toward an end to all theological teaching, both Jeremiah and Barth deliver what for them is an indispensable piece of theological instruction, a decisive lesson about the purposes of God: one day, they say, no such lessons will be necessary.

Finally, regarding Barth's theological work, his keen emphasis on the Jeremiah covenant may provide a glimpse into the unwritten fifth volume of *Church Dogmatics,* "The Doctrine of Redemption," and it may also allow for a kind of retrospective rereading of important themes in his theology. For example, we may reread Barth's famous emphasis on "the command of God" and the "obedience and disobedience" of humanity from a new angle. Indeed, considered apart from Jeremiah 31, Barth's perspective of God as characteristically "commanding" and humanity as characteristically obliged to "obey" may conjure up a picture of sovereign and subject, czar and serf — or worse, tyrant and tyrannized. But if we reread Barth's command-obey formulation of the divine covenant with Israel in light of his ultimate emphasis on Jeremiah's account of the "real purpose and nature" of divine covenant, we may be more alert to how both command and obedience are situated and relativized within the whole sweep of Barth's thought.

For Barth, in the context of separation and sin, of *leitourgia* and violence, the apparently heteronomous divine command — most famously in Barth, the divine "No!" — is properly prominent in Christian theology.

In the context of God's reconciliation of human beings in Christian life, Christian theologians may properly accent how the divine command manifests itself to human beings as heteronomous, but also in a sense as autonomous, since God the Spirit's conspiracy and God the Son's solidarity with human beings means that they now may live *ec*-centrically in Christ's body, "hidden with Christ in God" (Col. 3:3) (*CD,* IV.1, p. 8). In this theological register, human beings may faithfully discern the deeper divine "Yes!" simultaneous with the abiding "No!" This is because, for Barth, Christian pilgrims live *simul iustus et peccator.* However, in the context of God's redemption of human beings — that is, in the context of the *eschaton,* what Barth calls "the completely changed conditions of the last time" — the divine command is revealed to be what it actually was and has been all along: the resounding divine "Yes!" to humanity, an event of radically intimate friendship and love. The theology of Karl Barth, so well known for its account of God's commanding "No!", in fact decisively points to the divine "Yes!" behind every divine command, even the divine "No!"

These commands are indeed heteronomous, inasmuch as they issue from a partner external to the addressee; otherwise, intimacy would collapse into solipsism, and thus into solitude. And these commands are also autonomous, inasmuch as they resound from within the addressee as "the law of his own freedom" (*CD,* III.2, p. 268). Otherwise, friendship would collapse into mere duty, and thus into loneliness and religion. Of course, applied to friendship, the term "command" now begins to seem strained, since we typically do not speak of friends commanding one another. And in any case, the so-called commands of friendship seem a long way from the apparently strict heteronomy of the earlier divine commands, especially the divine "No!" — but also the no less sovereign divine "Yes!"

But this is precisely the point. The commands of friendship certainly are a long way from the commands of a monarch. And by highlighting Jeremiah 31 as the picture of the last form of divine covenant, the "new and eternal form" that reveals the substance and real purpose of the divine covenant itself, Barth argues in effect that, most fundamentally, God does not command as a monarch, much less as a tyrant, but rather as a friend, a partner who desires loving intimacy with human beings. This is clear, first of all, in the accounts of creation in Genesis: in *Romans,* Barth writes of an original, mythic time when God and humanity lived and walked together "freely in the garden in the cool of the day, as though in the equality of friendship."[29] And this is also clear, last of all, in Jeremiah's prophecy of the new covenant of friendship, according to which God issues divine law not as "an alien law imposed from without," but rather as a radically inward and intrinsic law, resounding from without but also from within.

Applying the terms "command" and "law," and even "covenant," to the reality of friendship is, to be sure, stretching each term beyond its typical semantic range. But for Barth, this kind of language — and this kind of stretch — best conveys the heart of divine covenant, and thus the heart of God's love for humanity. Like any good poet, Jeremiah takes up common terms like "law," conventionally understood as externally imposed obligation, and "covenant," conventionally understood as a legal contract between parties with at least potentially competing interests, and he redefines them in ways that challenge these conventions. First, he prophesies a law that issues not only from without but also from within; second, he prophesies a new covenant in which the parties' interests and purposes, far from competing or even potentially competing, perfectly converge. In both cases, conventional understandings of law and covenant are stretched to the breaking point, radically recast into a glimpse of something new. Redefining law and covenant entails redefining human "obedience" as well. Now the human covenantal role emerges not as submission to divine fiat but as spontaneous commission to purposes at once divine and human: divine because they are written by God, human because they are written, intimately and indelibly, on human hearts.

In this way, Barth argues, Jeremiah unveils "what the divine covenant with Israel had been in substance from the very first." In the beginning of all things, God created humans in order to live with them as intimate friends. At the end of all first things, this friendship will flourish. And now, in the interim that at once spans and includes this beginning and this end, God works out with us the history of human reconciliation and the return to this friendship, this redemption, this final Sabbath and celebration. Thus I would argue that Barth's well-known theology of "command and obedience" is properly read and understood within this framework, and especially in light of Jeremiah's eschatological picture of the "new and eternal" covenant to come. The prophet's recasting of law, covenant, and obedience, with its near-oxymoronic reversals of convention (internal law; noncompetitive covenant; spontaneous obedience), verges on rede-

29. Barth, *Romans*, p. 247.

fining these terms altogether. But this rhetorical, or poetic, recasting may itself be read as a picture of God's ongoing and promised redefinition of creation. Therefore, we may read Barth as pointing through Jeremiah to a kind of ultimate, eschatological redefinition — even abolition — of divine command, law, and covenant as we commonly understand them. In the *eschaton*, we might say, human beings will not speak of divine commands, laws, and covenants any more than we speak of them today with regard to our closest companions. We will speak and sing only of intimacy and friendship with God and one another. We will speak and sing only of love.

Thus the idea that liturgy will end is consistent with the biblical portraits of the original creation; the new creation promised at the end of all first things; the prophetic polemic against worship; and the complex history of God's covenant with Israel, culminating in the new covenant prophesied by Jeremiah and proclaimed, sealed, and promised in Jesus Christ. But the idea that liturgy will end is not only consistent with these features of the biblical account, it is also consistent with the theology of invocation that I have sketched in this book, following and building on the work of Barth and Luther. First, in this view, humanity's redemption means the end of our separation from God, the end of human sin and alienation, and thus, according to Barth's perspective on worship as fall, the end of *leitourgia*. In God's redemption of humankind, the work of people will not only be covered and lifted, it will be swept away once and for all. Humanity and God will live as intimate friends, in joy, delight, and celebration, precisely as God originally and ultimately intends.

But the "end of liturgy" follows theologically not only from Barth's account of worship as fall; it also follows from his account of worship as reconciliation. For once alienation itself is undone, once God is again and decisively "all in all" (1 Cor. 15:28) and the intended intimacy between Creator and creation has begun in earnest, then the work of reconciliation is complete — or rather, has already been completed. Once reconciled, friends no longer require reconciliation. They only require one another and a new creation within which to live out their mutual care and mutual joy, their "music and dancing" (Luke 15:25), their common life and their "delicious freedom of intercourse."[30]

In short, once God and humankind live together in communion, the divine work of reconciliation will be obsolete. No enemies will remain to

30. Barth, *Romans*, p. 249.

be reconciled. On that day, human beings will no longer live *simul iustus et peccator,* since intimate friendship knows neither the separation of sin nor the necessity of justification. They will no longer work to stand aright before God or one another, because they will live in righteousness, and righteousness will live in them, "written on their hearts," and also because, in love, friends stand not only outside but also with and within one another. In Barth's terms, humanity and God will be radically "inward and intrinsic" to each other "even in their otherness." In the end, the call will give way to the kiss: God and humanity will live face to face. Christian pilgrimage, the divine work of reconciliation, the work of people-with-God in Jesus Christ and the Holy Spirit — all will give way to an altogether different form of life.

Now the long-awaited feast will begin. Now the triune God will "dwell among mortals," celebrating with all creation, and the true heavenly banquet will commence at last, the feast promised and given as a foretaste in the eucharistic meal, but also marked in that ceremony as absent and forthcoming, since every eucharistic liturgy is also initially a record of "the night he was betrayed." Now friendship, the perfect reversal of betrayal, will reign supreme. And now all work, human and divine, will come to its finale. For what feast, what party, what celebration, and even more clearly, what joy and what delight can properly be called "work"? Rather, these things are properly called rest, play, peace, and *shalom.* In short, they are called *sabbath,* the end and completion of all work. In this light, the story of creation in Genesis 1:1–2:3 may be read not merely as a retrospective account of "the beginning," but also as a paradigmatic account of the whole history of creation, which culminated in the promised seventh day, the Sabbath, on which God "rested from all the work that God had done in creation" (Gen. 2:3). As in the case of the eucharistic supper, the Christian observance of the weekly Sabbath may give human beings a glimpse and foretaste of this ultimate Sabbath, but also a weekly reminder of its absence and a weekly provocation to pray for its arrival. According to this view, Christians today should observe the Sabbath, celebrate Communion, and pray for an end to this observance and celebration, that is, pray for the beginning of the final Sabbath and Communion to which all excellent Christian liturgy points and calls.

Christian worship itself, properly understood, always takes place under the sign of its own provisional character, for two reasons: first, it is provisional because *leitourgia* — as the work of people apart and away from God, the original and ongoing fall of humanity — one day will be swept aside. God will end it. The separation and bondage of sin will be transformed into the intimacy and freedom of friendship. Second, Christian liturgy is provisional because, as the work of people-with-God, the reconciling and ongoing work of Jesus Christ and the Holy Spirit to undertake, overcome, and lift *leitourgia* into participation in divine life, it will one day be unnecessary. God will end it. The divine work of reconciliation will give way to the divine play of redemption, and Christianity, along with all other "first things," will pass away.

On that day, God's new covenant of friendship — joy and celebration, intimacy and delight, love and new life — will flourish between human beings and their Creator. In this new and eternal scenario, there will be no temple (Rev. 21:22), no liturgy, no work of people, and no work of people-with-God. There will be only the rest and play of redemption, the delightful and beautiful communion of friendship. Humanity and God — as indeed the wolf and the lamb, the leopard and the kid (Isa. 11:6) — will at last walk together through Jerusalem in the cool of the day.

Reforming Worship

What difference might this view of worship — as both fall and reconciliation — make for Christian liturgical design and practice today? I will give two answers, from two different angles: first, no difference at all, and second, all the difference in the world.

1. "No Difference At All"

If by "difference" we mean "righteous advantage" (as in, what righteous advantage lies in store for us if we reform Christian worship according to this argument?), we can only answer, again and again, "No difference at all." Indeed, the crux of the case here is that Christian worship is not a matter of human beings acquiring righteous advantages. Quite the contrary, the very work of seeking and claiming this sort of advantage is itself the religious catastrophe, the work of people toward a separation from God. If God saves us from this work by taking it up with us, and thus transforming it into work toward communion, we have cause to rejoice; but we have no cause to then turn around and reinterpret or reconfigure an allegedly improved *leitourgia,* proclaiming anew our righteous advantage. Soteriologically, such a reinterpretation or reconfiguration makes no difference. After all, God can just as well undertake and transform Lutheran worship as Congregationalist worship, Pentecostal as Roman Catholic, or for that matter, the "work of people" of non-Christians as of

Christians. There is nothing we can do, not one thing, to facilitate our liberation by rearranging our prison furniture. Salvation is divine work. Every righteous advantage belongs, as it always has, to God alone.

And yet the religious urge to justify ourselves through some new (or fashionably old) religious reform persists, a permanent temptation to claim and supposedly carry out the work of salvation as though it were the work of people. And, in Barth's view, this temptation lurks not only on the shadowy periphery of religion but also at its focal point, well lit and in full view. That is, the temptation lurks at the altar and table of the Christian sanctuary. Accordingly, accounts of Christian worship (including the one in this book) are often picked up and wielded as soteriological techniques — formulas, in Luther's terms, for "obtaining righteousness in the sight of God" — and thus as Christian answers to the basic religious question, What then must I do? What is the proper work of people? Or, as a lawyer puts it to Jesus at the heart of Luke's Gospel, "Teacher, what must I do to inherit eternal life?" (Luke 10:25).

And why not? Why not ask just this question, and ask it of just this teacher? After all, don't Christians require sound advice regarding salvation, and thus precisely regarding *what I must do*? Isn't this our most prized topic of discussion? Indeed, from a Christian point of view, can we imagine a more apparently natural and pressing question to ask? And that is precisely the point. The question is all too natural and all too pressing. Accordingly, Luke tags the lawyer's question as an effort to "test" Jesus (NRSV), to "tempt" him (KJV). Here Luke returns to the same Greek root *(peirazo)* that he uses for the testing and temptation with which the devil confronts Jesus in the wilderness (Luke 10:25; 4:2).[1] And so we may say,

---

1. Indeed, the verbal link *(peirazo,* to "test" or "tempt") between the two confrontations (Luke 4:2; 10:25) raises the question: Is this an "opportune time," as Luke puts it, for which the devil has been waiting since the encounter in the desert (Luke 4:13)? And if it is, what exactly makes the time "opportune"? According to Luke, Jesus has just "appointed seventy others," sending them into the countryside ahead of him, with instructions to heal and preach (Luke 10:1ff.). Is this new organizational flurry what makes the time "opportune" for a temptation to religion? Is the devil, in other words, daring Jesus to match his bold new organizational strategy with an equally bold new religious doctrine? Or again, immediately preceding the lawyer's test, Jesus takes the disciples aside, rather dramatically telling them that they are blessed because "many prophets and kings desired to see what you see, but did not see it, and to hear what you hear, but did not hear it." And just then, Luke reports, precisely in this newly rarefied atmosphere of explicit privilege — an atmosphere in which spiritual pride, no doubt, is "lurking at the door" (Gen. 4:7) — exactly then, "a lawyer stood up to test Jesus" (Luke 10:23-25).

with Luke, that the lawyer's question is the devil's question, a question meant to provoke anxiety and, in turn, to invite spiritual pride. It provokes anxiety because the question presupposes that our salvation is our work to do; it invites spiritual pride because it makes it possible for us to imagine that we are doing it (and that others, alas, are not).

Recognizing the lawyer's question as a demonic question, Jesus does not answer it directly; instead, he reverses the exam. He counters the question with a question of his own and thus ironically tests the legal specialist who is trying to test him: "What is written in the law?" (Luke 10:26). The lawyer responds quite ably: "You shall love the Lord your God with all your heart, and with all your soul, and with all your strength, and with all your mind; and your neighbor as yourself." He thereby sums up both "the right answer," as Jesus goes on to call it, and precisely what he himself has failed to do in asking his treacherous question in the first place (Luke 10:27-28). That is, the lawyer has failed to "love God and neighbor," because posing a demonic test or temptation *(peirazo)* is by no means an act of neighborly love, but of love's reversal. The lawyer thus simultaneously completes the exam and delivers an unwitting confession — again, with perfect irony.

But this exchange also makes clear exactly what is at stake in the test the lawyer poses, and thus, by extension, what is too often at stake in Christian religious and liturgical reform. The question is not merely meant to probe Jesus' legal virtuosity, his ability to recite the law. If that were the case, the lawyer would hardly be so quick to give away the correct answer. Rather, with this question the lawyer invites Jesus to go beyond the familiar law and unveil a new one, a new teaching, a new religion. In a word, he invites Jesus to innovate, to proclaim a new path: "Teacher, what must I do? I know what the law says. But what does it fail to say? What new law, what new saving instruction, what new work of people can you provide?"

But Jesus does no such thing. He refuses to do so. Instead, he presses the lawyer into citing Deuteronomy and Leviticus himself: he thus demonstrates to his listeners, as well as to Christian readers today, that the Deuteronomic-Levitical "great commandment" formula is no Christian innovation but a widely known piece of Jewish exegetical wisdom in Jesus' day.[2] In other words, Jesus refuses to unroll a new "Christian" scroll of

2. The formula is a combination of Deut. 6:4-5 and Lev. 19:18; see also Mark 12:28-31 and Matt. 22:23-40.

soteriological instructions for holy human life; rather, he says, in effect: "We already have the scrolls we require. You have them, and can recite them with ease — and yet you ask for a new one. You hypocrite: start by following the scrolls you already have." God has not come in Jesus Christ in order to found a new religion. The lawyer tests him, tempting him to strike out in this direction, but Jesus will not do it.

By the end of the exchange, this all becomes clear: the lawyer, we learn, can already provide the correct legal answer to his own question, and thus his question is revealed to be, at best, an invitation to declare a new law, a new product in the emporium of religion. The fact that Jesus rejects this invitation, plainly approves of the answer cited from Hebrew Scripture, and then decisively cites Leviticus himself ("do this, and you will live" [Luke 10:28; Lev. 18:5]) is a standing rebuke to the lawyer's devilish test. That is, it is a standing rebuke to any attempt to set up a Christian *torah* above or beyond the Jewish one. And it is also a standing rebuke to the incessant Christian effort, alive and well today, to embrace the saving difference — that is, the soteriological "righteous advantage" — that Christians have over Jews, or over non-Christians generally, or, indeed, the advantage that some Christians have over other Christians. Jesus is quite plainly uninterested in this kind of righteous differentiation; in fact, he stands against it, continually pointing us — today's Christians no less than the lawyer of his day — back home, that is, back to verses from Deuteronomy and Leviticus and to a standard piece of Jewish scriptural interpretation.[3]

3. Some may object that, on the contrary, in the Sermon on the Mount, for example, Jesus seems quite interested in sketching the outlines of a new Christian *torah,* not least because the basic rhetorical pattern of that sermon may be read as a format for new instruction: "You have heard it said . . . but I say unto you. . . ." But this reading, common as it is among Christians today, misses at least two crucial features of the Sermon: first, according to Matthew, Jesus foresees that his teaching may be misunderstood as a new law, and so he excludes this interpretation at the outset: "Do not think that I have come to abolish the law or the prophets; I have come not to abolish but to fulfill" (Matt. 5:17). Thus the whole Sermon, and indeed the whole of Jesus' teaching and preaching, takes place under the sign of "fulfillment," that is, under the sign of deep and abiding continuity with foregoing Jewish tradition, even when he interprets and clarifies it, as every rabbi does. Second, the Sermon on the Mount is less a "ratcheting up" of ethical-religious standards and more a focused attack on ethical-religious pride, as Luther would insist. The discourse ultimately amounts to a call to repentance, for who can withstand the divine searchlight described here, if even "anger," "looking with lust," and "hating persecutors" are prohibited (Matt. 5:22, 28, 43-

This Christian appetite for righteous differentiation is at the heart of works righteousness, and thus it is at the heart of religion. For whoever asks the lawyer's question ("What must I do to inherit eternal life?") quite bluntly zeroes in on how *I* might myself inherit salvation, on precisely what *I must do* to come into such an inheritance. This presupposes, of course, that my salvation lies within the reach of my own work. Indeed, lest we miss the point here, immediately after Jesus' response and implicit rebuke of the lawyer, Luke editorially adds that the lawyer persists in "wanting to justify himself," thus clarifying that he is not only asking the demonic, religious question but is also driven by the demonic, religious motive (Luke 10:29). He wants to justify himself. He wants to *do* works that will secure his allegedly rightful (and indeed righteous) inheritance of eternal life. And in religion — and thus in much Christian liturgical reform — we desperately, doggedly do likewise.

Wanting to justify ourselves, we assiduously design and execute whatever liturgical work we suppose necessary for standing aright before God. We ceremoniously drape ourselves in vestments; or, just as decisively, we conspicuously cast such vestments aside. Either way, we make pretentious, prodigal claim to our "share of the property" (Luke 15:12), setting out to seize our own inheritance and accomplish our own salvation. And thus, implicitly or explicitly, we pronounce woe upon those who differ from us and blessing to ourselves. After all, if *we* are the ones carrying out the proper work of people, then we can only, alas, quite earnestly pray for — or when we deem it necessary, zealously condemn — those who do other work.

When it comes to reforming worship, that kind of spiritual pride is always lurking at the sanctuary door (Gen. 4:7). It is the permanent, quintessential religious temptation. Thus we do well to insist, again and again, that regarding salvation — and indeed regarding any difference whatsoever that is understood as righteous advantage — there is between liturgical forms "no difference at all."

---

44)? Indeed, precisely because of their stringency, these clarifications of the law are primarily designed to expose and subvert legal pride, self-righteous pretense, and judgmentalism. In short, they are designed to interrupt "seeing the speck in your neighbor's eye" and not "the log in your own" (Matt. 7:3). If the Sermon on the Mount calls its listeners to a fundamental form of life, that form of life is repentance, that is, the penitent's "pure humility" and "holy pride" (Luther). This is finally to say that, once the penitential form of life is unpacked and specified, the Sermon calls its listeners into a life of justice, kindness, and walking humbly with God (Mic. 6:8).

The point is crucial, and it is one that has often been missed. The historical proliferation of Christian liturgical practices is riddled with just this kind of self-justification, and it is significantly constituted by it. In a tragic, cascading refrain, one Christian group reforms its liturgical life in order to set itself apart from and against another group, proclaiming, in effect, "This worship service has a righteous advantage over that one!" Therefore, beneath a dazzling Christian variety, the religious catastrophe replicates itself with virus-like efficiency. Reformations beget counter-reformations, which beget reformations. High church begets low church, whose adherents energetically declare, "We are certainly not high church!" Low church begets high church, whose adherents solemnly intone, "We are certainly not low church!" And today, if we but listen for it, we can clearly make out in much Protestant worship the implicit or explicit claim, "We are certainly not Roman Catholics," and in much Roman Catholic worship, "We are certainly not Protestants." And so on. This chorus resounds across Christendom, this allegedly certain (and deeply anxious) claim of righteous advantage over other Christians, and over non-Christians besides. The history of Christian liturgical plurality is not strictly reducible to this kind of self-righteous religiosity, of course, but there is nary a Christian denomination free of it, and its power to shape sectarian identity cuts deep and wide. The devil gently leans in over every Christian shoulder, whispering, "You, good Christian, *you* are the true heir."

And so, as we view it from this angle, we must respond to the question, What difference might this account of worship make for Christian liturgical design and practice today? with a clear answer: No difference at all. We may interpret or reform Christian worship according to this evaluation, to be sure, but by so doing we advance not one step closer to accomplishing our salvation. On the contrary, our very striving to accomplish it — the religious striving to stand aright before God, and thus, at its heart, the liturgical attempt to adore and present God with suitable gifts and offerings — is the scenario within which our alienation from God originally and continually takes place. In other words, our lonely labor to accomplish our salvation, that is, religion, is exactly what gives rise to our need for rescue. Like someone caught in quicksand, we can attempt to escape, but our very attempts only deepen the trouble.

As we have seen, the crux of Karl Barth's critique of religion is that worship — preeminently Christian worship, in all its various and shifting forms and reforms — is the fundamental venue for humanity's "terrible and presumptuous" work of separation from God.[4] Again, it is not worship done poorly that is the issue, but rather worship done all too well. With respect to our salvation, then, no liturgical reform on our part can help, neither a fine-tuning nor an ambitious overhaul, since such reforms make "no difference at all." They only continue the crisis. It is as if a ship is sinking in the ocean, a gaping hole in one side of the bilge, and the crew works frantically to patch the hole — with planks they have torn out of the other side of the bilge. As one breach is closed, another opens. The sea rushes in. The ship is lost.

2. "All the Difference in the World"

The ship is lost, that is, but for the grace of God. For in Barth's view, as we have seen, a critical word about worship and religion is by no means God's final word. Through God the Son's solidarity and God the Spirit's conspiracy, the ship is saved. Or, to express the metaphor more meaningfully, the crew and passengers are saved definitively, the ship only provisionally, because one day it will run aground and be retired.

In the meantime, however, the ship is saved. It is still certainly a ship of fools, but now, miraculously, God the Son *(Immanuel)* is on board with us, God the Spirit is in our sails, and the ship has received divine orders to be decommissioned — once and for all. For we live "in the evening," we might say, and Noah's dove has come back, "and there in its beak [is] a freshly plucked olive leaf" (Gen. 8:11). We are still aboard the boat, adrift and surrounded by water as far as the eye can see, but the "fresh olive leaf" testifies that, despite appearances, the tide has decisively turned. The ordeal now comes to an end, and one day we will all leave this ark behind, high in the mountains, and go down to live in the green valleys below.

Thus our salvation, while by no means our own work, is for us the most radiant good news. It arrives entirely from outside, like a dove appearing on the horizon far off, gradually coming near, and at last alighting on our own hand. We cannot conjure it, or hasten it, or improve on it. But we do witness it, God willing, and we can proclaim what God has done. We can spread this good news throughout the ship in clear and compel-

4. Barth, *The Epistle to the Romans*, p. 247.

ling terms, in vividly symbolic acts and images, and in vibrant communal patterns of life. And this homiletical and sacramental mission provides the proper charter, of course, for Christian churches today.

But again, if we work to carry out this mission, we thereby gain no righteous advantage whatsoever. With respect to righteousness, our situation — with all its disadvantages — has not changed. Even in our preaching, our sacraments, and our communal life, we are still embroiled in religious work, in elaborate attempts to justify ourselves, in "deeply curving inward" (Luther), in *leitourgia* unto separation from God. If salvation comes to us, it comes not because our situation has changed, but because our situation needs changing, and God lovingly and decisively and continually moves to change it. In a word, salvation means *rescue.* The dove appears on the horizon, to our great benefit but in no way to our credit. In Luther's terms, we live *simul iustus et peccator,* as justified and as sinners at the same time. And indeed, in Christian preaching and Christian churches today, the signs of ongoing *peccatum* are legion.

But the dove does appear. The Holy Spirit, Christians confess, is not merely a topic mentioned from time to time in Christian worship; rather, the Spirit participates in it, conspires with it, and thus lends it an entirely new, simultaneous voice (Rom. 8:15-16). Jesus Christ, Christians confess, is not merely a founder and teacher recalled from time to time in Christian worship; rather, he participates in it, stands in solidarity with the gathered assembly, the body of Christ, and thus lends worship an entirely new, simultaneous standing. God is against religion. But God neither displaces nor destroys religion; rather, God meets us in it, at once preserving it (thus *leitourgia* continues apace) and transforming it decisively — from the inside out, so to speak.

And so Christians may and should describe Christian worship — even at its very best — in clearly critical terms: as mixed in motive, prideful in practice, narcotic in effect. Bold and rigorous Christian theological criticism of the best Christian worship and religion should flourish, and it should replace the sentimental, uncritical liturgical theology that too often prevails today. In individual Christian worshiping communities, and in the whole fractured landscape of Christian liturgical variation, we have as revealing a picture of human sin as one could hope to find. A Christian worship service is not a hiatus from corruption, but rather an epitome of it. And so on.

But from the point of view of God's saving action in Jesus Christ and the Holy Spirit, Christians must also describe Christian worship — even at its worst — in equally clear terms of faith and hope. "This morning," we might say, "we are surely a gathering of sinners, carrying out *leitourgia* in our own names and as our own corrupt collective body; but we also confess, in faith and hope, that this morning God simultaneously gathers us in Jesus' name and as the body of Christ. Likewise, this morning's Scripture and sermon are highly questionable affairs, fundamentally presumptuous human attempts to interpret God and proclaim God's word, to write and speak 'words of my mouth' that are 'acceptable in [God's] sight' (Ps. 19:14).[5] But we also confess, in faith and hope, that the Spirit simultaneously conspires with these words, that Jesus Christ simultaneously stands with the reader, the preacher, and the celebrant, so that God may speak to us through even these words, even this morning, even now."

5. This prayer formula, which introduces so many Christian sermons today, is nothing if not an ironic overture to Christian preaching. In the first place, it is a brazen bid for divine acceptance of the "words of my mouth," thus effectively announcing (and maintaining) the supposed separation over against God that is implied by the religious task of offering God "acceptable" works of our own. In this way, the prayer introduces the sermon as a consummately religious act, with us looking on from one side and God looking on from the other ("your sight"). But further, this formula cites a psalm in which, in the immediately preceding verse, the psalmist implores God to "keep back your servant also from the insolent," for the explicit reason that "then I shall be blameless" (Ps. 19:13). But what could be more insolent, we may ask, more audacious and questionable, than clearing one's throat and purporting to proclaim "the Word of God" for all to hear? And to do so, no less, in connection with the idea that "I shall be blameless"? In this sense, then, the preacher's prayer is an ironic bit of self-incrimination, an implicit and perhaps unwitting confession, just before acting, to the stark impropriety of the act.

On the other hand, however, exactly because of this impropriety, what could be more appropriate than to begin a sermon with, indeed, a prayer, and in particular, to begin with a plea for God to transform "the words of my mouth"? What could Christians require more urgently than just this transformation? Thus the ironic ambiguity of Christian preaching, prayer, and worship generally: it is both supremely "insolent" and, we hope and trust, nonetheless made "acceptable" by divine conspiracy, solidarity, and transformation. Therefore, Christian preachers should by no means discontinue the traditional use of this opening prayer, but they should continue it afresh in constant view of its ironic ambiguity. In other words, this prayer may remind preachers (and, with lay education, it may remind listeners, too) of (1) the sheer insolence of "interpreting the Word of God," both as a preacher and as a listener, and (2) our consequent need for God to work in and through this insolence, that is, for God's transformative work of reconciliation to break out here and now. The prayer must become a *penitential* prayer, spoken in humility and holy pride, desolation and hope. Not "I pray that you find this sermon (and me) to be a blessing," but "I pray that you transform this sermon (and me, and even this very prayer) into a blessing."

In concrete cases, then, and without withdrawing the critique of worship for an instant *(semper peccator),* and in fact depending on it, Christian worshipers should listen for God's Word of good news in Scripture, preaching, and sacramental life. We may hope for and expect God's word and presence in *leitourgia,* not because *leitourgia* is "sacred," but precisely because it is "profane," and thus requires divine transformation: "Those who are well have no need of a physician, but those who are sick" (Luke 5:31). Or better, we may hope for and expect God's Word and presence in *leitourgia* because exactly there, in Christian worship, we find the disastrous human work of setting up and maintaining a spurious divide between sacred and profane in the first place.[6] God is against this divisive work, for God actually desires thoroughgoing communion with all creation, "so that God will be all in all" (1 Cor. 15:28). God's opposition to *leitourgia* takes place not as brute annihilation, but as transformative accompaniment: the Spirit's saving conspiracy and the Son's saving solidarity. Thus, in a kind of divine judo, God undertakes worship in order to overcome it. God joins it, and thus God subverts it. God occupies religion and worship, the very locus and source of the fatal divide, and thus carries out the work of reconciliation. On this basis, in faith and hope, we may also describe worship as this loving reversal: abiding sin *(semper peccator)* lifted and turned by God into abiding salvation *(semper iustus).*

It is possible, of course, to misunderstand this position as a flat paradox, a merely doctrinal dialectic by which we alternately affirm contrary accounts: fall, then reconciliation, then fall again, and so forth. But, for Luther, the *simul* is best understood not as mere doctrine but as doctrine manifest in a concrete way of human life, the way of the penitent. Precisely as *semper peccator* and *semper iustus,* Luther argues, a Christian is properly *semper penitens* ("always a penitent"), and thus the doctrinal dialectic issues in an ongoing, comprehensive stance and carriage, a life lived out in simultaneous pure humility and holy pride. At every turn, the genu-

---

6. Indeed, the construction of a temple (i.e., a privileged liturgical site) effectively renders the outside world "profane" (from *pro,* "outside," or "in front of," and *fanum,* "temple"), or gives concrete expression and apparent reality to the presumption that the world already is "profane." This critique of worship and religion, the idea that religion seeks to construct and establish a divide between "sacred and profane," a divide actually at odds with the communion God intends with all creation (1 Cor. 15:28), is continuous with Barth's critique, and it may also be found in Orthodox Christian thought. See, e.g., Alexander Schmemann, *For the Life of the World* (Crestwood, NY: St. Vladimir's, 1995), e.g., pp. 16ff.

ine penitent understands her work, including her penitence, as no reversal of her separation from God, but as a continuation of it, both a cause and a sign of its ongoing reality *(semper peccator)*. As she moves along the pilgrim road, from cathedral to cathedral, she is no less a sinner at one confessional than she was at the last. After all, the instant she considers herself otherwise, she ceases to be a penitent. And in Luther's view, a penitent is exactly what she must, as a Christian, "always" be; furthermore, Luther insists, a community of repentance is exactly what the church, as a Christian assembly, must always be, always praying along with Jesus, "Forgive us our debts as we forgive our debtors. . . ."

At the same time, however, both the Christian and the church, as penitents, must live out lives of holy pride. Referring to their own resources, they can only confess their sin; but referring to God's resources and gracious promises, they can — in faith and hope — be consoled, encouraged, and above all, jubilant. "Penitential jubilation" may seem to be a strange idea at first, but it is nonetheless indispensable: if penitents are not consoled, encouraged, and joyful, if they are instead merely disturbed, ashamed, and gloomily preoccupied with their offenses, then they are not truly penitent at all. For as we have seen, in Luther's terms, true repentance issues not only in profound contrition but also in profound consolation, not only in pure humility but also in pure and holy pride. And so we may add, following this line of thought into Christian sanctuaries today, true repentance issues not only in deep solemnity but also in celebratory joy. Strictly on the basis of what they trust that God has done, is doing, and promises to do, true penitents not only remain prostrate, confessing their sin; they not only cry, *Kyrie eleison* ("Lord, have mercy"); they not only continually die in the turbulent waters of their ongoing baptism. They also rise. They also stand and act and live out that baptism and new life. In a word, they also cry, "Hallelujah! Praise God!"

Considered apart from God's saving solidarity and conspiracy, of course, these very acts, as the *en*-centric and isolated work of people, only repeat the fatal separation. But insofar as God the Son and God the Spirit also conspire and stand with human beings, these very acts, as the *ec*-centric work of people-with-God, are events of gracious dignity, reconciliation, and communion. Most fundamentally, this saving resurrection and doxology is divine work; but in this work God does not labor alone — apart from or over against human beings — but rather with us, precisely as *Immanuel*. Accordingly, though penitents never initiate these saving events, they do participate in them, *simul iustus et peccator*. It is the Spirit who cries out, but she cries out in and through the cries of human beings (Rom. 8:15-16). It is Jesus Christ who rises, but in baptismal life he rises with human beings (Rom. 6:4). In individual cases (including the case of humanity as a whole), whether God actually cries and rises in this way can only be a matter of trust and testimony; for human beings, there are no proofs available, no infallible signs of God's reconciling work; or, if there are, human beings are in no position to interpret them infallibly. For us, there is only "hope for what we do not see" (Rom. 8:25).

Therefore, from at least two directions, Christian triumphalism — or, as Paul puts it, Christian "boasting" — is emphatically ruled out: first, because salvation is divine work and thus cannot be crassly guaranteed or even definitively identified by us, but only humbly hoped for and, in faith, trusted; and second, as Luther insists, boasting is ruled out because, even where God's saving reconciliation actually does occur, it does so simultaneously with the disaster of sin, not instead of it.

According to this view, then, human beings can neither lay hold of salvation as a possession nor properly understand it as an escape from sinful territory. On the contrary, we can only receive it again and again, and call for it as an ongoing gracious gift, given in the face of our ongoing rebellion. It is a miraculous cool glass of water, but we are still deep in the desert. If we boast about it, raising our glasses triumphantly high, we only betray an absurd and tragic ignorance of our actual situation. But if we reverse such boasting, or if God the Son and Spirit reverses it in us, then we are "always penitents." Then the whole of our Christian life is lived under the sign of baptism — this penitential humility, this penitential joy.

And so this baptismal posture, this simultaneous contrition and dignity, pure humility and holy pride, provides the proper basis for Christian religious and liturgical reform, whether such reform seeks to change liturgical actions, or simply our interpretations of them.[7] That is, for the re-

---

7. In many cases, applying this book's argument to Christian worship will mean not remodeling familiar liturgical actions, but reconceiving them and understanding them differently, and to that extent experiencing them differently. As extensive and apparently fixed as much Christian liturgy is ("fixed" by either denominational fiat or local custom), exactly how the gestures of worship are understood — and thus the whole ethos, tone, and style in which they are inflected and carried out — is remarkably supple and open. Hence this argument may be applied fruitfully without changing a letter, not one stroke of a letter, of a given liturgical protocol, while still making "all the difference in the world" for how that protocol

former of Christian worship, this baptismal posture is both goal and way, both the key criterion and the *modus operandi* of her work. On one hand, then, the reformer seeks to renovate Christian worship by making it more clearly and deeply baptismal, and thus more truly penitential, and thus more humble and joyful. On the other hand, in keeping with this goal, she herself carries out her reform baptismally, and thus penitentially, and thus as humbly and joyfully as God provides. As long as a baptismal posture is the aim and standard of her liturgical design, she cannot do otherwise. She cannot claim that her reforms, understood as her own work, make possible any triumphant righteous advantage whatsoever. Indeed, she can at any moment properly point out that her efforts are open to divine judgment, that they are presumptuous, quixotic, detrimental, and so forth *(semper peccator)*. But, equally at any moment, she can describe her efforts as open to God's saving work. She can carry them out as a prayer for God to work through them, to transform them, and thus to make them a blessing. In faith and hope — and thus in holy pride — she trusts that God will do so. But at the same time, in pure humility, she never crassly guarantees or triumphantly declares that God will do so, or has done so. She can only humbly attribute every gift in her life, and in all creation, to God (James 1:17). As the author of her reforming work, we might say, the reformer prefaces her proposals, as indeed her whole life, with the author's familiar acknowledgment at the beginning of a book: "Whatever is of value here, credit goes to my benefactor; whatever here is in error, the errors are mine."

Strictly on the basis of the Christian gospel — the radiant good news that God has acted, is acting, and will act through human beings in order to reconcile them to God — the true penitent, confronting both her sin and her inability to escape it, does not simply throw up her hands. She does not resign herself to sin, however inevitable and inescapable it appears from her point of view. Though she can by no means help herself up and out of sin, she can never rule out the possibility that God will work in her, lifting her at any given moment, in any given act. In Jesus Christ — and preeminently in the Christian cross, that consummate instrument of death and ruin graciously lifted and remade into a tree of life and salva-

---

is grasped and experienced by those who undertake it. In what follows below, however, I experiment with not only reconceiving Christian worship but also redesigning some of its key patterns.

tion — God has accomplished, proclaimed, and promised this transformation. And in her ongoing baptism, as the penitent herself is continually lifted from the waters of her dying, she receives this promise afresh, again and again.

And so the penitent, precisely as a hearer of this divine proclamation, stakes her life on this promise. In faith and hope, she is continuously open to its fulfillment here and now, to God's actual conspiring and standing with her in her work, even the disastrous work of *leitourgia*. As long as she holds to this divine promise of conspiracy and solidarity, she can neither seek sin nor surrender to it (Rom. 6:1-2). She can only act and live with pure humility, openly acknowledging her ongoing sin, and with holy pride, boldly trusting God to live and move through her, so that she might truthfully say, with Paul, "I live, not I, but Christ in me" (Gal. 2:20). On this *ec*-centric basis, then, and on this basis alone, she not only carries out Christian liturgy, but she interprets it anew; in some cases, she reconfigures it. She renovates both its ceremonial and its broader, basic form: the work of people to stand aright before God.

The reformer of Christian worship finds herself in a strange position: she sets out to reform something disastrous, yet recognizing at the same time that her renovations alone will not alleviate the disaster, but only continue it. She nevertheless sets out in the hope and trust that God will act through her work, taking it up into the divine work of reconciliation. She cannot guarantee this. Nor can she definitively point to it in any given case. But she has heard the promises of God and the testimony that God acts in and through human beings, so that the divine work of salvation is labor in which we may, by God's gracious gift, actually participate.

On closer inspection, then, this "strange position," in all its *ec*-centricity, is not hers alone. It is the Christian position. Without exception, our work of people — interpretive, ceremonial, moral, or otherwise — takes place in the shadow of our ongoing sin *(semper peccatum)* and in the light of God's promised salvation *(semper iustus)*. Thus Christians properly live and act in the half-light of dawn *(semper penitens),* always humbly acknowledging our implication in catastrophe and always living and acting in the hope that God will nonetheless make our work God's own.

When it comes to Christian worship services, then, the crucial question is always how to more effectively emphasize and clarify this "strange position," in both of its aspects. That is, Christian worship must become more clearly dialectical, though certainly not by speaking and preaching about "dialectics" and the *simul*. On the contrary, the liturgical language for articulating and embodying this strange position must be much more concrete, more widely accessible, more narratively cast, more emotionally resonant, more vividly and tangibly engaging. In a word, it must be *sacramental* language. Christian worship must become more clearly and deeply baptismal and eucharistic, that is, more truly penitential, simultaneously more humble and more joyful.

In broad strokes, this is my second answer to the question, What difference might this account of worship make for Christian liturgical design and practice today? In brief, the difference it might make is to ground and facilitate a more profoundly sacramental liturgy, bearing in mind that in this view, the Christian sacraments themselves (in the Reformed tradition, baptism and Communion) are fundamentally dialectical in character in that they simultaneously replay both fall and reconciliation. This reform may take shape in new sacramental liturgies or in new interpretations of long-standing ones. Either way, I suggest, this kind of renovation may make "all the difference in the world" for Christian worship.

3. Christian Baptism

In the case of baptism, this basic dialectical structure is quite clear, however frequently it may be de-emphasized or overlooked. Christian baptism is, after all, both a "dying" and a "rising" (Rom. 6:3-4). It is a going down to death and a coming up and out into new life. Indeed, it is no semantic accident that the Greek word in question *(baptizo)* means not only "to dip" but also "to be drowned." Christian baptism, in the first place, is a kind of death. And note that it is not, therefore, a "good" kind of death, as Christian interpreters sometimes characterize it, as if death comes in good and bad varieties. On the contrary, death is, for Paul, the mode of being that follows from sin, the form of dominion through which sin is manifest in the world (Rom. 5:21). In biological terms, of course, I may be very much alive; but sin is nevertheless "working death in me," Paul says, corrupting both personal and social bodies of life, so that I may well cry out, "Who will rescue me from this body of death?" (Rom. 7:13, 24). From Paul's view in Romans, death is a power to be conquered, and thus Jesus Christ died not because death was somehow good or helpful or necessary in the divine work of salvation, but rather because the divine work of salvation is to defeat death, to co-opt and confound and surpass it, so that at last "death no longer has dominion over him" (Rom. 6:9).[8]

Here again we have a kind of divine judo: God the Son submits to death precisely in order to subvert and overturn its dominion. And in Christian baptism, Paul says, "we have been united to him in a death like his" (Rom. 6:5), that is, a death for the sake of undoing death. The rite itself sacramentally portrays this dying and rising by trading on the biblical motif — traceable from Genesis to the Psalter, from the Gospels to Revelation — in which water (typically the sea) is a figure of chaos, destruction, and adversarial power. Thus the one who is baptized "dies" in these turbulent depths. And since humanity's fall is both a fall into death ("you shall surely die" [Gen. 2:17]) and a fall into the ways of death ("Cain rose up against his brother Abel" [Gen. 4:8]), we may also describe baptismal "dying" as falling: that is, a sacramental repetition of fall carried out for the sake of standing anew in Christ, "so that we too might walk in newness of life" (Rom. 6:4).

In Christian baptism, first of all, we replay the plunge into sin and death: we drown *(baptizo)*. But this mortal plunge is not only a fall into a figurative sea of ruin; it is also quite concretely a fall, appropriately enough, into religion. For when it is considered strictly as *leitourgia,* the Christian baptismal rite is the consummately religious act of Christian initiation, the inaugural gesture of Christianity, and as such it is open to strong theological criticism. We may point out, for example, the cere-

---

8. Here is one fundamental reason (among others) why Anselm's atonement theology of the cross, and the various versions of "penal substitution theory" that have followed from it, must finally be rejected. In the last analysis, Anselm's view casts death — and indeed, death by torture, humiliation, and public execution — as a necessary (and, in that sense, "good") constituent in God's economy of honor and salvation. This idea, abhorrent on its face, is also foreign to Paul and, even more decisively, to the authors of the Gospel passion narratives. On the contrary, both Paul (e.g., in Rom. 5 and 6) and the Gospel writers depict death not as a necessary and liberating power, but rather as an insidious "dominion" from which we require liberation (Rom. 5:21; 6:9). Thus in baptism, as on the cross, the case is not so much that we join Christ in his saving death (i.e., the theology of baptism that follows from Anselm), but that Christ joins us in our catastrophic death — and thus saves us by incorporating us into his subsequent resurrection. It is God the Son, after all, who in the Incarnation decisively moves toward us, becoming "a curse" (Gal. 3:13), "sin" (2 Cor. 5:21), and "a slave" (Phil. 2:7). We may say that, most fundamentally, *Immanuel* does not mean "We with God" (the slogan of religion), but "God with us."

mony's implication in an alleged economy of purity, by which some individuals (the baptized) are deemed to be "washed clean," saved, forgiven, publicly committed to Christ, bound for heaven, and so on — while others (the unbaptized) are not. The rite only too easily encourages claims to righteous advantage and disadvantage, and in fact seems expressly designed to produce such claims, since it marks out a clear, tangible threshold between two classes (unbaptized and baptized, "not church" and "church") and a clear, practical program — a rite of passage — for crossing over from one to the other, from "unclean" to "clean," outsider to insider. In short, the Christian baptismal rite is a prime example of religion's clannish work of producing such boundaries and classes, and of investing them with an enchanting aura of sacred legitimacy. As such, Christian baptism is a stark miniature portrait of Christian works righteousness: "If you do the work of crossing this threshold, you will enter the ranks of the righteous. . . ."

Of course, it is possible to argue that, while some (or indeed many!) Christians do understand Christian baptism according to this kind of clannish interpretation, nonetheless their understanding is a misunderstanding, an unfortunate distortion of proper baptismal doctrine and practice. But it would seem both more forthright and more theologically fruitful to recognize that this clannish interpretation is actually an integral aspect of Christian baptism and its religious work on the ground today, and that, as such, it is the very kind of thing that God sets out to oppose and transform in the divine work of reconciliation. For God is against religion's clannish choreography. And so God disrupts it — by entering it.

In the Synoptic Gospels, the inaugural event in Jesus' public ministry is his baptism. God the Son approaches John the Baptizer on the banks of the Jordan: that is, God the maker of heaven and earth, God the author of all righteousness, God the judge of the quick and the dead begins the divine work of salvation by being baptized "with water for repentance" (Matt. 3:11). The sheer incongruity of this situation — an incongruity by no means lost on John, who is understandably taken aback, and at first refuses to comply (Matt. 3:14) — is an opening signal, enacted at the very outset of Jesus' public ministry, that, in Christ, God means to revolutionize religious life, beginning with its inaugural gesture. Imagine the Jordan River, a line of unwashed sinners on one side, waiting anxiously for baptism, and a line of those newly washed clean on the other. And now comes

God the Son, Jesus of Nazareth, the only one among them all who might truly claim to be clean and pure, and he proceeds to get in line with the sinners. He stands with them. God, too, will be "initiated."

Through this simple, stunning act of divine solidarity, the entire sacramental structure is turned upside down. For John the Baptizer has it right: according to religion as he knows it, he protests to Jesus, "I need to be baptized by you" (Matt. 3:14). But Jesus refuses and reverses this choreography, and thus he throws the baptismal caste system into question. First, he crosses the Jordan, so to speak, in the opposite direction: from "clean" to "sinner," from inside to outside. Second, he confirms his solidarity with sinners by submitting to baptism, and thus to religion, precisely in order to expose and transform it. God enters religion by the front gate. And to the prophet's baffled objections, Jesus responds with an overture for his whole public ministry, the divine work of undertaking and reversing religion: "Let it be so now; for it is proper for us in this way to fulfill all righteousness" (Matt. 3:15).

Thus foreshadowing the cross, Jesus enters and submits to catastrophe in order to subsume, transform, and overcome it. God the Son enters religion's exclusive ranks, and he calls that exclusion into question. Thus the heavens being "opened," as Matthew records it, immediately following Jesus' baptism — and indeed as part and parcel of it — is no mere announcement of his special identity (Matt. 3:16). It demonstrates and prefigures the reconciliation God is accomplishing in Jesus Christ: the opening of heaven, the tearing of the temple curtain, and thus the end of religion (again, preeminently Christianity) once and for all (Matt. 27:51). By personally submitting to baptism, God gives the ceremony a second, simultaneous character and direction: it remains our procedure for producing "insiders" and "outsiders," but now, we hope and trust, the rite is also taken up into God's work of indicting and reversing just this procedure, that is, it is taken up into God's life of continually moving into solidarity with "outsiders." If we are truly and graciously baptized into Christ's baptism, and not only our own, then we are baptized into this indictment and reversal of religion, this remaking of a sword into a plowshare. Or, to borrow Joseph's words in Genesis, while in baptism we wittingly or unwittingly "intend to do harm," nonetheless we hope and trust that "God intends it for good" (Gen. 50:20). In faith, we hold fast to this hope, for every Christian baptism requires this transformation.

Christian baptismal rites today should emphasize this dialectical structure as clearly as possible. Standing alone, they are paragons of religiosity; accompanied and transformed by the Spirit's conspiracy and the Son's solidarity, however, Christian baptisms may become events of true penitence, vivid reminders of (1) our plunge into religion, sin, and death, and thus a cause for confession and humility, and (2) God's ongoing promise to lift us up and out of this deadly sea into new life, and thus a cause for joy, courage, and dignity. In short, the idea is to emphasize that *our liturgy itself,* the personal and collective work undertaken here and now by this gathered assembly, is in pressing need of divine transformation. On its own, it is not a holy thing, but quite the contrary. If it is to be made right, God must make it so, *iustificatio impii,* even today, even now.

For example, a priest or pastor presiding at a Christian rite of baptism might first recount the story of Jesus' baptism, emphasizing the divine reversal just described, and then pray:

> Living God, as we prepare for this ceremony of baptism, we call on your presence, forgiveness, and mercy, for without you, our work can only lead to harm. Be with us. Transform us, and remake the work we do today.
>
> God of life and justice, grant us a share in your baptism on the banks of the river Jordan. Make [name]'s baptism a new birth, not of a supposed "insider," but of your own beloved child, who lives in solidarity with every "outsider," seeking out the lost, the hungry, the sick, the poor, and the stranger (Luke 19:10; Matt. 25:31ff.).
>
> Without you, we know this is impossible. But with you, O God, if this baptism truly be in your name — the name of the Father, the Son, and the Holy Spirit, one God, Mother of us all — we boldly trust that all things are possible. And so we call on you now: Come, Holy Spirit. Lord Jesus, have mercy on us. Transform us, and make this baptism your own.

In other words, if Christians confess that God is active through liturgies of baptism, we nevertheless cannot take this for granted. God must grant it afresh. Thus, for our part, Christian baptism must be a clear and urgent *epiclesis,* a calling on the Holy Spirit to lift and remake our work. Note that this is not an *epiclesis* calling on God to join us in our already holy — or even acceptable — proceedings, but rather to deliver us from our present distress, our religion, our *leitourgia*. Just because we are Christians, we carry out the divisive liturgy of Cain, and just because we are Christians, we require the reconciling liturgy of Jesus Christ, beginning with his baptism.

But if particular Christian baptismal rites require this kind of reform, so does Christian liturgy as a whole, for the entire worship service should be profoundly baptismal. In practical terms, this task will manifest itself variously across church contexts. But baptismal waters should, in general, play a more central role in Christian liturgy: they should by no means be confined to particular ceremonies (baptismal rites and special "remembrance" services), but should feature prominently whenever Christians gather for worship. Architecturally, the pool or font should be front and center in Christian sanctuaries; if this is impossible, it should be visually emphasized in some other way (with lighting, color, or other means). Liturgically, baptismal waters should be touched, stirred, and vividly displayed throughout the service (e.g., during opening processionals, calls to worship, and benedictions), as liturgists take full advantage of the beautiful sights and sounds of water. In particular, liturgies of confession should highlight baptismal waters, because, as Bonhoeffer puts it, genuine confession is "the renewal of the joy of baptism."[9]

For example, introducing the rite of confession, the leader might stand at the pool or font, and with cupped hands lift waters high for all to see and hear, saying:

> In baptism, Christ dies with us in the waters of sin and death, so that we might rise with Christ in the waters of birth and freedom. Brothers and sisters, do not be afraid, for where we stumble God will reach out and catch us, and where we fall into death, God will lift us up again into newness of life. Remembering this, God's gracious mercy, let us confess our sins with honesty and courage. . . .[10]

Then, after the prayers of confession, the leader might introduce the "words of assurance" with the same gesture, this time lifting the water higher and with more exuberance, saying:

9. Bonhoeffer, *Life Together* (New York: Harper and Row Publishers, 1954), p. 115.
10. For "reach out and catch us," see Matt. 14:30-31; for dying and rising into "newness of life," see Rom. 6:3-4.

In baptism, we rise with Christ from death into new life, peace, and justice, and God says to each one of us, "You are my beloved son; you are my beloved daughter; in you I am well pleased." Friends, God invites all of us to rise into newness of life: lift up your heads, stand as you are able, and receive the good news of the gospel. . . .[11]

The assuring words are then delivered (e.g., Rom. 8:38-39), though their successful delivery finally depends on whether they are successfully heard and believed, and thus this reception must also be given liturgical form. Baptismal contrition and humility must now be matched and surpassed by baptismal joy, for this joy is itself the form of tangibly receiving the good news of the gospel.

In other words, while confessing sin is a necessary condition of true penitence, it is by no means a sufficient condition. It is quite possible — and, I dare say, quite common in Christian circles — to confess our sins as a kind of dutiful chore, an anxious propitiation, or a debilitating expression of shame. And yet, in Luther's view, such confessions are not actually penitent at all. On the contrary, they are reversals of penitence, since true penitence is a continual pilgrimage from contrition to consolation, a walk infused with not only humility but also holy pride, dignity, courage, and above all, abundant joy. If it is merely humbling, or indeed merely humiliating, it is not true penitence; rather, it is the very devastating guilt that so concerned Luther in his theological work, the original shame that leads *'adam* to hide and thus to compound humanity's estrangement from God (Gen. 2:25; 3:7-10). This is the permanent, clear, and present danger of Christian liturgies of confession: the insidious way in which the direction of the penitent's pilgrimage can all too easily double back on itself. The true penitent, in contrast, is not only contrite; he is also profoundly consoled. He hears the promises of God, and by the Spirit's conspiring gift, he receives them with thanksgiving and joy — the "renewed joy" of his baptism.

Therefore, Christians of every stripe would do well to name the penitential rite the way Roman Catholics, increasingly since Vatican II, have named it: the "liturgy of reconciliation." The "confession" and "words of assurance," as many Protestants call the penitential rite, are really constituent parts of a larger, unified baptismal movement, the divine work of rec-

---

11. For "you are my beloved," see Luke 3:22; for "lift up your heads," see Ps. 24:7.

onciling human beings to God and one another. Therefore, in order to further clarify the shape and bearing of this choreography, I propose that "confession" and "words of assurance" should explicitly culminate in a third step: "celebration," in which the gathered assembly, buoyed by the Spirit, responds to the merciful good news their confessions have received. A proper liturgy of reconciliation in Christian worship, then, should take three distinct turns, each marked by beautiful words, music, and gestures: confession, words of assurance, and celebration — in other words, truth-telling, comfort, and joy.

This three-part unity is the basic form of Christian life, *semper penitens,* always being reconciled by God, always being baptized anew. As such, it should frame liturgies of baptism, reconciliation, and indeed the whole arc of Christian liturgy and life as a whole. Celebration, in this view, is the proper culmination of every Christian worship service. Note that this is not because we are duty-bound to celebrate God's gifts, but rather because the actual, full, and genuine receiving of those gifts — gratuitous and unmerited as they are — can only take the form of celebration, of joy and delight. Our celebrating constitutes our receiving. Here on the ark, we can only truly witness the dove's telling olive leaf if we witness it as good news for us, and thus as a cause for jubilation. If we do not rejoice in it, then we quite plainly have not yet truly seen and understood it. Likewise, if we grimly or flatly or casually announce the good news of our salvation, then we quite plainly have not yet truly heard it, and so our alleged proclamation amounts to an admission that we ourselves require a good sermon. To put it succinctly, by the Spirit's conspiracy and the Son's solidarity, Christian worship is a journey into joy. In this sense, it is an answer to the psalmist's poignant call, the call of someone who is already reconciled with God by God's grace but who has somehow lost track of this good news along the way: "Restore unto me the joy of your salvation" (Ps. 51:12).

4. Christian Communion

This brings us, at last, to the table. The Communion rite is the quintessential, climactic celebration in Christian worship: the joyous thanksgiving feast ("Eucharist" is from the Greek *eucharistia,* "thanksgiving"), the reinterpreted Passover meal of liberation from bondage, and the foretaste of the messianic banquet that will be a culmination of all things. At the same time, of course, Communion is the meal of solemn remembrance that re-enacts Jesus' Last Supper and the night of his arrest, that is, the night he was betrayed and deserted by his disciples, the original Christians. Thus the dialectical structure so evident in baptism (dying and rising) is no less evident here (betrayal and communion, sorrow and joy). In the same meal we take our place at God's table of reconciliation — and at our own table of desertion. The more strongly we deny that we will abandon Jesus ("I will not!"), the more clearly we confirm our role in the narrative, for "they all said the same" (Mark 14:31). On the other hand, the more deeply we doubt that we betrayers and deserters are already forgiven, embraced, and reconciled by God, the more clearly we confirm that this Communion in-vitation, as Jesus delivers it, is indeed addressed directly to us.

Insofar as Jesus stands with us, hosting the meal, the Communion ta-ble is a table of consolation. If we doubt our own worthiness for a divine supper, we may be assured by our presence here, since our doubt itself confirms our place on the guest list. Indeed, as Matthew, Mark, and Luke report it, the Lord's Supper is no gathering of the faithful and true; on the contrary, it is a meal for the unfaithful and false, the lost and the wayward, the betrayers and deserters, that is, it is a meal for Judas and Peter. Jesus is well aware that this table is "prepared in the presence of my enemies" (Ps. 23:5), a situation he emphasizes repeatedly, beginning at the outset: "Truly, one of you will betray me, one who is eating with me" (Mark 14:18). Only then, after this charge and the flood of sorrow it produces, does Jesus break the bread and share the cup. And finally, at the end of the meal, as if to head off the possibility of the eleven closing "faithful" ranks against the one, Jesus predicts Peter's desertion, setting off a second round of consternation and passionate denial. Peter is heroic in protest, and his colleagues quite convincingly follow his lead when they perceive that Jesus' charge is also meant for them (Mark 14:31). It is only a few hours later, of course, that Peter does desert Jesus, as do all the rest. The men disappear; the women look on "from afar" (Mark 15:40). In retro-spect (indeed, "in remembrance"), then, the meal is revealed to be a sup-per of devastating sorrow, divine indictment, and Christian duplicity.

To sacramentally replay that meal, as Christians often do, ritually po-sitioning ourselves as "disciples around the table" in the unfolding drama, is to confess our ongoing implication in this duplicity (a confession that is all the more true to the narrative if it is unwitting). That is, our participation in these proceedings, far from demonstrating our admirable devotion, in fact showcases our Christian hypocrisy, our only too eager efforts to pass off our thin commitments as fidelity and adoration. To claim otherwise, as Christians often do, is to promote ourselves over the original disciples — as if our sincerity surpasses theirs — and thus to separate ourselves, by way of this boastful claim, from the New Testament accounts we are supposedly remembering and re-enacting.[12] Indeed, the biblical accounts themselves are quite clear: at the brink of his ordeal, Jesus shares this meal with his betrayers and deserters. He goes out of his way to identify his companions as such: he offers himself to them, in advance of their betrayal and desertion, and thus in the shadow of the cross. Therefore, if we seek to accept these gifts — bread and wine, body and blood — in faithful remembrance of the meal we find narrated in the Gospels, we can only do so by inhabiting these disgraceful roles. Or we can only do so by recognizing that we indeed already inhabit them, betrayers and deserters all, *semper peccator*. Communion is thus properly a confessional meal of contrition and humility.

But in the midst of this disgrace, alongside and simultaneous with it, God's grace abounds, and so Communion is ultimately a meal of celebration and joy. We must remember this as well, and this most of all. Bracketed by the devastating charges of betrayal and desertion, Jesus blesses the bread, breaks it, and presents it to us as a gift for us, the very ones he has just accused — and will accuse again. It is as if he is saying: "You will abandon me, but do not be afraid, for I will not abandon you. You will break my body and spill my blood, but look, I have already broken it for you, and poured it out for you, and I freely give them to you now, as a sign of my covenant of forgiveness and liberation. You will carry out your abysmal sacrifice, but look, I have already lifted it up into a sign that there shall no longer be sacrifice. My grace has outrun your sin. You come to the end of your way of death, and I am already there, the living God."[13]

12. Or again, such boasting may be read as a poignant replay of Luke's account, where, immediately after the meal, still at the table, the disciples begin a spirited debate over "which one of them was to be regarded as the greatest" (Luke 22:24).

13. It is worth underscoring Jesus' compassionate *defiance* here vis-à-vis sin, his preemptive and decisive transformation of it, lest his strategy be understood as a merely passive form of accepting and forgiving abuse. Like an elegant martial artist, Jesus defies sin and death by co-opting and subverting its power. Moreover, his submission to torture and execution (again, the sort of "submission" found in judo, "giving way" as part of a strategy

Such is the duplex, unified story we recall and replay in Communion: the story of God's reconciling forgiveness precisely in the face of our ongoing turning away. But again, as in the case of baptism, if we consider the Communion rite without reference to this divine solidarity, conspiracy, and transformative co-option — that is, if we consider it strictly as *leitourgia,* the work of people — then we can and must critique Communion as another paragon of religiosity. However, here the accent is not on initiation, as it is in baptism, but on sacrifice, the alleged act of "making sacred" (Latin *sacer,* "sacred," and *facere,* "to make") by way of a "holy offering" to God.[14] The details of what exactly is made sacred in Communion, what exactly is offered to God, and how these things are supposedly accomplished, vary significantly across Christian sectarian accounts; but these variations should not distract us from what is fundamentally and invariably at stake. That is, by partaking in this meal, Christians seek and claim to commune with God, engaging the divine "real presence" in a special, matchless way. Whether the technicalities of this presence and engagement are explained primarily in terms of ingesting God's body and blood (as according to doctrines of transubstantiation and consubstantiation, among others), or in terms of faithfully obeying Christ's ordinance to "do this in remembrance of me" (as according to doctrines of "mere memorial"), the meal is, in any case, primarily an act of alleged community with God. As such, it is exalted above all other meals: it is the holy feast celebrated at Christ's table. If we participate in it properly, Christians claim, then precisely to that extent we enjoy special access to divine

---

of subduing an opponent, in effect turning the opponent's own power against him) is by no means a simple endorsement, model, or instruction for human beings to follow. When it comes to his passion, a strict *imitatio Christi* does not apply. On the contrary, Jesus' passion and death on the cross takes place exactly "once and for all," as the Epistle to the Hebrews puts it, precisely to liberate human beings from the bloody bonds of our sacrificial economy. To imagine that we are required to imitate this liberating passion, repeat it, or somehow add to it amounts, in the end, to a denial of its once and for all character. Christ "offered for all time a single sacrifice," and by so doing "abolished" all other sacrificial forms (Heb. 10:8-13). As a compassionate savior (in the root sense of *compassion,* i.e., "suffering with"), Christ joins us in our suffering (see, for example, Ignacio Ellacuria's idea of the "crucified peoples" in Latin America and elsewhere); but we need not then turn around and join Christ in his. Divine compassion for humanity is sufficient. When it takes self-destructive forms, human compassion for God is unnecessary and mistaken.

14. These two aspects of religious life — "initiation" and "sacrifice" — often converge, as in the common Christian practice of allowing only the baptized to receive Communion.

presence and favor, a singular intimacy often figured as mutual incorporation: Christ into our bodies and we into Christ's body. Thus, in the end, the "making sacred" in Communion comes down to this: via this work, Christians are allegedly transformed, renewed, graced, strengthened, and incorporated into God's body, and thus are themselves "made sacred."

If the *leitourgia* of Christian baptism is the supposed rite of passage from sin to divine favor, the *leitourgia* of the Eucharist is the ongoing, repeatable maintenance and exploitation of this alleged favor, the offering by which we maneuver to come near and commune with God. Again, the technical details of what is allegedly offered in Communion vary across the breadth of Christian accounts. Some consider the bread and wine themselves to be initially offered to God, even processing these elements forward as part of the assembly's "tithes and offerings" (as Cain did!). Others conceive of the consecrated elements, that is, the putative body and blood of Christ, to be a sacrificial offering to God the Father, the church's participation in God the Son's self-offering on the cross. Still others explicitly reject these alternatives and instead emphasize the memorial dimension of the meal. Yet even here, solemn Christian obedience to the divine ordinance ("Do this in remembrance of me") is itself no less an offering, no less a presentation to God of a precious good (obedience).

All of these varieties of Communion make an offering to God, and in Barth's words, this work is both "terrible and presumptuous."[15] We endeavor to give gifts to God, to become God's benefactors, to intimately commune with God at the divine table, and thus, in various ways to be, as the serpent expressed it to Eve, "like God" (Gen. 3:5). We dutifully bring sacrifices of bread and wine, of obedience, of thanksgiving, of praise, and so on; we quite earnestly "honor God" with these gifts, and we hope, explicitly or implicitly, that our works of honoring God are themselves eminently honorable and will not go unrewarded. In short, we give in order to receive.[16] We sacrifice in order to be made sacred.

---

15. Barth, *The Epistle to the Romans*, p. 247.

16. Communion liturgies that place the financial "tithes and offerings" collection immediately before the Communion rite, and indeed under the same rubric, manifest quite starkly a picture of this attempted exchange: this "offering" given in order to acquire a gift from God. On its face, this sequence gives the impression of a bargain, a quid pro quo, though many Christians naturally would be at pains to protest and deny this, no matter how plain the appearance of an exchange may be. My own position is that such appearances actually help to bring to the surface dynamics that are always already at play in Christian reli-

We can deny all of this, of course. Surely Cain would deny it. We might even take offense that our humble piety could be so crudely called into question, an indignation that would serve as our own taste of Cain's religious rage, a clear sign that our humility is not quite so humble after all. Indeed, in the face of this critique, even our Christian resentment itself evokes J's narrative, where Cain's liturgical motive is precisely this giving-in-order-to-receive, and where God debunks the inaugural human offering *(minchah,* "gift"),[17] and thus every offering that follows, as complicit in a sacrificial economy of exchange, obligation, anxiety, and violence.[18] Like Cain, we offer up our bread and cup, our obedience and praise, our sacrificial fruit that we hope will not only be accepted but remade into a means of our own acceptance, forgiveness, and "uplift" (Hebrew *se'et,* Gen. 4:7): our own approach toward intimacy with God, our own atonement, and, finally, our own way back into Eden.[19] Thus, like Cain's, our thankful offering *(eucharistia),* despite its guise of generosity and gratitude, is at bottom a bid for acquisition (true to Cain's name).[20] The origi-

---

gious life, and that the stronger and more fruitful theological response to any semblance of liturgical bargaining is not piously to deny it, but fully to admit that we Christians bargain with God all too frequently, that such maneuvering is at the heart of the religious predicament from which we require salvation. And, I hasten to add, in these cases it will do no good to shift the "tithes and offerings" collection to some other portion of the service. At most, doing so would only obscure a relatively clear sign of Christian worship's religiosity. Indeed, as *leitourgia,* Christian worship is precisely an exercise in bargaining: it is the liturgy of Cain *(qayin),* a strategic offering in order to acquire *(qanah)* divine respect and acceptance (Gen. 4:1, 5, 7).

17. As we have seen in Ch. 2, *minchah* ("gift") appears in three stories in Genesis, and each time it applies to a gift given expressly in order to appease and atone, and thus as part of an implicit exchange (Gen. 4:3ff.; Gen. 32:13ff.; Gen. 43:11ff.). In reverse order, these are: (1) the "gift" of "choice fruit" Jacob sends with his sons to Pharaoh's governor (who is actually Joseph), a gift given in order to appease the governor by compensating for the appearance of theft; (2) the "gift" of livestock Jacob sends ahead to his approaching brother, Esau, a gift given in order to appease Esau, whom Jacob fears is planning to kill him; and (3) the "gifts" of fruit and livestock Cain and Abel bring to God (see Ch. 2, note 22).

18. For resonance between this view and recent anthropological and critical theories on gift-giving in the work of Pierre Bourdieu, Jacques Derrida, and others, see above, pp. 43ff., 86ff.

19. See above, pp. 85ff.

20. As we have seen in Ch. 2, with the name "Cain" *(qayin),* J points to a cluster of ideas: the word's Hebrew root, *qyn,* is linked to both metallurgy and music; accordingly, J reports that Cain's descendents pioneer these arts in human history (Gen. 4:21-22), and that

nal human maker and acquirer of things, Cain puts his ingenuity to work in an attempt to secure divine respect, to stand aright on his own two feet before his Creator, and thereby be accepted (Gen. 4:5, 7). Cain is an artisan, the builder of the first city, and his labor is epitomized by his first masterpiece, his sacrifice to God, his "making" that is also "making sacred." As exactly this sort of extraordinary project, the Eucharist is consummately Christian, religious work.

But if Communion's sacrificial dimensions recall the liturgy of Cain, the rite's form as a supper recalls the deeper, more fundamental, original liturgy of his parents. Cain eventually elaborates the human lunge for autonomy over against God by masking it as an offering, but he does not invent the lunge in the first place. His parents did, as J tells it, by way of a disastrous meal in Eden. And so we may say that, every time we participate in the Eucharist, we repeat and extend that original meal, even as we repeat and extend the meal shared by the disciples in that upper room. Like 'adam and Peter, we take and eat; also like 'adam and Peter, we betray and hide, deserting God out of fear for our own well-being. The Last Supper has become a tragic continuation of the first meal in Eden.

Therefore, God graciously moves to deliver us at exactly this crucial point of rupture and shame: God is against Communion's choreography of sacrifice, and so God disrupts it — by entering it. God hosts the meal and thus reverses and transforms the supper of betrayal and desertion — 'adam's and the disciples' — into a supper of reconciliation, of meeting again. In other words, Jesus Christ *(Immanuel)* takes up our sacrifice *with us.* He does not do away with Passover, nor, in Christian terms, with Communion. On the contrary, Jesus enters it and celebrates it, reframes it and reinterprets it, and thus calls Christians to observe it with him, *simul iustus et peccator,* in remembrance of him and his reconciling, transforming work.[21]

Cain himself builds the first city (Gen. 4:17). From this angle, then, "Cain" is the name of the first human artisan, the first builder, smith, and maker, the founder of human ingenuity, and the inventor of the human "gift" *(minchah).* Moreover, J punningly links the name *qayin* to the word *qanah,* "gain," "acquire," or "possess": "she conceived and bore Cain [*qayin*], saying, 'I have acquired [*qanah*] a man with the help of the LORD'" (Gen. 4:1). And so the first human being who gives a gift to God is marked, paradoxically and tellingly, as a virtuoso of acquisition. See above, pp. 82ff.

21. There can be no question of Christianity superseding Jewish Passover, much less Judaism. Rather, Christians should consider Holy Week, and indeed the Eucharist itself, as a Christian interpretation of Passover, an interpretation at once distinct from, parallel with,

Just as Jesus begins his public ministry by entering religion at the baptismal front gate, so he takes his leave of human life by way of his religion's most exalted meal, on the highest holy day of his religious calendar: "the first day of Unleavened Bread, when they sacrifice the Passover lamb" (Mark 14:12). He begins with initiation and ends with sacrifice. In Christian terms, he begins with baptism and ends with Communion. He hosts the holy eucharistic feast, yesterday and today; and, as in the case of baptism, his participation exposes and reverses the rite's basic sacramental structure. It does so in at least three ways.

First, Jesus' participation scrambles and transposes the sacrificial rite's key roles, for this host portrays *himself* as the Passover lamb. His companions at the table, he insists, are betrayers and deserters. There will be a sacrificial death here, to be sure, but now the victim presides at the table, and the unwitting priestly perpetrators surround that table. A priesthood — of all believers! The violence at the heart of worship and religion, so clear in Cain's crime, is now again laid bare. So desperate are we for divine favor, or in any case for righteous advantage, that we are willing to take life for it, even our own life, and even divine life, strung up on a cross. For this preeminent Lamb, Christians confess, is both Son of humanity and Son of God, our own true life and indeed the "son of the householder," about whom we whisper, with the voice of Cain, "This is the heir; come, let us kill him and have his inheritance" (Matt. 21:38). Jesus exposes sacrifice in general and Christian Communion in particular, as it is caught up in an economy of exchange and acquisition, a vicious circle of rivalry, anxiety, and violence. Jesus takes up the position at the center of this sacrificial circle — that is, the seat at the head of the Christian Communion table — in order to unveil sacrifice once and for all, to lay out its deadly consequences for his own body, and to achieve and proclaim its ultimate defeat by an empty tomb.[22]

---

and dependent on Jewish interpretations of Passover. If the Eucharist involves a "new covenant," it is certainly new in the sense of being a distinct Christian alternative; but this by no means entails that the original divine covenant with Jews is somehow foreclosed, demoted, or left behind. On the contrary, since Christian interpretations of Passover rely on Jewish interpretations (the Jewish idea, for example, of the meal as a meal of liberation) for their own intelligibility and force, we Christians should give Jewish interpretations of Passover, different from but parallel to ours, the utmost honor and interest, as one would the work of a close relative.

22. There are significant points of contact between my position here and René Gi-

Second, Jesus reverses the meal's sacramental structure by virtue of the fact that now God the Son plays host. According to the liturgy of Cain, humanity brings an offering to God, a gift given to acquire forgiveness, acceptance, and intimacy with God, but it is giving-in-order-to-receive. To the extent, however, that this act is now presided over and carried out by God, the One who gives all things, lacks nothing, and so needs nothing in return, Jesus in effect co-opts Cain's liturgy of humanity-giving-gifts-to-God and lifts it into a simultaneous God-giving-gifts-to-humanity. Now God the Son, as host of the meal, gives the divine body and blood to humanity, and the liturgy of Cain is thus joined and transformed by the liturgy of Jesus Christ. Insofar as Jesus actually hosts the meal and the Holy Spirit actually conspires with it, our giving-in-order-to-receive is simultaneously reversed and transformed into a receiving-in-order-to-give, that is, a receiving of God's blessings in order to share them with our neighbors and with all creation — in abundant love and joy.

Third, by entering and presiding over the Communion meal, Jesus transforms 'adam's supper of death into God's supper of life with 'adam. The first couple in Eden, moving against and thus apart from their Creator, prepare and serve a meal contrary to their own vocation and being, a meal carried out as though without God. They act surreptitiously, as if they are out of God's sight, and they take and eat — that is, steal and devour — the one fruit in creation not given to them as a blessing, the one food they may not "freely eat" (Gen. 2:16; 3:6). The woman — the first and original priest acting on behalf of herself and her husband — takes, eats, and gives the illicit fruit to the man in Eden, the first and original parishioner, who just as disastrously receives, takes, and eats on behalf of himself and his wife (Gen. 3:6). But now Jesus, preempting, co-opting, and transforming exactly these gestures of death, lifts them into his choreog-

---

rard's (the ideas, for example, that violence is at the heart of "the sacred," that Jesus exposes sacrifice by taking up the sacrificial victim's position, and that the Gospels' passion narratives portray sacrifice in order to unveil and oppose it); Girard's work has certainly stimulated my thinking in important ways. But I do not intend to endorse Girard's wider position (his analysis of *mimesis* and violence, his repeated emphasis on scapegoating, and so forth). See René Girard's books *Violence Unveiled* (Baltimore: Johns Hopkins University Press, 1979); *Things Hidden Since the Foundation of the World* (Stanford, Calif.: Stanford University Press, 1993); *I See Satan Fall Like Lightning* (Maryknoll, N.Y.: Orbis Books, 2001); see also Gil Bailie, *Violence Unveiled: Humanity at the Crossroads* (New York: Crossroad, 1996); and S. Mark Heim, *Saved from Sacrifice* (Grand Rapids: Eerdmans, 2006).

raphy of reconciliation and new life. "Take, eat," he says to *'adam,* to his disciples, and to us. "This is my body, broken for you. This is my blood of the covenant, which is poured out for many for the forgiveness of sins" (1 Cor. 11:24; Matt. 26:26-28). Thus humanity still takes and eats. But insofar as Jesus reframes these gestures, now their plunder is also a gift; now their accursed theft is also a receiving of blessing, for God the Son himself bids them take and eat. The abysmal Mass, the continual beginning of exile, is thus lifted into the Mass of reconciliation, the continual ending of exile, the continual "meeting again." God is against religion, and thus takes it up with us in conspiracy and solidarity, so as to turn its fatal strokes against itself and fashion a plowshare from a sword.

As in Christian baptism, however, whether this renovation actually takes place is God's prerogative, not ours. We can only cling to this possibility in faith and hope. Moreover, just as in baptism, even when God does lift Communion into a simultaneous meal of reconciliation, the feast nonetheless also remains *leitourgia,* and so at best we participate *simul iustus et peccator.* Every Christian Eucharist, everywhere, is still a meal of shame "on the night of his arrest." It is still an attempt at sacrifice and offering, and thus it is still implicated in an exchange economy of obligation, acquisition, and violence. Just because God's transformation of the rite occurs again and again in the face of our ongoing religiosity and sin, and thus is an entirely free, entirely gracious transformation — for just these reasons, Christian Communion can and should result in Christian joy. This is indeed the holy feast, precisely because it is unholy and yet lifted and saved by God. That is what Christians hope, trust, and testify. To put it another way, in Communion Jesus interrupts and transforms our specious attempts to divide between "holy" and "unholy": Jesus interrupts and transforms our religion. By joining and hosting the meal, God at once exposes the liturgy of Cain, the give-in-order-to-receive liturgy, and institutes the simultaneous liturgy of Jesus Christ, the receive-in-order-to-give liturgy. One day, of course, God will end Cain's liturgy once and for all; that day, not yet fully arrived, has already dawned in Jesus Christ. Once Cain's liturgy is no more, the reconciling liturgy of Jesus Christ will be unnecessary, and thus liturgy itself will come to an end. In the end, all our work of people will give way to play, rest, Sabbath, *shalom,* and thus to music and dancing, to celebration, joy, and life without end (Luke 15:25).

In Christian Communion, then, we properly get a foretaste of this joyful celebration and vitality. For if the rite is (1) a remembrance of the

Last Supper, and (2) a present-day participation in God's reconciling work, it is preeminently (3) a tangible anticipation of the messianic banquet, the music and dancing that awaits every prodigal on his or her return home. And so the act of celebration, of enjoying what God has done and is doing and will do, is the proper crescendo and goal of Christian worship. Ultimately, God saves human beings for joy — our joy and God's joy. And so this mutual jubilation, this human and divine community of delight, is the proper goal and basis for proclaiming and receiving the good news of human salvation.

To return once more to the image of Noah's ark, we *witness* the dove's olive leaf, if we genuinely witness it at all, as a cause for rejoicing; therefore, any *witnessing to* it should likewise resound in joy and for the sake of joy. That is, the witnessing-to should be a continuation, an overflow of the original witness (Ps. 23:5). Familiar analogies abound: if we suddenly see a beautiful landscape, for example, we may almost instinctively feel moved to share it by pointing others toward it or describing it later in vivid detail. And if we do these things out of love and delight, that is, out of a desire to increase and impart joy and good pleasure to our companions, then we relay the kind of news Christian proclamation must always aspire to become. For the Christian gospel is nothing if not, as the angels sing, "good news of great joy for all people" (Luke 2:10).

Great joy, as everyone knows, can make "all the difference in the world." Christian worship should be, finally and fundamentally, celebration. It should issue from joy — and for joy. Infectious delight should be its characteristic mark. Christian preaching, prayer, sacrament, song — every liturgical element should be designed and coordinated for the sake of jubilation. But note that not every liturgical element itself need be happy, or even upbeat. Christian liturgies should not be manic jamborees. Rather, the point is that every liturgical element should be designed and coordinated for the sake of jubilation, for the sake of joy. This will invariably mean that many liturgical elements will be characterized by other emotions and postures: sorrow, reflection, anger, longing, courage, and so forth. But these elements should have an arrangement, a clear overall pattern, direction, and purpose. In its own way, each liturgical part should advance the project of the whole, a coordinated movement toward genuine celebration, that is, toward corporate, tangible experiences of delight. An authentic "Hallelujah!" is the culminating response that every Christian worship service, without exception, should finally and most basically elicit from the congregation.

Of course, in order for this "Hallelujah!" to be real and sincere, it will have to emerge as an authentic response within a broad liturgical design sensitive to local circumstances and cultural conventions. That is, there are different forms of jubilation available to different assemblies at different times. However, even on the most discouraging days of sorrow and anxiety — indeed especially on those days — "Hallelujah!" must ultimately arise in Christian worship. In extreme cases, this enjoyment may be radically implicit: simply being with one another, for example, in support and shared bewilderment, may be all we can enjoy at such times. But especially in these cases, the ultimate "Hallelujah!" should be clear, no less beautiful and true for its resounding through tears or in a whisper.

And likewise, variation according to local circumstances is matched by variation according to local cultures. Celebration need not be manifest as, say, shouting and applause (although it certainly might). For some communities, the cultural marks of genuine celebration are indeed music and dancing, but for others, joy takes different forms, from a quiet, stirring encounter with beauty to a boisterous shared meal. And well it should, not only because different temperaments and cultural conventions demand different modes of joy, but also because this diversity itself is marvelous and makes for a more resplendent chorus. The key question for leaders and designers of Christian worship, then, is not *whether* to create conditions for genuine celebration, but rather, first, *which* local cultural forms generally mediate celebration for a given congregation, and second, *how* to create conditions in which these local forms may flourish in a given service of Christian worship. There are a thousand ways to authentically say "Hallelujah!" so the liturgical designer's first question is always an ethnographic one: How do we best say "Hallelujah!" around here?

Finally, some proposals for eucharistic practice. First, Christian liturgical leaders may help clarify the penitential, dialectical structure of Communion — sorrow and joy, *Kyrie eleison* and Hallelujah! — by more explicitly grounding the meal in the New Testament narratives it is meant to remember. For example, introducing Communion, a lay leader might read Matthew 26:17-19:

> On the first day of Unleavened Bread, the disciples came to Jesus, saying, "Where do you want us to make the preparations for you to eat the Passover?" He said, "Go to the city to a certain man, and say to him,

'The Teacher says, My time is near; I will keep the Passover at your house with my disciples.'" So the disciples did as Jesus had directed them, and they prepared the Passover meal.

A brief musical interlude might follow, as the table is set and prepared. Then the celebrant, standing apart from the table, might say:

The hour has come for the sacred supper, the meal in which we celebrate God's gift of liberation. Jesus called on his disciples to prepare the feast, and we have done so here this morning. In faith and hope, we now await his arrival. Let us pray.

Come, Lord Jesus. Take your place as our host, so that we may be your guests. Call us again to your table, not bearing our gifts for you, but empty-handed and open to your gifts for us. For we can only come to you as broken people who need your healing touch, children who need your loving care, sinners who need your sweet forgiveness, and pilgrims afar off, restless until we rest in you.

Loving God, we call on your presence, forgiveness, and mercy, for without you, our work can only lead to harm. Without you, this meal can only be yet another first supper in Eden, a feast of fear, distrust, deception, and sin. But with you, gracious Lord, this meal may instead be your Last Supper in Jerusalem, and a foretaste of that glorious banquet in the New Jerusalem, for which we wait and call.

Come, Lord Jesus. Make this table your table, this meal your meal. Come, Holy Spirit. Transform this bread and cup, and this whole assembly gathered here this morning, into your body and blood, your life for the world. Amen.[23]

Here the celebrant might move to the Communion table or altar, saying:

And so we remember that on that night when he took his place at the table, the Good Shepherd called together his sheep. They were not "the faithful and true." They were his friends. Judas was there, the betrayer. Peter was there, the denier and deserter. As he did so often in his ministry, Jesus ate that night with sinners, and he bade them, "Come, all you

23. For "Come, Lord Jesus," see Rev. 22:20; for "restless until we rest in you," see Augustine's *Confessions,* Book I.i; for "your life for the world," see John 6:33, 51.

who are hungry, thirsty, weary, and I will give you rest. I will give you peace. I will give you life."

Then Jesus took a loaf of bread, and after blessing it, he broke it....

I will make three observations about this proposed Communion invitation. First, by framing the rite in the Gospel narratives, the meal takes place more clearly as a meal of forgiveness and care, an event of love, acceptance, and blessing precisely in the face of betrayal, desertion, and stark human needs. Thus the thematic atmosphere of the sanctuary may become more clearly one of *divine mercy*. And thus the role inhabited by congregants in the ceremony becomes more clearly a *penitential* role, an empty-handed posture of contrition and admitting of need on the one hand, and joy at being invited, accepted, and nurtured on the other. Thus the sacrament's dialectical structure — sorrow and joy, *Kyrie eleison* and Hallelujah! — is given practical, tangible form as a penitential encounter with divine mercy. The penitent's path *(semper penitens)* is at once a way of sorrow and a journey into joy, and here that path takes place as a pilgrimage to the table.

Musically, then, this feast should by no means have the feel of a slow and solemn march (much less a dirge). Instead, the musical setting should be suitable for penitential practice: full of joy and beauty, but avoiding mere "cheerfulness"; appropriate for a prayer of confession, but not for anything dreary, dull, or despondent. The music itself may build over the course of the meal, of course, ascending in mood, tempo, or theological theme; familiar tunes, with their emotional and lyrical associations, can be particularly conducive to widespread engagement by the congregation. In any case, however, the musical task is to provide support and space for Communion's dialectical character to flourish, leading us anew along the way of the penitent, a path brimming with both pure humility and the dignity of holy pride.

Second, the proposed Communion invitation takes advantage of the fact that, according to Matthew, Mark, and Luke, the disciples prepare the supper before Jesus arrives to host it. By taking up a position of prayer at precisely this point in the narrative, we are able to emphasize the idea that even here, in this familiar meal, we may not take divine presence for granted. God must grant it afresh. Jesus must arrive again in this upper room, and so we pray for this arrival, calling for it again and again. As in the case of baptism, Communion must always take place as an *epiclesis,* a calling on the Holy Spirit, and as a cry, *Maranatha!* ("Come, Lord Jesus").[24] Our worship itself is in pressing need of divine transformation. And so we call on God, here and now, to lift our liturgy of *'adam* and Cain into the liturgy of Jesus Christ.

Third, precisely because this invitation frames the meal as an encounter (we hope and pray) with divine mercy, it lays the groundwork for genuinely felt celebration. If Communion is actually experienced as a meal of divine forgiveness and care in the face of our sin and creaturely need, it can only take place as an occasion for joy. Likewise, if divine presence is actually understood as gracious, free, and impossible to take for granted, but nonetheless granted afresh here and now, then the rite's participants can only become celebrants. Or, to make the same point from the opposite direction, the conditions that would foreclose or obstruct the possibility of joyfully celebrating the Eucharist are: (1) that we understand ourselves to somehow *deserve* the divine forgiveness and care manifest in the rite (here the thematic atmosphere of divine mercy is replaced by an atmosphere of our own entitlement and therefore of our own triumph); (2) that we understand divine presence as something to be taken for granted in the rite, as, say, an extension of our own impeccable liturgical technique, and thus after all as a banal, routine, or otherwise rather unremarkable thing; or (3) that we deny or question the reality of divine forgiveness, care, and presence in Christian Communion in the first place.

---

24. *Maranatha* (Aramaic words transliterated into Greek) appears once in the New Testament (1 Cor. 16:22) and was likely a common greeting/farewell for early Christians, perhaps a widely significant liturgical formula. The same idea, expressed in Greek, ends the New Testament (Rev. 22:20: "Come, Lord Jesus!"), and thus it is a continual testimony to the invocational openness, insufficiency, and unfinished character of every Christian work, and indeed of Christian life as a whole. At the close of the New Testament, the place where we might well expect to find a satisfied summing up, we instead find ourselves standing at a precipice, calling out for God. Thus the doctrine of the *Parousia* (the "Second Coming"), so often thought today to be the exclusive territory of so-called right-wing Christians fascinated with apocalypse, is in fact an indispensable idea for all forms of Christian theology, since it should be understood as a culminating, standing rebuke against Christian triumphalism — including the triumph of understanding Christianity as a totally closed or settled system of thought and practice. The doctrine of the *Parousia,* in effect, puts everything in Christianity under the sign of transience and open expectation. When the last page of the New Testament is turned, Christians can only, here as always, take up the empty-handed, hopeful position of invocation. As Luther would put it, "We are beggars," living only on the grace of God.

If any of these conditions arise, joyful celebration will not. The ceremony will take place as a dull, solemn, or empty affair; or it might be quite a festive display of self-congratulatory, triumphant good cheer. In contrast, however, genuine and joyful eucharistic celebration requires the reverse set of conditions: (1) that we understand that we in no way deserve the divine forgiveness and care manifest in the rite (thus a clear thematic atmosphere of divine mercy); (2) that we understand that divine presence is never something to be taken for granted, and that if God grants it here and now, God does so against and even despite our liturgical technique (thus a provocation to wonder and joyful astonishment); and (3) that we feel — personally, corporately, and vicariously — the assurance of divine forgiveness, care, and presence in the rite, indeed, well beyond it. If these conditions arise, joyful celebration will be there as well.

And through this jubilation, Christian Communion — the church's meal remembering the Last Supper narrated in the Gospels, and as such, participating here and now in Christ's transforming work — may also become a tangible and compelling foretaste of the messianic banquet that will be a culmination of all things. That is, by way of joy and wonder, the meal may become a glimpse and taste of the kingdom of God coming into the world here and now, a sumptuous table in the New Jerusalem, where humanity and God feast together in friendship. Accordingly, it may become a glimpse and taste of the end of worship once and for all; as such, it may make "all the difference in the world" for Christian worship.

For here, in the eschatological dimension of the feast, we may anticipate and lay claim to the day when no more sacrifices are made, no more atonements attempted, no more offerings presented to God — in other words, the day when no temple will be found in a new creation (Rev. 21:22). "Death shall be no more," and thus the Christian sacraments — whether as liturgical paragons or divine transformations of death — will likewise pass away (Rev. 21:4). For on that day there will be no *leitourgia*, no work of people, indeed no work at all, but only the rest and play of friendship and love, intimacy and celebration, Sabbath and *shalom*. In a word, there will be a banquet. And in the Christian Eucharist, by the grace of divine solidarity and conspiracy, human beings may have a foretaste of that great feast to end all feasts, that playful meal to end all liturgical meals, and thus that new beginning, for humanity and God, of genuine communion without end.

Bibliography

Althaus, Paul. *The Theology of Martin Luther.* Philadelphia: Fortress Press, 1966.

Aristotle. *Nicomachean Ethics.* In *The Basic Works of Aristotle.* New York: Random House, 1941.

Augustine. *Confessions.* New York: Penguin USA, 1961.

Baker, Mark D. *Religious No More: Building Communities of Grace and Freedom.* Downers Grove: InterVarsity Press, 1999.

Balthasar, Hans Urs von. *The Theology of Karl Barth.* San Francisco: Ignatius Press, 1992.

Barth, Karl. *Prayer.* Louisville: Westminster John Knox Press, 2002.

————. *The Christian Life.* Grand Rapids: Eerdmans, 1981.

————. *Ethics.* Edinburgh: T&T Clark, 1981.

————. *Church Dogmatics.* Edinburgh: T&T Clark, 1936-1975.

————. *Theology and Church.* London: SCM, 1962.

————. *The Humanity of God.* Richmond, VA: John Knox Press, 1960.

————. *The Epistle to the Romans.* London: Oxford University Press, 1933.

————. *The Word of God and Word of Man.* New York: The Pilgrim Press, 1928.

Bass, Dorothy C., ed. *Practicing Our Faith.* San Francisco: Jossey-Bass Publishers, 1997.

Bell, Catherine. *Ritual Theory, Ritual Practice.* New York: Oxford University Press, 1992.

Biggar, Nigel. *The Hastening that Waits: Karl Barth's Ethics.* Oxford: Clarendon Press, 1993.

Bonhoeffer, Dietrich. *Life Together.* New York: Harper and Row, 1954.

Boulton, Matthew. "Forsaking God: A Theological Argument for Christian
Lamentation." *Scottish Journal of Theology* (Jan. 2002): 67-83.

————. "We Pray By His Mouth: Karl Barth, Erving Goffman, and a Theology of Invocation." *Modern Theology* 17:1 (2001): 67-83.

Bourdieu, Pierre. *Outline of a Theory of Practice.* Cambridge: Cambridge
University Press, 1977.

Braaten, Carl E., and Robert W. Jenson, eds. *Union with Christ: The New
Finnish Interpretation of Luther.* Grand Rapids: Eerdmans, 1998.

Brecht, M. *Martin Luther.* Philadelphia: Fortress Press, 1985.

Busch, Eberhard. *Karl Barth: His Life from Letters and Autobiographical
Texts.* Philadelphia: Fortress Press, 1976.

Calvin, John. *Institutes of the Christian Religion.* Edited by John T. McNeill.
Philadelphia: Westminster Press, 1960.

Cavanaugh, William T. *Theopolitical Imagination: Discovering the Liturgy as
a Political Act in an Age of Global Consumerism.* London: T&T Clark,
2002.

————. *Torture and Eucharist.* Oxford: Blackwell Publishers, 1998.

Condivi, Ascanio. *Vita di Michelangelo Buonarroti.* Translated by A. S.
Wohl; edited by H. Wohl. University Park, PA: Pennsylvania State University Press, 1999.

Derrida, Jacques. *The Gift of Death.* Chicago: The University of Chicago
Press, 1995.

————. *Given Time: I. Counterfeit Money.* Chicago: The University of Chicago Press, 1992.

Di Noia, J. A. "Religion and the Religions." In *The Cambridge Companion to
Karl Barth,* edited by John Webster, pp. 243-57. Cambridge, UK: Cambridge University Press, 2000.

Ellul, Jacques. *Perspectives on Our Age.* New York: Seabury Press, 1981.

————. *Living Faith.* San Francisco: Harper and Row, 1980.

Fishbane, Michael. *Biblical Text and Texture.* Oxford: Oneworld Publications, 1998.

Fowl, Stephen E., ed. *The Theological Interpretation of Scripture.* Malden,
MA: Blackwell, 1997.

Freedberg, Sydney J. "Michelangelo: The Sistine Ceiling." In *Michelangelo:*

The Sistine Chapel Ceiling, edited by Charles Seymour, Jr. New York: Norton, 1972.

Frei, Hans. *The Eclipse of Biblical Narrative.* New Haven: Yale University Press, 1974.

Geller, Stephen. *Sacred Enigmas: Literary Religion in the Hebrew Bible.* New York: Routledge, 1996.

Gerrish, B. A. *Grace and Gratitude: The Eucharistic Theology of John Calvin.* Minneapolis: Fortress Press, 1993.

———. *Grace and Reason.* London: Oxford University Press, 1962.

Goffman, Erving. *Forms of Talk.* Philadelphia: University of Pennsylvania Press, 1981.

Gorringe, Timothy J. *Karl Barth: Against Hegemony.* Oxford: Clarendon Press, 1999.

Green, Garrett. "Challenging the Religious Studies Canon: Karl Barth's Theory of Religion." *The Journal of Religion* (Oct. 1995).

Hibbard, Howard. *Michelangelo.* New York: Harper and Row, 1974.

Holl, Karl. *What Did Luther Understand by Religion?* Philadelphia: Fortress Press, 1977.

Hunsinger, George. *Disruptive Grace: Studies in the Theology of Karl Barth.* Grand Rapids: Eerdmans, 2000.

———. *How to Read Karl Barth: The Shape of His Theology.* New York: Oxford University Press, 1991.

Jehle, Frank. *Ever Against the Stream: The Politics of Karl Barth, 1906-1968.* Grand Rapids: Eerdmans, 2002.

Jenson, Robert W. *A Religion Against Itself.* Richmond, VA: John Knox Press, 1967.

Johnson, Elizabeth. *She Who Is: The Mystery of God in Feminist Theological Discourse.* New York: Crossroad, 1992.

Josefson, Ruben. *Luther on Baptism.* Hong Kong, 1952.

Jüngel, Eberhard. "Invocation of God as the Ethical Ground of Christian Action." In *Theological Essays,* translated by J. B. Webster, pp. 154-72. Edinburgh: T&T Clark, 1989.

———. *Karl Barth, A Theological Legacy.* Philadelphia: The Westminster Press, 1986.

Kierkegaard, Søren. *Philosophical Fragments.* Princeton, NJ: Princeton University Press, 1985.

King, Ross. *Michelangelo and the Pope's Ceiling.* New York: Penguin Books, 2003.

Lathrop, Gordon W. *Holy People: A Liturgical Ecclesiology.* Minneapolis: Fortress, 1999.

———. *Holy Things: A Liturgical Theology.* Minneapolis: Fortress Press, 1993.

Locke, John. *The Reasonableness of Christianity.* Bristol, UK: Thoemmes Press, 1997.

Lohse, B. *Martin Luther's Theology.* Minneapolis: Fortress Press, 1999.

Luther, Martin. *Three Treatises.* Philadelphia: Fortress Press, 1970.

———. *Luther's Works.* Edited by Jaroslav Pelikan and Helmut Lehmann. Saint Louis: Concordia Publishing House, 1960-1974.

McCormack, Bruce L. *Karl Barth's Critically Realistic Dialectical Theology: Its Genesis and Development 1909-1936.* Oxford: Clarendon Press, 1995.

McFague, Sallie. *Models of God: Theology for an Ecological, Nuclear Age.* Philadelphia: Fortress Press, 1987.

McGrath, Alister E. *Luther's Theology of the Cross: Martin Luther's Theological Breakthrough.* Oxford: Basil Blackwell, 1985.

Oberman, Heiko A. *The Dawn of the Reformation.* Grand Rapids: Eerdmans, 1992.

———. *Luther: Man Between God and the Devil.* New Haven: Yale University Press, 1989.

———. *Werden und Wertung der Reformation.* Tübingen, 1977.

Pickstock, Catherine. *After Writing.* Oxford: Blackwell Publishers, 1998.

Ricoeur, Paul, and André LaCocque. *Thinking Biblically.* Chicago: University of Chicago Press, 1997.

Ritschl, Albrecht. *The Christian Doctrine of Justification and Reconciliation.* Edinburgh: T&T Clark, 1900.

Rosenzweig, Franz. *The Star of Redemption.* Notre Dame: University of Notre Dame Press, 1970.

Saliers, Don E. *Worship as Theology: Foretaste of Glory Divine.* Nashville: Abingdon, 1994.

Schleiermacher, Friedrich. *The Christian Faith.* Edinburgh: T&T Clark, 1989.

———. *On Religion: Speeches to Its Cultured Despisers.* Cambridge, UK: Cambridge University Press, 1988.

Schmemann, Alexander. *For the Life of the World.* Crestwood, NY: St. Vladimir's, 1963.

Seitz, Christopher, and Kathryn Greene-McCreight, eds. *Theological Exegesis.* Grand Rapids: Eerdmans, 1999.

Thompson, John. *Christ in Perspective: Christological Perspectives in the Theology of Karl Barth*. Edinburgh: Saint Andrew Press, 1978.

Tillich, Paul. "Moralisms and Morality: Theonomous Ethics." In *Theology of Culture*. Oxford: Oxford University Press, 1959.

————. *Systematic Theology,* Vol. I. Chicago: University of Chicago Press, 1951.

Torrance, Thomas F. *Karl Barth: An Introduction to His Early Theology, 1910-1931.* London: SCM Press, 1962.

————. *Karl Barth, Biblical and Evangelical Theologian.* Edinburgh: T&T Clark, 1990.

Troeltsch, Ernst. *The Christian Faith.* Minneapolis: Augsburg Fortress, 1991.

Vajta, Vilmos. *Luther on Worship.* Philadelphia: Fortress, 1958.

Wainwright, Geoffrey. *Doxology: The Praise of God in Worship, Doctrine, and Life.* New York: Oxford University Press, 1980.

Wallace, Mark I. *The Second Naivete: Barth, Ricoeur, and the New Yale Theology.* Macon: Mercer University Press, 1990.

Webster, John. *Barth.* London: Continuum, 2000.

————. *Barth's Moral Theology: Human Action in Barth's Thought.* Grand Rapids: Eerdmans, 1998.

————. *Barth's Ethics of Reconciliation.* Cambridge, UK: Cambridge University Press, 1995.

Zizioulas, John D. *Being as Communion* (Crestwood, NY: St. Vladimir's, 1985.

Index of Names and Subjects

Index of Scripture References

240

INDEX OF SCRIPTURE REFERENCES